THE MAKING OF THE MODERN MIND

THE MAKING OF THE MODERN MIND

PHILIP HODGKISS

THE ATHLONE PRESS
LONDON & NEW YORK

First published in 2001 by
THE ATHLONE PRESS
A Continuum imprint
The Tower Building, 11 York Road,
London SE1 7NX
370 Lexington Avenue
New York, NY 10017–6503

British Library Cataloguing in Publication Data
*A catalogue record for this book is available
from the British Library*

ISBN 0 485 00441 0   HB
       0 485 00629 4   PB

Library of Congress Cataloging-in-Publication Data
Hodgkiss, Philip, 1951–
  The making of the modern mind : the surfacing of consciousness in social thought /
Philip Hodgkiss.
      p. cm.
  Includes bibliographical references and index.
  ISBN 0–485–00441–0 (case : alk. paper) – ISBN 0–485–00629–4 (pbk. : alk. paper)
  1. Sociology–Philosophy. 2. Thought and thinking. I. Title.

HM511 .H63 2001
301'.01–dc21   00–067640

Typeset by RefineCatch Limited, Bungay, Suffolk
Printed and bound in Great Britain by
MPG Books Ltd, Bodmin, Cornwall

This book is dedicated to the memory of my mother and father.

CONTENTS

PART II

PREFACE

The aim of this book is to assess whether or not the concept of consciousness can be recovered to reveal its salience in *social* analysis, though it is not a systematic or comprehensive history of ideas of the period in question; excellent legacies exist of that type elsewhere as in H. Stuart Hughes (1958) or in Hawthorn (1976) or more recently in Morris (1991) or Tarnas (1996). In considering the prospects for a unified, naturalistic theory of consciousness Flanagan writes: "Besides the troika of phenomenology, psychology, and neuroscience, evolutionary biology and cultural and psychological anthropology will also be crucial players" (Flanagan, in Block *et al.*, (eds.), 1997, p. 101) Though sociology, significantly, is omitted, in many texts in this area it is often the author's aim to tightly argue their own case over and against the high points of the literature with which they assume such an intimacy on the part of the reader that nothing further needs rehearsal. The intention, here, is to show more courtesy to the reader by drawing connections of line and lineage, to chart sometimes divergent points of reference often by shedding light on tracts lately cast in shadow, with the aim of designating a thorough-going legacy of the concept of consciousness.

I trust that specialist colleagues across the disciplinary range will grant me licence to cover their ground, with only moderate levels of righteous indignation at the presumption. My reservation in this regard is only tempered by a growing sense during the writing of this book of the legacy to the account of mind and consciousness of countless, nameless authors from various ancient traditions whose insights have been co-opted by proxy into modern thought.

ACKNOWLEDGEMENTS

I would like to thank the following for their encouragement and support in the writing of this book: Stephen Edgell, Gary Littlejohn and the late David Boulton. Correspondence at various points from Paul Hirst, Margaret Archer and Chris Bryant encouraged me to approach the task in hand rather more critically. I am also indebted to Mary Searle-Chatterjee who endeavoured to get me to think more anthropologically! All the shortcomings of this monograph are, however, mine alone. I am grateful to Tristan Palmer, editor at Athlone, for his consistently sound advice and guidance and to Margaret Sugden who worked diligently and patiently in the production of the manuscript.

PART I

1

INTRODUCTION

POSING THE PROBLEM (AND STAGE SETTING)

What construction exactly are we to put on our title *The Making of The Modern Mind*? Precisely what might be signified by *making* or by *mind* for that matter? Certainly the modern mind was not formed from out of the void but was there at its own making. It did not arise fully fledged at the appointed hour but was the agent of its own creation. Yet life, too, fashioned the mind to order and conditioned its reflexive arc. Each of us lives out this contradiction but can seldom make sense of it unaided. Instead we have recourse to the available accounts – what has been 'made of' this process in the various reaches of social thought. The story of consciousness then becomes, in many senses, the story of competing paradigms and perspectives which, in their own terms, define it, or, conversely, define it out of existence. This will be reflected in this discussion where the legacy became not so much a question of the actual, ontological status of consciousness – albeit an Archimedean point – but rather whether it is thinkable or unthinkable according to the lights of a series of persuasive positions. Their parochial nature – with each going thus far and no further across the academic range – compounds the 'now you see it, now you don't' status of consciousness, as intellectual empires rise and fall in swift succession. But what of this legacy should we seek to retain? In his later work the great American sociologist C. Wright Mills believed that 'the sociological imagination' involved understanding the expansive historical picture expressed in its meaning for both the 'external career' *and* 'inner life' of individuals. Here, is thrown up the region where the intricate relations of history and biography intersect and where the *public issues* of social structure and the *personal troubles* of the private individual (the self) interact. Grasping this, Mills felt, was the means of making a difference to the quality of life in our time. He was undoubtedly right in that but, ironically, he himself was in part responsible for a retreat from ever imagining the relation of history and biography. Why this laudable project came to be endangered forms the substance of our story. We will have to thumb the historical record to piece together how and why 'inner life' and the 'external' world were to be so very nearly lost to the imagination and imagination itself to be allowed to flicker and all but die.

Firstly, and most straightforwardly, the intention is to re-cover the ground both theoretically and methodologically, suggested by the concept consciousness – whatever, at this stage, that is taken to mean. This endeavour is badly needed in the area of social science dominated by sociology because overviews of the meaning and significance of consciousness that have both an individual *and* social dimension are comparatively rare. Consciousness as a term is often used quite unproblematically to designate beliefs that are held – individually and/or collectively – at any one point in time and consciousness as a practical property or achievement is not at issue. The relative fortunes of a concept of consciousness in recent sociology, social-psychology, psychology and philosophy forms the immediate context for this discussion. Whilst consciousness has become inadvertently buried away in some areas of sociology, or sent hence unceremoniously in other areas such as social-psychology, it has undergone a surprising renaissance in recent popular psychology and philosophy. Others, have sought to demonstrate a connection between consciousness and mathematics and physics – in particular quantum mechanics (see Penrose (1995) and Zohar and Marshall (1993)) – and a concept of consciousness has also featured in popular texts in the area of physical science, particularly neurology (see Sacks, 1986 and Rose, 1993). Specialisms in the academic division of labour have lent the problem of consciousness the appearance of layers – much like an onion, where the peeling away of each successive layer does not reveal a fleshy inside or the essence of 'onionness' but more, and simultaneously less, of the same: all layers make it whole organically and without any one layer there would be an inevitable inward collapse. Choosing which layers will form the focus of attention is a value-relevant (in Weber's sense of the term) and, ultimately, practical consideration. In the case of consciousness there is quite literally an organic problem with the innermost layer for dissection being the brain. This is often couched in terms of the mind–body problem or the mind–brain problem as a relationship, to turn the couplings around, between the physical and (apparently) non–physical. Again, depending upon the academic division of labour, this question might become the preserve of philosophers, psychologists or neurologists. It will not be the purpose of this analysis to dwell here. How the water of the (physical) brain turns into the wine of consciousness (McGinn, 1993, p. 1) is a question that cannot detain this discussion long. Whether it is ultimately unanswerable as some appear to think (McGinn, 1993, Nagel, 1986) and which itself, as an issue, has now generated a great deal of debate, (Flanagan, 1992; Humphrey,1993; Searle 1994) will not be addressed.

It is easier said than done to range a discussion across several disciplines where the terms and points of reference might be divergent. Additionally the terminology in one perspective might mean something quite different elsewhere (for example, 'functionalism' in psychology where 'mind' is what the brain does and 'consciousness' is to some degree presence of mind as commonly understood and 'functionalism' in sociology where the social system coheres through shared values). In considering the currency of a concept of consciousness right across the social sciences the question arises as to whether or not this is actually, in any significant respect, always the same concept. Block (Block in Block *et al.*, 1997, p. 375), for one, has indicated the problem of cross-purposes attendant on the analysis of consciousness – though as a concept it is not unique in that. The problem of the prospect of cross-purposes is a very real one. Nevertheless, whilst many studies in the area do have their own idiosyncratic points of reference there is usually sufficient common ground and the marshalling of enough relevant data and evidence to come to recognise a centre of gravity forming in and around consciousness, though this is only half of the story because broad agreement about what consciousness might be develops at a tangent to considerations of whether or not it is at all the right quarry to pursue. *Secondly*, therefore, there is an attempt to inquire whether or not it is feasible, or advisable, to set about recovering consciousness from the premature obscurity to which it has been consigned in a great deal of social science and philosophy. Ironically whilst consciousness has been duly excised from the agenda of large areas of social thought, most recently in the cases of post-structuralism and postmodernism though the trend is not new, radical alternative versions of consciousness have begun to appear as the nostrums and noetics of 'New Age' insight into the human condition – many of which, in turn, are themselves not new. This indicates how wide, potentially, is the legacy and constituency of consciousness. It should be borne in mind that the western philosophical tradition draws on wider visionary and revelatory sources of knowledge which have been built into the literature on consciousness often without attribution. From the more centrally located neoplatonism there ranges out the influences of Hermes Trismegistos, Zoroaster, the Kabbalists, the Upanishads (influencing Schopenhauer), Paracelsus, Jacob Boehme (influences on Hegel and Nietzsche) and Swedenborg (whom Kant admired). There are, of course, others. In the twentieth century there has been rich cross-fertilization of ideas, ranging from literature to politics and philosophy, that have connected thinkers from differing traditions. Whilst this analysis will remain in the mainstream such contributions need to be recognized tributaries.

Thirdly, consciousness is explored as an issue pertaining to actively becoming conscious of the social and historical world. Here, the focus of attention is perhaps best captured by the expressions 'consciousness raising', at an individual and inter-group level, and 'class consciousness,' for example, at the level of state and society. An obvious complexity in the concept consciousness stems from its equal utility in describing the awareness of the individual *and* the group. As Hobbes recognised: 'When two, or more men, know of one and the same fact, they are said to be CONSCIOUS of it one to another; which is as much as to know it together' (Hobbes, 1968, pp. 131–132). It could be that consciousness considered first individualistically then collectively is not, in fact, the same kind of concept in both cases. That possibility has to be considered seriously but should there be grounds for consistency across the board in consciousness conceptually, the connections between the two aspects (individual and collective) becomes a substantive issue. In various strains of social determinism and social behaviourism, ranging from Marx and Durkheim, in their different ways, right up to Mead, an hiatus or lacuna between collective and individual consciousness is hardly conceivable. Consciousness *is* a social product and that's that. The dualism of the collective and individual disappears altogether and there is no separation when communication and language are seen as the essentially social precondition for what takes place in individual consciousness.

The first part of this discussion, comprised of four chapters, sets the scene and is meant to be informative and descriptive rather than critical and analytical whilst the second part is much more interrogative of positions and perspectives considered. In a loosely chronological way, Chapter Two explores the legacy of philosophical thought to the investigation of consciousness. The three enduring themes that undoubtedly form a contribution are what the self and consciousness are taken to be, the subject–object relation and whether anything ranging from existence (ontology) to reality can be established with anything like certainty. Practitioners new to the field might not be looking for reality to be doubted or for the individual, *per se*, to be called into question, but such uncertainty inevitably attends consciousness, which has to be approached by way of other uncertainties – reality and the individual. There is a need, then, to review the way in which philosophy since the seventeenth century has struggled to establish the indubitability of reality whilst perpetuating the division of subject and object with a consequent failure to find adequate grounds for belief in the existence of either. The points of reference are obvious ones: Descartes and rationalism, Hume and empiricism, Kant and Hegel and idealism. Chapter Three is, in many senses, a pivotal chapter covering as it does the paradoxical position of consciousness in the thought of classical Marxism. The issues considered here include Marx's concept of 'Man', the role of praxis, what might be meant by ideology, reification and hegemony and the contribution of the classical Marxists to the materialist conception of consciousness. In fact, this analysis of consciousness emerged from a concern with mainstream sociological questions: why do men obey?; what is social change and what are its processes?; and, most informatively, do concepts like ideology, reification and hegemony in the lexicon of Marxism explain the persistence and acceptance of a self-evident social order? It becomes apparent from all the relevant sources that the authors of the classical literature concerned with these questions were themselves steeped in the tradition of the problem of consciousness – particularly in their reaction against idealism in philosophy – and that the answers to the above questions, such as there can be any, still seem to hang on what is made of consciousness. We need to renew a dialogue with the concept of consciousness that was second nature to the authors of the classical literature in this area. Chapter Four considers late nineteenth- and early twentieth-century social thought where the concern with consciousness – even in its outright repudiation – becomes heightened. Here lie the origins of irrationalism with Schopenhauer and Nietzsche, the contributions of empiriocriticism and pragmatism and the work of Mach, James, Bergson, Dilthey and the *Geisteswissenschaften* tradition in particular which bridge over into the twentieth century. After reviewing a variety of perspectives including structuralism and logical empiricism the discussion, in Part Two, Chapter Five, then concentrates upon the contribution of phenomenology, which feeds eventually into sociology. Contained here, in juxtaposition with the central review of phenomenology, will be an outline of the contribution to the debate on consciousness of Durkheim, Pareto, Weber, Schütz, Mannheim, the Sociology of Knowledge and the Social Construction of Reality perspective, Simmel and the Chicago School, Mead and symbolic interactionism, C. Wright Mills and ethnomethodology.

It is the purpose of Chapter Six to review the contribution of Wittgenstein and Ryle and, in juxtaposition with Heidegger, the contributions of Sartre and Merleau-Ponty are considered as are the contribution of Foucault and post-structuralism. Quite new and radical interpretations of the thought of Marx form the counterpoint to the chapter. Recent developments in sociology and anthropology that touch on the question of consciousness are considered in Chapter Seven. An additional level of analysis is that of comparatively recent psychology which has distanced itself from the erstwhile behaviourist rejection of consciousness. Whilst having itself unique insights to offer, this approach, outlined in Chapter Seven, ironically enough, often uses the philosophical literature in the area as a point of reference for its own endeavours. Most of the 'new' psychologists of consciousness have been influenced by the pioneering work on consciousness of the psychologist and philosopher William James. Here, related concepts such as the self have been discussed in relation to consciousness and the idea of the narrative self has emerged which has lead to an emphasis on language. In the case of Dennett this, in turn, evokes the insights of Wittgenstein. That consciousness may be inessential, not entering into intelligent activity at levels of self-awareness and self-monitoring, or that it may be an epiphenomenon, merely the escaping 'steam' from the 'engine', has exercised the minds of the new philosopher – psychologists of consciousness. So, too, has the temptation to deal with consciousness by reference to computational models. Some of the recurring reference points in the literature of this type are generically alien to sociology. Self-conscious bats, brains in vats, zombies, conscious computers, blindsight and perceptual conundra, (such as whether the world is experienced by each of us the same, often using the instance of perception of colour), whilst perfectly legitimate lines of non-social enquiry, do not resound with history. In the analysis attempted here, for the same reason, there is no engaging with thought experimentation as is the case in some philosophy. In addition at this point the academic areas designated by 'social constructionism' and 'discursive psychology' are reviewed to assess the significance of their much more socially minded approach.

Chapter Eight forms the conclusion. Here, there is reflection on the merits of concepts out of favour in certain quarters: memory, imagination and emotion. At this stage there is also consideration of in what sense we can conceive of collective consciousness. What are taken up for discussion are those issues and theoretical questions with most obvious relevance to a socially and historically informed analysis, though, ironically, any specific instances of social and historical transition remain, as such, beyond the bounds of the present remit. An ideal account of consciousness would trace its evolution over historical time in juxtaposition with the emergence of a concept of consciousness. The role of consciousness in child development and the life-course more generally would also need to be considered. Sociology, too, in its own way, has explored the relationship between phylogeny and ontogeny but seldom to the degree of speculation that might suggest that the stages of cultural or cognitive evolution of our human ancestors is reflected in the phases of mental development of the child (phylogeny recapitulated in ontogeny). In fact, evidence and data of this order garnered in the writing of this book will have to be left to a subsequent volume concerned specifically with those ideas.

CONSCIOUSNESS – DEFINING THE CONCEPT

Whether consciousness always accompanies mental states has per-plexed philosophers and is indicative of their more traditional con-cern with mind rather than consciousness. The philosophical study of mind seeks to account for what mind is and for mental functioning and has been preoccupied historically with the relationship between body and mind (the classic instance being Descartes). Nevertheless, whether it be in emphasising mind as the domain of the association of ideas, as in Hume, or mind actually structuring experience, as in Kant in the tradition of German idealism, the philosophical emphasis has been upon mind as private and covert. If we reflect on having been asleep or 'knocked out' we would undoubtedly concede to a loss of consciousness but not to the loss of our minds. Mind seems to con-note a more permanent and enduring inclusiveness – tied to the ongoing project of the person – that survives the fleeting moment. This state in itself has come to be referred to as *intransitive* con-sciousness, whilst, following James, *transitive* consciousness connects with cases, states, objects and things in full flow. It is this conscious-ness that is awake to the transient states of the here and now. But this is not as straightforward as it might seem, as the philosopher Leibniz (as reported in Bourdieu, 1986, p. 474) concluded that 'we are automatons in three-quarters of what we do' and William James that 'a good third of our psychic life' consists of not-yet-articulate inten-tions and schemes of thought (premonitions). Leaving on one side whether the ratios posited here are invariable properties of physi-ology and psychology, the point to be taken is that the plane of men-tal life is, most of the time, on auto-pilot. In contrast, when the mind *is* focussed upon something it is so to the exclusion of all other pos-sible directions of attention. The conscious mind cannot, as it were, chew gum and walk at the same time; that is, there are high levels of isolation of, and concentration upon, the issue as defined by the sub-ject. 'Auto-pilot' mode, it has been suggested (Jaynes, 1990), allows the organism not to be tripped up by its own self-consciousness. The range of things human beings can accomplish that do not enter into consciousness has been logged by psychologists and it is undoubtedly the case that consciousness constitutes only a comparatively small part of mental life. In fact, Jaynes has contended that most reasoning is not conscious (for example Einstein, whose discoveries often flitted into his mind whilst shaving) and that consciousness is not necessarily the medium for thinking or learning – i.e., consciousness is not primarily conceptually based.

We cannot ignore the tensile nature of consciousness: sometimes slack, sometimes taut, sometimes tied in knots. We are in and out of consciousness with great rapidity: from automaton into consciousness; from one exclusive focus of intentionality to another. Referring to Husserl's unpublished writings Merleau-Ponty remarks that '[c]onsciousness is in the first place not a matter of "I think that" but of "I can"' (Merleau-Ponty, 1962, p. 137). According to phenomenology, the person is given over to the object rather than thinking themselves thinking it, as it were, inwardly. Consciousness cannot be ignorant of its intentions and Merleau-Ponty concludes that 'all consciousness is consciousness of something' (p. 5). This remains consistent with the inner perception of rationalism and, for that matter, empiricism, and with the outer perception of phenomena anticipated in the synthesising activity of the subject, as in Kant's idealism. What is different with phenomenology, Merleau-Ponty would claim, is that *it* remains with the object to which consciousness is perpetually directed in unity. This process of intentionality might be compounded by a process identified by the French philosopher Bergson that the mind exhibits a 'reducing valve' filter to prevent itself becoming overwhelmed by all possible sources of perception. Consciousness, then, concentrates attention on a process of perception. Examples from ordinary experience are insistent and fascinating: to be unable to recall a 'fact' for it then to be tickertaped into consciousness hours or days later; to come to one's 'senses' after a long period of absorption in something; to remember a loved one after hours of forgetfulness when busy at work – shocked by the scale of neglect; to look back on oneself as a stranger, hardly the same 'you' at all, and; to 'make up' one's mind. We may turn away from ourselves and witness the rapt inattention and lack of eye contact in our compatriot when they stare, not into the middle distance, but, somehow blankly, into an inner distance to grapple with what they are after. We can recognise this for what it is: thought, reflection, musing, and so on and can construe, further, this activity as distraction, boredom or extra special insight depending upon our reflection on its merits when it is eventually made public. We tend to assume that something approximating our own experience of introspection is going on but without a great deal of actual evidence for it.

There is evidence that consciousness is actively future oriented. Mill remarked in the 1850s that '[t]he human faculties of perception, judgement, discriminative feeling, mental activity, and even moral preference, are exercised only in making a choice' (Mill, 1991, p. 65). William James's early psychological definition of 'mentality' also emphasised the choice of means to attain future ends. There is subsequent data from a wide range of sources that consciousness is most clearly demonstrably engaged when there is a novel choice to be made between various possible courses of action, i.e., as solutions are sought to problems of a non-routine kind. As Jaynes remarks: 'If consciousness is the mere impotent shadow of action, why is it more intense when action is most hesitant?' (Jaynes, 1990, p. 11). James a century earlier, had raised this very same question. Human consciousness seems to be there to recognise a critical crossroads for the individual themself and for others. Consciousness is being equal to that situation as the medium for assessing the possibilities of how to get to grips with the world. According to Bateson (1987) the mind is primarily a purposive power of discrimination motivated to make connections and aggregate differences, thus creating order in the world as a product of a state of mind. Nonetheless, consciousness is highly contingent in the human condition and only prevails when not overridden by more physical or emotional automatic 'systems'. Schopenhauer provides us with a catalogue of human failings and James, who had read his Schopenhauer, adds further dimensions to the inventory of fallibility. This creature, the human being, now hating, now loving, now willing, now reasoning has, as we know, a frame of mind alternately engaged. Around this, James arranges other foibles: we change with the time of day, the seasons, with age and when we are tired, hungry and frustrated; our moods 'colour' what we see, what we favour and from what we turn away. James says that we see things in new lights from one year – perhaps one moment – to the next: friends and lovers, the beauty of nature and the life of the mind can all lose their appeal. The quality and intensity of the given reality undergoes change. In addition, as we have seen, the mind is necessarily selective about what it chooses to consider at all, i.e., that which will become *real*, at the expense of the rest, through perception and definition. Experience is, thus, manufactured. Not only *can* such characteristic features be exhibited in the view of James (and that of his recent adherent's) but *will* be in any number of given social, historical circumstances. Dennett's 'multi-drafts model' of consciousness, an attempt to sell out the 'Cartesian Theatre', is a variation on this theme of competing voices trying to get heard above the general din of proto-consciousness so that they alone become the spokesperson at the present-ation of consciousness. Although Dennett's model might seem a radical departure from James's stream-of-consciousness idea when it substitutes implicit discontinuity and a plurality of streams, it has a great deal in common with the original position in stressing an 'in' channel of a range of possibilities out of which is selected *the* performance (for example, is this the 'confident me' for public consumption today?).

In St Augustine's terms consciousness 'anticipates', 'attends' and 'remembers' so that what consciousness 'anticipates passes through what it attends into what it remembers; and what it remembers then provides the substratum for what it anticipates. Here are three modalities of our conscious experience, an orientation to past, present and future, the three always existing in a relationship of tension but always forming a cognitive whole' (Cohen and Rapport, 1995, p. 8). Foucault says that ' Condillac defined the necessary and sufficient operations for representation to deploy itself as knowledge: reminiscence, self-consciousness, imagination, memory' (Foucault, 1974, p. 318). Consciousness appears to have been transformed over historical time from existing coextensively with being in the world, to becoming the medium for being present with a whole range of qualities that transcend the moment – self, identity, imagination and memory, and so on. It is almost as if over time consciousness assumed tacit responsibility for these other properties, i.e., it had acquired content and depth and also echoed through the outer reaches of social and historial space. The legacy from sources stretching from Kant to Dilthey reveals a range of 'consciousnesses': the unbridled experience of life itself; the content of experience; the psyche and individual subjective consciousness; transcendental consciousness and so on (see Volosinov,1973). In anticipation of what is outlined in subsequent chapters, it is possible to identify in a programmatic way three major dimensions pertaining to consciousness. The first dimension, if it is conceded that consciousness can be isolated in this manner at all, is the unique *capacities* that are present if consciousness is in evidence. Examples, here, would be 'tensions' of consciousness as in Bergson, 'intentionality' inherited from phenomenology and the 'multi-drafts' model of consciousness devised by Dennett which all indicate, as will be seen, what consciousness is doing at any one point in time. The second is comprised of a whole range of ancillary states and concepts without which consciousness would be inconceivable. They are in some sense the 'shape' which consciousness takes and the means by which we could recognise it at all. Included, here, are those properties very similar in kind to the capacities of consciousness, such as memory and will, but which themselves act as vehicles for the articulation of that person's sojourn in the world, such as the self, identity and personality. These interrelated aspects of consciousness are inseparable from language and the corporeality of the individual within the matrix of social and historical time including the maturation of the subject during the life-course. The third dimension is the crucible of consciousness in the social and historical world, the complexity of which is hard to distil in a short passage but would certainly encompass the determination of social structure, social relations and social forms based on the mode of production in the creation of material life; the making of a real world and one appearing also distorted and thing-like (the workings of ideology, reification and hegemony), and the coexistence of 'multiple realities' competing for attention. Here, too, is evidence that the experience is not subjective and singular but objective and collective in a shared orientation to the world. Whether there is a common understanding of that experience, a common identity and will to act in common is, however, an uncertain confluence in practice.

Both Marx and Nietzsche concluded that consciousness emerged out of the need for communication and 'new' psychologists of consciousness such as Jaynes and Ornstein have described how consciousness evolved over millennia. In the main these psychologists see consciousness as having emerged as adaptive to a stable, though confrontational, world. From detailed historical case studies (Hirst, 1994) sociology has provided insight into how social and cultural experience filters what human beings are able to recognise as relevant. Consciousness for Hirst is 'the capacity to construct and narrate courses of action' (Hirst, 1994, p. 47) – the capacity for social and practical action – which 'enables us to "place" ourselves, to reflect and review our performances and our relation to others' (p. 51). Consciousness, then, can be defined as a present juxtaposition where narratives and discourses of what is understood about the world are brought into play with things past, said and unsaid, to orient the future project. The present 'juxtaposition' (as capacity) *is* consciousness; the 'narratives and discourses' import meaning; 'the world' and the 'past' are social and historical containing the 'future project' which is, itself, the culmination of the momentum of the selves of the life-course. There is sufficient evidence to suggest that consciousness has evolved in human beings over millennia as a result of the acquisition of language and increasingly proficient adaptation to the environment. But, unlike natural selection, the creation of different cultural forms and cultural interpretations of reality, both natural and social, has bounded the possibilities of consciousness. This might be interpreted in terms of 'historicism', or what can be seen as the 'horizon' of the possible in any specific time or place, or, what can be *said* about the world in one given time or place. But there are other interpretations along these lines not at all sympathetic to consciousness which, too, indicate the 'time–space-boundedness' of meaningful human experience. Althusser's 'problematic', Foucault's 'episteme' and Habermas's idea of ideology as 'systematically distorted communication' each stem from a recognition of historically specific systems of power and interests forming the web of categories which constitute the limits of what it is possible to imagine and mean at a given historical moment (it is debatable in the work of these theorists the extent to which this is an unconscious process).

In fact, terms of reference which signal the centrality of consciousness are, to critics of this position, merely empty and superfluous rhetoric. Indeed, there is a line of argument that considers consciousness a gloss term for a wide range of modalities and, as such, quite useless. There is not, therefore, an *it* to be explained; thinking is a polymorphous activity by this light. Interpreting such activities as understanding and memory as mental (even present in the arch anti-Cartesian Ryle) is, in itself, misleading. Avoiding this mentalistic legacy, in consequence, means having immediate recourse – in Ockham's razor fashion – to language. After having mentioned Ryle, to make play on his illustration of a collegiate university is helpful. In this view the alleged capacities of consciousness are the colleges but there is no university (i.e., consciousness itself) to ask after. Moreover, the colleges themselves can only be construed as they give publicly confirmed accounts of themselves. Hence, what is surplus to requirements is a mental entity which is different in kind to the actions and words that are actually actively constituting thinking. In addition, it has now been observed in text books in sociology (for example, Bradley, 1996) that in postmodern thought, identity, untainted by any association with 'grand narratives', has supplanted consciousness – itself formerly viewed as the vital, if problematic, link between structure and action. Although it *is* possible to argue in Sartrean fashion that identity, rather than replacing consciousness (both theoretically and ontologically), is, in fact, *for* consciousness like any other object in the real world, it would appear that after centuries of being held fast in the opposition of body and soul, mind and body, consciousness is now to be found caught firmly on the cleft stick of meaning and materiality. The relationships between percepts and concepts, a world of 'blooming, buzzing confusion' and a world of 'things said' has always been at issue but, it was assumed classic-ally, the former was being incrementally transformed into the latter in the life-course of individuals and, over time, historically. But now the world, apparently, has ceased to bloom, buzz *and* confuse – it is a nonentity apart from meaning. It is to that prospect that this discussion now turns.

2

THE COMING OF AGE OF CONSCIOUSNESS IN PHILOSOPHY

Without consciousness there is no person.
(Locke, 1977, p. 170)

THE SELF AND IDENTITY - INTRODUCTION

Although the following discussion begins with modern philosophy, its reference points lie, inevitably, with the Ancient Greeks. Heraclitus, for example, contended that everything is in a state of flux, where permanence is an illusion – so, reality differs from the appearances we observe. His contemporary, Parmenides, concluded that thought and reality are the same, whilst a later thinker, Protagoras, concluded that things actually are as they appear to different individuals. The problems of change, appearance, reality and relativism still form the cornerstones in this area of social thought. When it came to the self, Plato and Aristotle each embodied divergent positions. Generally speaking, Plato begins a tradition that insists that there is a composite of a corporeal body and an incorporeal – and immortal – soul that is contained within the body of human beings. What has to be conceded in this Platonic view is that the soul is, or is identical with, the person: I am my soul. Though there is little squaring off of the soul against the self in modern social science this is the corollary of Plato. If Plato can be described as a 'dualist', Aristotle is, by the same token, a 'monist'. For Aristotle, for something to have a soul is for it to be alive – the form of a particular living body. The soul cannot be separated from the body and, by implication, is not immortal. Although Aristotle's overall view is less clear cut – he contends at one point that Abstract Intellect is eternal – and the differences between the two philosophers is complicated by their different terms of reference (for example, the meaning of 'form' in the two philosophies), this is where the scene is set. A concern with the self, identity and consciousness *was* the legacy of the ancient Greeks but took a particular turn in the early modern period with the view of Descartes, of Hobbes, of Locke and that of his critic Butler, and of Leibniz.

RATIONALISM AND EMPIRICISM – DESCARTES TO HUME

After resolving to doubt everything, Descartes had believed that the only thing of which he could be certain was that he was a thinking being ('I think therefore I am'). The conclusion at which Descartes arrived led him to believe that the world of matter, including the body, had no part to play in mind or consciousness. He then spent a great deal of time trying to establish how one affects the other. Cartesian dualism of body and mind – 'the ghost in the machine' – constitutes an ultimate separation of the physical and the mental; soul and mind are equated and the human mind is what he calls a 'thinking thing' which is not extended in length, width and depth and does not participate in anything pertaining to body. For him, the idea he possesses of the human mind is incomparably more distinct than that of any corporeal thing. In sum, he says that he had concluded that he 'was a substance the whole essence or nature of which is to think, and that for its existence there is no need of any place, nor does it depend on any material thing; so that this "me", that is to say, the soul by which I am what I am, is entirely distinct from body, and is even more easy to know than is the latter; and even if body were not, the soul would not cease to be what it is' (Descartes, 1997, p. 92). He continues in this vein as he considers that 'our soul is in its nature entirely independent of body, and in consequence that it is not liable to die with it. And then, inasmuch as we observe no other causes capable of destroying it, we are naturally inclined to judge that it is immortal' (p. 109). Elsewhere, though, he is more equivocal about what this means for the body and at one point says that it is not sufficient that the 'rational soul' 'should be lodged in the human body like a pilot in his ship, unless perhaps for the moving of its members, but that it is necessary that it should also be joined and united more closely to the body in order to have sensations and appetites similar to our own, and thus to form a true man' (p. 109). Indeed, experience, as Descartes defines it, depends upon mind and body in intimate union and to be a substance whose whole essence or nature consisted in thinking within which truths inhere as Descartes held, has more complex properties and locations than might be thought on first acquaintance. Whilst self-conscious reflection is the preserve of the mind, memory, imagination and the passions are incorporated in the body and are dealt with on materialist–mechanical lines, and the impression is given that there is a need for the inner domination of passion by thought. But by this time Descartes's identification of himself with a 'thinking thing' had already begun to tantalise.

Hobbes thought he detected in Descartes a return to the scholastics when he saw him apparently identifying thought with the thinker, the exercise of understanding with that which understands, the use of intellect with the intellect itself, and so on. All philosophers, Hobbes contends, distinguish a subject from its faculties and activities. To this reproach Descartes responds by saying he intended nothing of the kind and that he does not deny that the thinker is distinct from their own thought. Nevertheless, it is clear in Descartes what attracted Hobbes's criticism in this regard. Total identification of the human subject and thinking leads to obscurity in Hobbes's view. For him, that which is conscious – 'I', 'myself' – is distinct from consciousness. The idea that mind construed as a spiritual substance is, in fact, as such meaningless can be traced back to Hobbes's *mechanism* with the mind being viewed as simply a body in mechanical motion. Human beings, for Hobbes, are self-moving machines directed towards self preservation and the possession of power. Interestingly enough, too, Hobbes might be viewed as a precursor of a tradition, culminating in Wittgenstein as we shall see, which stresses the linking together and conjoining of names for things as the real ribbon of reason. Though, Hobbes confirms that the Greeks had just one word for both speech and reason 'not that they thought there was no Speech without Reason; but no Reasoning without Speech' (Hobbes, 1968, p. 106) he, himself, remarks: 'Whosoever looketh into himself and considereth what he does when he does think, opine, reason, hope, fear &c. and upon what grounds, he shall thereby read and know what are the

thoughts and passions of all other men upon the like occasions'
(quoted in Evans and Deehan, 1990, p. 148). Although a great deal of
emphasis is placed on memory and imagination in Hobbes – the former being linked to experience, the latter being the train of thought
which, as mental discourse, is distinct from verbal discourse –
humans are essentially machines and consciousness is determined.
Things are connected in thought or our memory because they were so
connected in our original experience of them (though, qualities of
experience do not inhere in the object but, rather, *in* the experiencing
person). In turn, voluntary acts are associated with the will and,
ultimately, with the body. Similarly, Spinoza (1992) so closely identifies mind and body that there can be no survival of the mind
beyond the lifetime of the body. They are one and the same substance and ideas are connected in the way they are because of the
actual connection of things. Whilst Spinoza does not see the world
from the point of view of an 'I' he still regards self-seeking and self-
preservation as the guiding threads in human behaviour, holding that
volition, striving or desiring is the supreme human faculty. Reference
to Descartes, Hobbes and Spinoza is enormously helpful but it is
really with Locke that this discussion of consciousness *per se* begins
in earnest.

Locke divides our ideas (i.e., understanding) into *sensations* and
reflection. The former are the impressions made on our senses by
external material objects from without whilst the latter draws on that
which the senses have provided. In fact, *reflection* is variously
described as being conscious of observing in ourselves, a view turned
inward upon itself and the notice the mind takes of its own operations – ideas and the passions arising from them, i.e., emotional
states. This is, in fact, contemplation of prior content garnered from
experience; *reflection* on a repository of relations to the world. The
mind is actively directed towards the object for perception to occur
and simple ideas from perception become complex through associated experience and memory. In drawing a distinction between primary and secondary qualities Locke, in prescient fashion, introduces
the prospect of a world different to our everyday perceptions opened
up to us by science but, at the same time, problematises our relation
to that fine-grained world. Primary qualities are in things even when
not being perceived or taken notice of and on which depend the
secondary qualities which have the power to produce ideas in us via

our senses and as such they do not exist if there is no perceiver. The catch-22, however, is that we must remain blissfully ignorant of the connection between primary and secondary qualities. Like Berkeley and Hume on their own accounts after him, Locke observes drily that the world of common sense and commerce should not be much affected. In fact, Locke theorises an interface between ourselves and the world hinging on what is real or unreal or what can or cannot be known and thereby is the inception of a trend. To Berkeley (1983), in criticism of Locke, a separate world of material objects is literally unthinkable it being totally incoherent to distinguish a mind-independent world from the contents of mind. Dualistic talk about such a mind-independent world is, in fact, of nothing at all – it is empty and meaningless, i.e., it is about the literally inconceivable, signifying nothing. Thoughts, which cannot, of course, exist outside the mind, are exhausted by their relation to sensations. Experiences are, in fact, of other experiences. His entire account hangs on this presupposition. Congeries of experience compose an immaterial world and the twofold distinction deployed by Locke of primary qualities of the material world becoming the secondary qualities of private experience is collapsed. Maintaining belief in the former for Berkeley amounts to what we might call today a 'useful fiction'.

Locke's analysis of the self emerges from a discussion of the question 'does the soul always think?' and is largely a first person account, i.e., of my self. Locke held, unlike Descartes, that it was mistaken to believe that the soul always thinks which also suggested fallaciously, that there is something else, besides me, that does the thinking. It is the very awareness in the act of thinking that operates in awareness of the self, and the person or self consists in the thoughts and actions which the individual *appropriates* through their consciousness. Thoughts and actions, then, are *appropriated* to form a concept of self. Locke might be described as a 'continuity theorist' (Flanagan, 1992, p. 187) or a 'successionist'. He declares : 'For, since consciousness always accompanies thinking, and it is that that makes every one to be what he calls *self*, and thereby distinguishes himself from all other thinking things: in this alone consists *personal identity* i.e. the sameness of a rational being. And as far as this consciousness can be extended backwards to any past action or thought, so far reaches the identity of that *person*: it is the same *self* now it was then, and it is by the same *self* with this present one that now reflects on it, that that action was done' (Locke, 1977, p. 162). He continues along these lines and summarises quite conclusively: 'This may show us wherein *personal identity* consists: not in the identity of substance, but, as I have said, in the identity of *consciousness*' (p. 168). Both body and mind, in this view, inherit the past as they inherit the future. The conscious self thereby has continuity as benefactor and beneficiary. For Locke, the human personality was an essential psychosomatic unity of mind and body which he saw as having identity as both a bodily organism and as a person. The former is participation in the same continued life whilst the latter depends on the reach of consciousness. Butler disputed the claim, apparent in Locke, that consciousness constitutes or makes personal identity. For Butler, consciousness of personal identity *presupposes* personal identity; self and personal identity is substance which endures and to which consciousness refers. He is convinced that 'though present consciousness of what we at present do and feel is necessary to our being the persons we now are; yet present consciousness of past actions or feelings is not necessary to our being the same persons who performed those actions, or had those feelings' (quoted in Flew, 1964, p. 167). If Locke is right, Butler argues on what grounds could it be imagined that our present self cares what befalls 'It' tomorrow? This acute problem of personal teleology has haunted this approach. All the implications of Locke's position of accountability before God and life after death focus Butler's mind wonderfully. Leibniz, too, was sufficiently engaged to put pen to paper in rejoinder to Locke.

In response to Locke's view of the soul, Leibniz volunteers that he is of the opinion that there is nothing in the intellect that has not been before in the senses, except the intellect itself and the forms of the intellect. In doing so, he erases the inevitable logic of Locke's *tabula rasa* marked upon by sense perception and experience, and simultaneously etches out the system inherited by Kant and which came to figure in his epistemology. Leibniz links souls with memory which provides them with *consecutiveness*. The rational soul or mind is when we are raised to knowledge of ourselves in the grasping of necessary eternal truths. The soul, then, when raised to the level of reason is reckoned a mind. He says that it is well 'to distinguish between *perception*, which is the inner state of the monad [i.e., soul] representing external things, and *apperception*, which is *conscious-*

ness, or the reflective knowledge of this inner state, and which is not given to all souls, nor at all times to the same soul' (Leibniz, 1973, p. 197). Souls, it appears, are capable of performing acts of reflection. Each soul knows the infinite and knows everything – but 'confusedly'; the result of the impressions which the whole universe makes on us. In answer to Locke maintaining that the mind does not always think and is without perception in dreamless sleep, Leibniz maintains that death is but a sleep and that the mind is always 'awake' – at least to minute perceptions which also figure in personal identity. He says:

> These insensible perceptions are also the signs and constituents of personal identity: the individual is characterised by the traces or expressions of his previous states which these perceptions preserve by connecting them with his present state . . . though the individual himself may not be conscious of them, that is to say though he may no longer expressly recollect them.
>
> (Leibniz, 1973, pp. 156–157)

HUME'S EMPIRICISM

Of all possible witnesses to the import of the issues of self and identity, questions should perhaps be asked at this turn of David Hume. But what and who would be forthcoming? The pregnant pause may be imagined but something like the following might be occurring. Hume says: 'For my part, when I enter most intimately into what I call *myself*, I always stumble on some particular perception or other, of heat or cold, light or shade, love or hatred, pain or pleasure. I never catch *myself* at any time without a perception, and never can observe anything but the perception . . . the rest of mankind . . . are nothing but a bundle or collection of different perceptions, which succeed each other with inconceivable rapidity, and are in a perpetual flux and movement' (Hume, 1962, pp. 301–302). For Hume perception is whatever can be present to the mind, through the senses or through thought and reflection. Perceptions, in turn, are divided into *impressions* and *ideas*. Hume seems to resolve the legacy of Locke's ambiguous view of the location of ideas – i.e., in the mind or between subject and object – by drawing on the term *impressions*. Images of an external object conveyed to the mind by sense perceptions is an *impression* whilst an *idea* is when the object itself is not present. He describes *impressions* as 'lively' and 'strong' and *ideas as* 'fainter' and 'weaker' perceptions. Interestingly, he remarks that the distinction is as that between feeling and thinking (he distinguishes between memory and imagination in the same fashion). Quite crucially, Hume concludes that all *ideas* are derived from *impressions* and thinking from external sense perception and feeling. *Impressions* are made up of sensation and reflection which go to make up *ideas*. Reflection is derived from *ideas* which when returned to the 'soul' (Hume's term here) produces a new *impression* of reflection. When copied by memory and imagination further ideas are produced and so on. Hume believing that all our knowledge was based on sense *impressions*, came to the conclusion that we cannot have anything like an *idea* of self, therefore, there cannot be any such thing as the self. The logic goes: from what *impression* could this *idea* possibly be derived? It could not possibly *be* an *impression*, in empiricist terms, therefore never an *idea* – at least not one that does not embody a manifest contradiction and absurdity according to him. The reality of *impressions* is taken in through the 'filter' of a conceptual apparatus that mediates *ideas*, but the intensity and primordiality of *impressions* should not be underestimated: 'In terms of both content and energy, mediated or interpreted experience involves loss – of the unique, mind-stunning power of originality. Inasmuch as our ideas are ciphers of knowledge, human knowledge itself stands under the sign of deprivation' (Appelbaum, 1996, p. 13). There is wonder and awe in the vital spark of immediacy which is lost when awareness is turned into meaning as twentieth-century existentialists recognised. The squandering of Hume's insight became evident within a generation: 'That a primacy Hume accords to immediacy is immediately lost to Kant and succeeding generations reminds us of the evanescent nature of Hume's discovery. An impression is a momentary energy configuration. It is of the moment. To form or formulate its content is to distort its identity and to obscure the awareness needed to register it' (p. 21).

Hume's view of the mind as a 'bundle', 'heap' or 'collection' of perceptions, often taken as everything he has to say on the issue, is, as such, misleading. Whilst human beings have a propensity to imagine the simplicity and continuity of identity according to Hume, it is *successive* perceptions that constitute the mind. In our common way of thinking we confound the two, but enduring identity ascribed to the mind of man is a fiction. The measure of the difference between Locke's idea of the self being carried forward and that of Hume's is that in the latter's view there are no grounds for believing in a permanent self apart from the succession of inner perceptions. It is successive perceptions that constitute the mind. Nevertheless, belief in an external world and in an integrated, substance self, seems, in Hume's view, a quirk of inference inimical to logic but indispensable to life. Indeed, Hume was concerned with human subjects not only as rational beings but also as active social beings. Unlike Descartes, for whom we just *are* selves with the self as the bearer of subjective states which generate all else, for Hume, it is history, politics and morality comprising the world of *sensibility* – both shared and public – that provides the source of the self. He distinguishes between the self as it concerns an inner-realm of the 'imagination', where it is at best something we have to go on, though ultimately fictitious, and the self as it concerns the 'passions' or the concern we take in ourselves. In Hume's view we *become* selves, so what he has to say in Book I of the *Treatise*, most often construed as the embodiment of scepticism and the entirety of a negative doctrine on the self, is modified if Book II (*The Passions*) and Book III (*Morals*) are taken into account bringing into focus a much more positive position. What begins to come together, here, with Hume is the recognition of the mythical status of the claim that the sequence must go from, first, an individual subjective experience of how it is for us (I think, therefore, I am) to, second, a construction of a shared, public world – though Hume and Kant, as will be seen, tend to arrive at this conclusion by different routes.

The question on personal identity that Hume poses for himself is this: 'What then gives us so great a propension to ascribe an identity to these successive perceptions, and to suppose ourselves possessed of an invariable and uninterrupted existence through the whole course of our lives?' (Hume, 1962, p. 303). He indicates how the trick is done in the following way: 'The reason can plainly be no other, than that the mind, in following the successive changes of the body, feels an easy passage from the surveying its condition in one moment, to the viewing of it in another, and in no particular time perceives any interruption in its actions. From which continued perception, it ascribes a continued existence and identity to the object' (p. 306) and, again, 'identity is nothing really belonging to these different perceptions, and uniting them together, but is merely a quality which we

attribute to them, because of the union of their ideas in the imagination when we reflect upon them' (p. 309). Our idea of personal
identity proceeds from a smooth, uninterrupted progression of
thought along a train of connected ideas in Hume's view and he
draws on several different analogies including, significantly as it will
turn out, that of a river to capture continuity not identity. Hume's
position here refers to other eighteenth-century philosophical points
of reference (for example, the soul) but also points forward in time
to the late-nineteenth-century psychology of William James: 'we feign
the continued existence of the perceptions of our senses, to remove
the interruption; run into the notion of a *soul*, and *self*, and *substance*, to disguise the variation. But, we may further observe, that
where we do not give rise to such a fiction, our propension to confound identity with relation is so great, that *we are apt to imagine
something unknown and mysterious, connecting the parts, beside
their relation*' (p. 304, emphasis added). Nevertheless, in this process
our distant perceptions influence each other developing in us a
present concern for our past or future pains or pleasures. But it is
memory, for Hume, that is the real source of personal identity as it
alone acquaints us with the continuance and extent of the succession
of perceptions. Although Aune (1970) suggests that a concept of
memory poses problems in the work of Hume, it would appear that
memory does not so much produce as discover personal identity by
confirming the relation of cause and effect amongst different perceptions. For Hume the soul does not remain unalterably the same for
one moment. He feels he may truly be said not to exist when he is
sound asleep and he can countenance personal annihilation without
compunction.

Hume is advising us that human beings are 'wired-up' to judge,
and looking for a customary connection is as unstoppable as is thinking whilst awake; being governed by the workings of the association
of ideas which impose a necessity on thought, minds are systems that
are essentially truth-seeking – they can do no other. Not only this, but
minds are also able to weigh up the balance of available evidence. For
him belief is more a part of the 'sensitive' than 'cognitive' parts of
human nature, leading him to the conviction that belief is never
rational since human beings can know nothing for certain. By this
token, belief in causality is a matter of learning rather than logic,
i.e., it is a psychological principle. Rational justification of the

expectation of a future occurrence being like one experienced in the past would have to proceed from the principle that those instances, of which we have had no experience, resemble those of which we have had experience – a principle derived not from reason, but from habit. Hume reflecting on the sceptical implications of his philosophy confirms that 'almost all reasoning is there reduced to experience; and the belief, which attends experience, is explained to be nothing but a peculiar sentiment, or lively conception produced by habit. Nor is this all, when we believe any thing of *external* existence, or suppose an object to exist a moment after it is no longer perceived, this belief is nothing but a sentiment of the same kind' (Hume, 1962, p. 348). The ultimate corollary of Hume's contention concerning the status of *external* existence is that we proceed as though it were there, even though there is no rational means of establishing it. The idea that lies behind this, of the 'veil of appearance', is that perception interposes between the external world and the individual. Hume's explanation of both sides of this equation attracted contemporaneous criticism. Reid claimed, quite cogently, that 'my personal identity . . . implies the continued existence of that indivisible thing that I call myself. Whatever this self may be, it is something which thinks, and deliberates and resolves, and acts, and suffers. I am not thought, I am not action, I am not feeling; I am something that thinks, and acts, and suffers' (Reid, quoted in Parfit, 1987, p. 223). Personal identity is thus construed as an all or nothing, deep further fact (see Parfit, 1987). In addition, the mind, in Reid's view, is active in perceiving both internal and external sensations; sensations – private and subjective – are the concomitant occasion of perceiving external, material objects. In Reid's common-sense realism it is possible for us to transcend a phantom world of ideas to have immediate contact with a mind-independent reality of which we are directly aware. Hume, it should be noted, remained unmoved and refused to rise to the bait.

The status of the external world and perception of it is worth remarking upon at this point, though it is a question to which this discussion will inevitably return. Notwithstanding Reid, theories of perception at this time assume that material objects in the world stimulate private sense data, but then deny that individuals are ever directly aware of public objects themselves. If the world is perceived through a 'veil of appearance' there can be no knowledge of the world. Seeds of doubt about the straightforward nature of the reality of the world had already been sown from Descartes onwards. Whether it be rationalist doubt from Descartes, or Humean (empiricist) scepticism there is a suspicion about whether reality actually exists and, should it, whether reason can do anything in its apprehension. Whilst formerly, absolute truths had been seen to exist in realms above experience, empiricism accepted truth as simply relative to the way individuals order the appearances of the world as they impress themselves on their minds. The assumption that lies behind empiricism is that the external world is only knowable through observation. This itself tends to be taken as a passive process of exclusion of those things eluding sense perception. This compilation of sense data becomes a very individual and private process, on which both truth *and* knowledge depend. In effect, this has unleashed a dogged subjectivism and solipsism on social thought: the insistence that the world exists in the individual's mind and their verbal evaluations. Experience tends to be associated with and imply private perception, i.e., how it appears to the subject – only provisionally linked to any implications for what may or may not be the case in the objective, external, material world. The paradox, here, is that although knowledge has its source in that world, for each individual certainty is possible only with regard to an individual's own private experience. Although experience is often taken in common sense to imply both that someone has come into contact with, encountered, or has been present with real, actual material objects and that the individual's awareness, perceptions or cognitions have been employed, experience in this tradition connotes how things appear to the subject rather than problematising how things may be actually ordered in an external, objective world. But the actual quality of one's own experience had already begun to figure in the Romantic tradition which, in turn, fed into idealism.

Taylor (1992a) claims that it is Montaigne, writing a generation before Hobbes and Descartes, who inaugurates a fundamental theme of modern culture by stressing that search for the self intent on coming to terms with oneself. This is not a radical disengagement of the self as in Descartes but, rather, a more profound engagement with our own particularity in a process of self-discovery. The goal is to achieve self-knowledge by seeing through everything that is self-deluding. Taylor senses that whilst the goal of achieving a disengaged grasp and, thus, control of our nature drove the enlightenment phi-losphes, Hume's inquiries were informed with a concern for coming to terms with what we really are in an engaged self-acceptance, fear-lessly taking our lives as they really are. Our lives have to be accepted and embraced for what they are in all their limitations and imper-fections and we have to be actively reconciled to the prospect of being human. Perhaps this 'squares' with Hume's epistemology when he refers to us chasing our imagination to the heavens or the utmost limit of the universe and never advancing a step beyond our-selves or our own narrow compass. Nevertheless, drawing on pre-Renaissance thought Hume in his moral philosophy utilises the idea of *sympathy*, which, in his hands, is a power that transcends habit in an imaginative leap outside of the isolation of the ego and the separ-ateness of subjectivity. Sympathy, in this view, is the prerequisite for common understanding amongst people whereby the minds of men can become mirrors to one another. Sympathy is feeling together with another human being as consciousness of our own person con-nects with that of others. Hume believed that the entire course of history had been concerned with an enlargement of our capacity to sympathise with Others very different from ourselves. Notwithstand-ing, Hume's recourse to sympathy seems to be at odds with his injunction to resist the temptation of positing a field of 'experience' beyond the physical realm. There is, in addition, always the prospect that when we turn inward we find not self-transparency but, rather, incomprehensibility and contradiction. Initiating, what would come to be described as the Romantic–expressivist tradition, Rousseau blames dependence on a world of appearance comprised of others' evaluations of us which prizes us away from (our) nature. We can no longer depend upon inner, authentic impulse and have trouble con-necting motives within ourselves. For Rousseau reason is subordin-ated to the rule of the heart and emotions and it is with them, by implication, that man's innate goodness must reside. Goodness is identified with freedom and it is discovered by turning within to tap an inner resource of sentiments, i.e., to be in touch with (one's) nature. Truth is thus found within us for Rousseau who is 'at the origin point of a great deal of contemporary culture, of the philo-sophies of self-exploration, as well as of the creeds which make self-determining freedom the key to virtue. He is the starting point of a transformation in modern culture towards a deeper inwardness and a radical autonomy. The strands all lead from him' (Taylor, 1992a, pp. 362–363).

A further strand, however, increasingly from the end of the eighteenth century, leads from the east and to trace the development of the philosophical interpretation of consciousness would not really make a great deal of sense without full acknowledgement of the infusion of eastern thought. The Ancient Hindu Scriptures and Buddhist sources are replete with dialogue and discussion concerning the nature of the 'I', self and consciousness in relation to each other and to the cosmic whole. The influence of the east on the classical world should not be underestimated with Gnostic ideas on the soul and inner life, for example, being influenced by Hindu and Buddhist thought. Plotinus, a formative influence on Christian neoplatonism, was also attracted by eastern ideas. In the Europe of the fifteenth and sixteenth centuries there was an influx of ideas not only from ancient Greece and Rome but from Jewish and Hermetic traditions. Jesuit missionaries as they moved both west and east, to the 'new' world and the 'old', became a conduit for the flow of ideas. They became the initial source of reportage on China, interpreting its culture and civilisation as they went. Whilst Montaigne, Malebranche, Leibniz and Wolff (the latter two in direct line of influence to Kant) were all influenced by Chinese philosophy, in the later years of the Enlightenment, Diderot and Helvetius, at one time greatly influenced by China, came to be critical, as did Montesquieu, Rousseau and Condorcet. Voltaire in this period used Confucianism as a stalking-horse for undermining both Catholic Church and state. Yet, the certitude of post-Enlightenment beliefs and epistemology eventually come to falter with the increasing recognition of the plurality of 'life-worlds'. Right from the eighteenth century, with the Enlightenment, to the present day, an equivalence with and, often, superiority to, the western tradition was recognised at every turn. First came a preoccupation with China, then at the end of the century attention turned to India and finally in the nineteenth century a concern with Buddhism took centre stage. Buddha taught that there is no such thing as 'self' but, instead, only an illusion of 'self'. At the moment of enlightenment, seeing into the mystery of things, Buddha understood the self was an illusion. If a real, eternal self were to exist, it was concluded, it would be the cause of eternal suffering. Recognition of the illusoriness of the self, in contrast, is the pathway to enlightenment and a step towards an end of suffering.

THE COMING OF AGE OF CONSCIOUSNESS

Western social thought has not been concerned directly with the potential of a 'selfless' consciousness to be both extended and altered, but the work of Hume, who concluded that a substantive and enduring self could not be seen to exist, is an echo of Buddha's conception of a 'bundle of elements' void of self. In fact, interspersing any reading of, say, Leibniz Hegel or Schopenhauer with the eastern texts would exhibit a surprising 'flow' of thought. However, it is to Kant that attention needs to turn initially as he builds on Leibniz, Hume, Rousseau and others to radically re-orient the direction of philosophical thought on consciousness.

IDEALISM - KANT AND HEGEL

Kant refers at one point to being awakened from his 'dogmatic slumber' by becoming acquainted with the work of Hume. Thus aroused, though, it is Kant (1959) who very largely sets the agenda for subsequent sociological thought (see Chapter Five) on the nature of human apprehension of the world without, ironically enough, resolving a great deal of the Humean legacy. Kant draws a distinction finer than that found in Hume's division between matters of fact to do with the evidence of memory and senses based on cause and effect, and relations of ideas determined by the nature of thought and not dependent on what is in the world and of which it is not revelatory. Where Hume thought that all relations of ideas are both analytic and *a priori* and all matters of fact are both synthetic and *a posteriori*, and that there are no other kinds of judgement, Kant substituted a double distinction for Hume's simple binary one. Kant's distinction is first a logical one, between analytic and synthetic judgements (in an analytic judgement the concept of the predicate is 'contained' in the concept of the subject of the judgement as in 'bachelors are unmarried'; in a synthetic judgement the concept of the predicate is combined with – synthesised with – the concept of the subject as in 'water solidifies when frozen') and then an epistemological one between judgements *a priori* (no conceivable experience could falsify the judgement) and judgements *a posteriori* (we could have an experience that would falsify the judgement). Kant maintained that some judgements are both synthetic and *a priori*, e.g., the truths of mathematics, but more importantly, in the process, paved the way to a revolutionary conception of the relationship between human subjects and the objective world. Where Hume placed a question mark against the status of an objective reality, Kant held that whatever lies beyond our experience is not accessible to us as knowledge. Kant's Copernican revolution amounts to a recognition of the primacy of our experience of reality as the problem over and above the questionable status of reality itself. In a complex argument, Kant contends that in so far as our experience can be ascribed to ourselves (that is, is 'self-conscious'), it has to embrace a distinction between subject and object – the latter being experience to which *a priori* concepts (space, time, causality) must pertain.

Apperception is a virtual synonym of consciousness for Kant for whom the senses intuit, the understanding thinks and thinking, in turn, unites representations in one consciousness. The forms of intuition and categories of understanding inherent in the mind actively create the phenomenal world as it is experienced. A consequence of this 'creativity' is that there is no one-to-one relationship between objects in the external world and, in apperception, the sensations we have of those same objects. Yet Kant circumvents the problem of the potential mismatch between synthetic *a priori* judgements and whatever the world might throw at us, by concluding that such concepts do not just describe possible experience (as it happens) but actually constitute it. Experience can, therefore, never out-run reason. Kant's ultimate reference point, and his first-order public realm, lies in the world of inanimate matter acting under causal laws in space–time as decreed by Newtonian physics. He overlays this by informing us that it is only possible to have an individual perspective on the world *because* we have experience of a shared, public world, in itself objective, upon the availability of which the subjective experience is contingent. Not only do we each have our own point of view because we share the world on which we have such a point of view, but there are no points of view at all without the co-ordinates from which these points of view are definable. For Kant, experience is an objective and structured realm shared (which we know *a priori* that we share) with other rational beings *not* a private, inner 'realm' of items of consciousness present to the mind. If we can show that we could not even have experience unless constitutive concepts were applicable to it, then we would have 'deduced' these concepts from the very possibility of experience. In fact, alongside the 'knowing' mind, Kant presents us with a distinction between the realms of the phenomenal

and noumenal duly compounded by the introduction of a phenomenal or empirical self in its passivity and a noumenal or transcendental self of rational will and moral agency. In consequence, the
noumenal or transcendental self – in common with other unknowable things – cannot be apprehended as a thinking subject and Kant,
thereby, seems to marginalise the constituency for the analysis of
consciousness. Although he *did* refer to it in these terms, being the
same person over time, for Kant, is not simply the ability to say 'I'
consistently as, in turn, personal identity is more than the persistence
of an inaccessible mental substance. Kant appeared to be persuaded
that personal identity depends on a flow of perception though he
does not allow the absolute divorce of being the same and sensing one
is. He appeared convinced of the hopelessness that any theoretical
assertion of personality could be at all certain for us.

The characteristic features of Kant's philosophy can be adumbrated,
though inevitably confounding its inherent complexity: he was not
prepared to accept that all knowledge is derived from experience, as
was supposed by empiricists, and knowledge conforming to objects
was replaced with objects conforming to knowledge, i.e., the way in
which we perceive and reflect actually structures the objects of our
experience; a distinction was drawn between sensibility and understanding, 'through the former objects are given to us: through the
latter they are thought' and it is only through the workings of understanding that sense experience is structured, ordered and classified,
i.e., we, ourselves, give order and regularity to objects of nature and
the idea of the accumulation of little pieces of sense data is rejected in
favour of the construction of consciousness; concepts utilised in our
knowledge of objects of sense experience were not applicable to
things that lie beyond such experience or transcend it, with any
such attempt leading to error, confusion and inconsistency, and phenomena and noumena (things in themselves) which are unknowable
(for example, God is not known from experience) are quite separate.
Kant declares that consciousness can only arrange appearances and
proceeds to distinguish ontologically between 'appearance' – producing a whole domain of categories where judgements (as functions
of human understanding) are possible – and 'real existence' of
unknowable 'things in themselves'. This distinction, perhaps more
than anything, galvanised those who came after Kant. Fichte, Kant's
pupil, discarded Kant's 'thing-in-itself' and, instead of deriving the

thinking self from experience, set out to deduce manifold experience from the activity of the ego; though consciousness could not be explained in terms of being, experience, though not the 'thing-in-itself,' *could* be constructed from datum of consciousness. Fichte contends that the thinking principle itself is the thing-in-itself of Kant, substantiated through reflection upon itself and its objects in a struggle to create both the world and itself, thereby realising an objectifying and sovereign ego.

In contrast to these endeavours, Hegel rejected as unintelligible Kant's idea of the 'thing-in-itself', which led him to contend that all that exists must be mental. This 'monism' leads to the all pervasive subject who thinks the object. Hegel, at one point, describes Reason as the certainty of possessing reality and 'what is not present for consciousness as something existing in its own right [*Selbstwesen*], i.e., what does not appear, is for consciousness nothing at all' (Hegel, 1977, p. 151). But, if everything is in the mind, how is truth to be identified or subject distinguished from object? At this point Hegel concluded that the 'true is the whole' and that nothing is real in isolation. For Hegel, recognition that finite, self-subsistent objects have no genuinely independent existence is the overcoming of an illusion – the estrangement of the mind's apprehension of the nature of reality and, therefore, its own nature. Hegel's is the dynamic 'big' picture whose perspective is expository. The subject, *and* object as it turns out, is Spirit as the agent of history whose goal is freedom. Hegel's system decries the abstraction of the individual with its inflated importance in the scheme of things. Whilst he implores human beings to 'know thyself', he, at the same time, recommends that the individual must all the more forget himself. What is to be remembered, rather, is the all-embracing, collective identity of spirit pervading history and suffused through us all. This was not self-knowledge to which the single self would come, but the acceptance of the self as Absolute Spirit – man's genuine reality and true and essential being. Spirit for Hegel is to be *realised* with the reality constituted by and revealed to the universal self – the thoughts of individual selves being only moments of it. Hegel located the fundamental structure of self-consciousness beyond the knowing subject unfolding in the realm of Absolute Spirit.

Hegel agreed with Kant that objects were constituted by consciousness but rejected the individualistic implications of this – each creating their own world. Unlike Kant, who sees a self-conscious solitary 'I' which refers back to itself as its sole object and recognises itself as self-constituting and Fichte's version of the ego positing itself as a being-for-itself locked in struggle to be realised in creating itself and the world, the young Hegel interprets the self as produced inter-subjectively. In Hegel's view, not only must the 'sullen tyrant' of the self perish for us to realise the prospect of freedom but once we are conscious of the fact of the coincidence of interest of ourselves and others – in the Other's relation to us as an individual – the Other disappears in our sight and we are set free. In the *Phenomenology of Spirit* Hegel develops a dialectical, social-psychological view of the emergence and maintenance of the self and consciousness. This is based upon mutual recognition, interdependence and the manu-facturing of meaning, where one consciousness – the victor in mortal combat – realises the need for the self-confirming witness of the vanquished. In this sequence he demonstrates that consciousness must – in a conflictual, primarily cultural context – become self-consciousness, and, in turn, self-consciousness become aware of itself *as* self-consciousness. He says: 'Self-consciousness exists in and for itself when, and by the fact that, it so exists for another; that is, it exists only in being acknowledged' (Hegel, 1977, p. 111). Yet, there is not for a moment an individual caring self anywhere to be found outside the stately procession of the Absolute Spirit, and, should there be, they would not anyway, know what was going on. For Hegel 'immediate experience is itself a kind of false or partial con-sciousness; it will yield up its truth only when it is dialectically mediated, when its latent manifold relations with the whole have been patiently uncovered. One might say, then, that on this view our routine consciousness is itself inherently 'ideological', simply by virtue of its partiality . . . one might say that a certain kind of false consciousness is for Hegel our 'natural' condition, endemic to our immediate experience' (Eagleton, 1991, pp. 98–99).

In the unfolding of his dialectic Hegel is displaying the active mode of the relation between mind and the world. Depending on the stage of the dialectic and the location in the development of Hegel's own thought there are different points of reference and terminology. Perhaps the clearest triadic movement is that from sensuous con-sciousness, to understanding and, then, to Reason. *Sensuous con-sciousness,* indicates a mind not separate from the world and incapable of reflection as the subject merges with the objective world; *understanding*, involves the subjective discriminating between itself and the object world which becomes divisible into separate qualities falling apart into form and content, universal and particular, and; *Reason*, whilst not reneging on the distinctions made by *understanding*, recognises deeper unities and releases the system of combination suspended by understanding. Though understanding has this inherent defect it is a necessary moment in the acquisition of *Reason;* stages of the dialectic are preserved and raised to the higher level (*aufhebung*). Reason is the purposive activity of self-knowing truth and self-cognising reason; it is the final result of the development of theoretical mind. Spirit is self-conscious Reason or Reason conscious of itself. Hegel attributes to Kant the distinction itself between *understanding* and *Reason*, though in his own thought it is of wider application. The world Spirit has to give itself objective existence as mind's awareness of itself comes about through projection into that which it is not. This priority of the objective existence of culture, religion and art will be encountered again the work of Dilthey (see Chapter Four). In turn, Hegel studies the mind of the individual in abstraction from his social relations (subjective mind), then assesses mind in its social context of civil society and the state (objective mind) and, finally, mind concerned with philosophy, religion and art (absolute mind – the highest stage). Hegel came to replace solitary reflection upon itself with a formative social process unfolding through three discrete media: linguistic (symbolic) representation, distinct processes of labour, and reciprocal interaction. Firstly 'the power of waking consciousness to represent objects symbolically is synonymous with its capacity to make distinctions and systematically recognise and remember that which it has distinguished. Through the employment of symbols, speaking consciousness experiences itself as subjective through its objectifications' (Keane, 1984, p. 125). Secondly, through artful consciousness, i.e. 'labour, and the fabrication of tools, the cunning subject makes itself an object for itself by outwitting and overcoming the power of natural processes. Thirdly, and finally, through interaction with others (for example, in the family), the individual subject learns to recognise itself in and through the eyes of another subject or "I" ' (p. 125).

Mankind finds that their own creations of culture and civilisation become objectified; what was once in their own hands is extruded to become simultaneously part and *not* part of them. This process of alienation is reflected in the young Hegel in his view of language. Language is our creation, but a sort of alien existence, in a realm of its own. Belonging and not belonging to us, language represents a specific mode of self-estrangement. Thus, Hegel stressed consciousness working collectively through a shared language, culture and society. But shared concepts are not the whole, universal truth but particular aspects of the truth for Hegel. He countenances the prospect of forms of life and consciousness which have alternative perspectives and truths – though some may be more true than others. In fact, the precise status of the symbolic in Hegel remains unresolved. At the very least, there is here ambiguity in the Hegelian *leitmotif* of language. He juxtaposes the trivialities of external existence and contingency with the truth of substantial and underlying essence, yet, he still feels confident enough to state elsewhere that '[w]e only know our thoughts, only have definite, actual thoughts, when we give them the form of objectivity, of a being distinct from our inwardness, and therefore the shape of externality, and of an externality too, that at the same time bears the stamp of the highest inwardness. The articulated sound, the *word* is alone such an inward externality . . . [it is] . . . ridiculous to regard as a defect of thought and a misfortune, the fact that it is tied to a word; for although the common opinion is that it is just the *ineffable* that is the most excellent, yet this opinion, cherished by conceit, is unfounded, since what is ineffable is, in truth, only something obscure, fermenting, something which gains clarity only when it is able to put itself into words. Accordingly, the word gives to thoughts their highest and truest existence' (Hegel, 1971, p. 221). What *is* a problem for Hegel, here, however, is the profusion and (over) familiarity of words used automatically and uncritically thus losing thought its objective purchase (the 'alienation of intelligence').

Mind is active and productive and as *will* mind steps into actuality. The world is made manifest through action and human beings come to know themselves in the prosecution of projects. Hegel convinces us that the true being of a man (sic) is his (sic) deed in which the individual is actual, doing away with something only 'meant' to be. Sounding so much a precursor of Wittgenstein, Hegel remarks that 'the deed equally does away with the inexpressibility of what is "meant", in respect of the self-conscious individuality. In such mere opinion the individuality is infinitely determined and determinable. In the accomplished deed this spurious infinity is destroyed. The deed is something *simply* determined, universal, to be grasped in an abstraction; it is murder, theft, or a good action, a brave deed, and so on, and what it is can be *said of it*. It *is* this, and its being is not merely a sign, but the fact itself. It *is* this, and the individual human being *is* what the *deed* is' (Hegel, 1977, p. 194). The deed alone, for Hegel, is man's genuine being though there is the risk of immanent change in the process. He says 'when his *performance* and his inner *possibility*, capacity or intention are contrasted, it is the former alone which is to be regarded as his true actuality, even if he deceives himself on the point, and, turning away from his action into himself, fancies that in this inner self he is something else than what he is in the deed' (p. 194). He contrasts the deed as an actual being that endures with a fancied performance – a 'nothing at all' – which passes away and he draws a distinction between the play of meaningless activity of the individual and the pure activity of mind. Subjective particularity or the main mass of singularities pale in comparison with the great events of an age. Hegel says, to the extent that the business of 'actuality appears as an action, and therefore as a work of *individuals*, these individuals, as regards the substantial issue of their labour, are *instruments*, and their subjectivity, which is peculiar to them, is the empty form of activity' (Hegel, 1971, p. 281).

CONCLUSION

The intention in this chapter has been to explore several related themes: the way in which 'consciousness' has featured in philosophy since the seventeenth century; how both the non-substance (unsubstantive) and disengaged self emerged as of enduring significance; the recognition of the problematic status of reality; the way language came to feature as of independent importance; and how a theory of action and experience emerged as a counterpoint to the critique of consciousness. Although different in many respects Descartes and Locke have in common, at very least, their support for a disengaged subject gaining rational self-control and thus able to stand back and take stock. Indeed, in Locke the capacity of *reflection* is crucial. Attaining the first person standpoint creates sufficient space to open up the prospect of self-remaking. Taylor (1992a) refers to this prospect in critical terms as the 'punctual' self where a radical objectivity can only be accessible and intelligible via a prior radical subjectivity. What was formerly seen as linking inseparably the existence of a human being and the object world, is newly localised 'inside' the human subject from where language itself is circumscribed. Locke held that we have intuitive knowledge of the existence of the self and that it is impossible to perceive without perceiving that we perceive. For him, consciousness always accompanies thinking; we cannot think without being conscious of it. Locke is certainly anxious to distinguish his position from Descartes, but he is also more of an under-labourer for the subsequent work of Hume than is often acknowledged. In Locke, consciousness appears to be that which actively retrieves the past and appropriates to the present self that about which it cares. In contrast, in Hume, consciousness is the appropriation process *per se* as one thought inherits the next, i.e., consciousness is that relation in itself. The difference is an emphasis on what consciousness *does* in a process (Locke) as opposed to actually *being* that process (Hume).

In the transition from Descartes to Hume and Kant a concept-fired, substantial self is replaced by a perception-driven self which 'ceases to be a premiss; instead, it becomes merely the location, or perhaps the name, for our ultimate data base' (Gellner, 1992, p. 20) and the hard, gem-like substantial self of Descartes disappears. But Kant's system cannot seem to contain a 'successionist-self' as might have been inherited from Locke or Hume. It is, in fact, Locke and, particularly, Hume who inherit the future with their minimalist self and consciousness without the need of an inner director of mental events. It is Hume who pre-eminently rejects the self as a possible object of experience and observation and, by that token, accounts the self as falling short of the status of a possible object of empirical knowledge. As Berlin has said of Hume, though giving short shrift to Locke: 'The nature of selves as opposed to things is something left undiscussed, save in very glancing terms, by Locke and Berkeley . . . the honour of exploding the dogmatic assumptions about substantive selves, timeless and unchanging, which were common to the theories of knowledge of rationalists and theists, belongs to Hume alone. His analysis of the self is perhaps the most characteristically devastating application of his empirical method, and has, in its own way, caused as much scandal during the two hundred years that followed as his undermining of the *a priori* basis of induction. Material objects are to Hume a harmless illusion, but an illusion nevertheless' (Berlin, 1956, p. 216).

Hume's view of the material world has not much more to commend it than that on offer via Cartesian doubt, for despite the emphasis on perception and sense experience acquaintance with the real world apparently remains beyond us. Experience, for rationalists like Descartes and Leibniz, remained deceptive and not the source of the formation of ideas; rather, innate, general ideas serve to interpret all experience. In Berkeley's account the possibility of a mind-independent world is subsumed under an experiential realm of thought relations. With empiricism, consciousness had become a property of experience but the corollary is that each of us has a 'view', which compounds the original retreat from the real. Reality *per se* cannot be confirmed by Hume so neither, ultimately, can a social, historical reality. Though for Hume history appeared to be about our increasing capacity to sympathise with others, he can provide us with no evidence for the existence of reality; it is Reid, uniquely, who seems to be persuaded of the incontrovertibility of reality. We find in Hume and Kant the initial inclination towards a conception of a public, historical world and in Kant an emphasis on language as not just a mere medium, as in Hobbes and Locke, but, rather, an existential limit beyond which we inevitably step over into error. The insight from Kant of the world being actively ordered by consciousness, is, however, counteracted by the positing of an unknowable thing-in-itself and a solitary ego destined to be detained in an 'unreal' world of appearance. Kant's method places in jeopardy not just what we are able to *know* about the world but also what we are able to *think* outrightly about it. The attempt by Fichte to define the thing-in-itself as the thinking principle itself only compounds the problem. It is left to Hegel to transcend the idea of the thing-in-itself and provide a social, cultural and historical dimension lacking elsewhere in German idealism, but in doing so he removes consciousness to the stratospheric working out of Absolute Spirit and denies mankind their feet of clay – individually and collectively. It has been remarked that Hegel 'is in truth as little interested in thought as a subjective phenomenon, perhaps as inadequately acquainted with it, as that other great dweller on words, Wittgenstein' (Findlay, forward, Hegel, 1971, p. xviii).

Hegel's depiction is of reality as a whole in its totality with a teleological property as its creative force – the evolution of the Absolute Idea. Throughout history and through human consciousness this has taken on different shapes or forms, in itself a reflection of the historical development of the world Spirit where earlier faltering steps of consciousness are raised up to a higher stage in a simultaneous moment of preservation and supersession (*aufhebung*). Consciousness has the capacity to recognise and recall systematically the distinctions drawn through the symbolic representation of the objective world and through its symbolic objectifications, comes to experience itself as subjective and the immediacy of the human condition may then be transcended through the power of consciousness to represent. It is, however, human practical and critical activity which actualises life out of this process of unceasing change, with the ultimate destination being self-consciousness of this active role whence alienation of consciousness and reality is broken down and consciousness appears to us self-evidently in the world through praxis. It is because man is a self-conscious being that he can be transformed by his own activity and *Reason* is described by Hegel as *purposive activity*. The opposition of subject and object is overcome when man produces and reproduces himself in practical–critical activity and comes to recognise himself in the process. The divorce of appearance from reality is also confounded in practice. After taking on a sequence of diverse configurations Spirit has finally travelled the road to a full and proper rational understanding of the world.

There is contained in the transition from Hume to Kant a movement away from the veil-of-appearance idea to a concern with ontology which in the Kantian categories is exemplified in the distinction between real existence and appearance. In a further step, Hegel concludes that thinking is the negation of that which is immediately before us and makes Absolute Spirit the subject of history and the hypostatisation of human mental life, but loses it any critical purchase on the objective world. Thought and reality, the identical subject–object of history, so fused in the Absolute, drift apart to reveal omnipotent thought leaving all things as they are. It is with Marx, in fact, that social and historical specifity comes to inform the lexicon of concepts encountered in this chapter: appearance and reality, as a relation, has restored to it dialectical properties; experience and action are judged by the yardstick of praxis; and the internal relations of the capitalist mode of production are a structured determination not open-ended or arbitrary – a lesson that Marx had learned from Hegel. In the period under consideration in this chapter there had appeared a cosmic shift in the guiding maxim: from Descartes's 'I think therefore I am' to Marx's 'social being determines consciousness' which itself now demands our attention.

3

MARX AND THE MARXISTS

Does it require deep intuition to comprehend that man's ideas, views and conceptions, in one word, man's consciousness, changes with every change in the conditions of his material existence, in his social relations and in his social life?

(Marx and Engels, 1968, p. 51)

THE POLITICAL ECONOMY OF 'CONSCIOUSNESS'

The precepts and tenets of Marxism are sufficiently well known in outline not to require repetition here. In the space available we cannot hope to trace every turn in what became the 'articles' of Marxism but can only draw parallels relevant to the present discussion. However, it is worth noting at the outset in juxtaposing Marx's view of consciousness with the discussion in Chapter Two that 'Marx's own philosophical culture was itself by no means an exhaustive one. Essentially steeped in Hegel and Feuerbach, it was not characterized by any very close acquaintance with Kant or Hume, Descartes or Leibniz, Plato or Aquinas, not to speak of other lesser figures. . . . Marx himself had never directly assessed or surpassed all previous ethics, metaphysics, aesthetics, nor even touched on numerous basic issues of classical philosophy' (Anderson, 1979, p. 60). Despite Marx's imperious, dismissive '[t]he philosophers have only *interpreted* the world in various ways; the point, however, is to *change* it' (Marx and Engels, 1968, p. 30) Anderson reckons, rightly, that 'a single sentence cannot dispose of centuries of thought'. In fairness,

Marx inherited a wider-ranging legacy than the philosophy of mind including the influences of the Romantic period, the Enlightenment and of developments in science and economics that comprize the source of a philosophical anthropology of human nature and society. In the Romantic reaction to the Enlightenment, consciousness and subjectivity come to be opposed to scientific reason and objectivity. Romanticism undoubtedly influenced idealism, as we have seen, and Marx's early philosophical adherence was to a Romantic-idealism drawing on Kant and Fichte before coming under the influence of Hegel. Marx did not engage with the legacy of the psychology of mind (and self) inherited from Locke, Hume and Kant that considered an unsubstantive or transcendent self but was saddled initially with empiricism (and materialism) and idealism at odds on the direction of influence of thought and matter. For Locke experience is the source of all understanding and only so because our minds reflect external sensible objects; an insight lost to subsequent empiricists where experience comes to equal a mentalistic activity. After Locke there is a glorification of appearance and a rejection of the real world and how it is reflected in the mind. From the empiricist stand point a metaphysical dualism is created between subject and object, experience and reason.

Under Hegel's influence, what Marx rejected in the materialism he inherited was the subject–object relation where the thought of the knowing subject passively reflects the object with which it is confronted. Without doubt it is the attraction and repulsion of Hegel for Marx that creates the force-field for his analysis of consciousness. Marx is intent on providing a masterkey to the riddle of Hegel's mysticism – the compendium of the illusions of speculation in Marx's view. He states that Hegel 'does not allow society to become a truly determining thing because this would require a *real* subject while he has nothing more than an abstract one, a figment of the *imagination*' (Marx, 1992, p. 192). In Marx's estimation what occurs in Hegel's system is that the subject comes into being only as the result of knowing itself as Absolute self-consciousness (i.e., Absolute Spirit; God) whilst real nature and real man remain mere predicates and symbols of this hidden unreal nature and unreal man. These forms of abstraction are, in their universality, indifferent to all content; being, in effect, logical categories and forms of thought torn away from both *real* nature and *real* mind. Hegel had denied that reality is external and other than consciousness – if anything, reality is consciousness objectified. The real world for Hegel is the phenomenal external form of the Idea. In Marx's re-interpretation the Idea is, in fact, the material world reflected by the human mind and translated into forms of thought. Hegel's system is indifferent to all specific, historical content in Marx's view and as he says in his later work:

> My dialectic method is not only different from the Hegelian, but is its direct opposite. To Hegel, the life-process of the human brain, i.e. the process of thinking, which, under the name of 'the Idea', he even transforms into an independent subject, is the demiurges (CREATOR) of the world, and the real world is only the external, phenomenal form of the Idea. With me, on the contrary, the idea is nothing else than the material world reflected by the human mind, and translated into forms of thought.
>
> (Second German Edition of *Capital*, Vol. I, p. 19)

In Feuerbach's critique of Hegel on which Marx came to draw, humanity is blessed with the power of reflection and capable of sympathy (both qualities we would recognise from our accounts of Locke and Hume respectively). However, Marx's exclusive focus of attention tends to remain Feuerbach's *transformative method* which holds that religious illusions once recognised as the dream of the human mind inadvertently ascribed to god will be abolished. To this Marx replies that religious illusions will only finally disappear when the social relations of mankind are transformed and self-evidently rational as a result of a programme for the reform of consciousness through analysis of 'mystical consciousness obscure to itself' – whether appearing in political or religious form. Not only is the object reflected in thought but so is its socio-historical context. In Marx's social materialism the problematic of theory and practice replaces traditional materialism's preoccupation with thought and matter. Thought for its own sake was rejected by Marx as was experience as subjectively conceived, i.e., experience that does not confirm external reality but which remains forever beyond our ken. Instead, Nature is viewed by Marx as an object world which develops but not as somehow eternally separate from the world of mankind.

After Marx's death Engels returned to the ground they had covered together more than forty years before in working out their opposition to the 'ideological view of German philosophy', i.e., the settling of accounts with their 'erstwhile philosophical conscience'. Once again the polarised disposition of idealism and materialism is rehearsed. Differences in the 'two great camps' on the question of the relation of thinking to being has, says Engels, yet another side to it: 'in what relation do our thoughts about the world surrounding us stand to this world itself? Is our thinking capable of the cognition of the real world? Are we able in our ideas and notions of the real world to produce a correct reflection of reality?' (Engels, in Marx and Engels, 1968, p. 594). In Engel's view the overwhelming majority of philosophers have given an affirmative answer to the question of the identity of thinking and being – Hegel's affirmation being self-evident according to Engels – whilst those who question the possibility of any exhaustive cognition of the world, in his view, have numbered among them Hume and Kant. Hegel, for Engels, provided a refutation of this latter position if from an idealist and, ultimately, illusory standpoint whilst Feuerbach's materialistic intervention is described as more 'ingenious than profound'. Feuerbach's mistake was not to conceive of man coming into being in a real world and being historically determined; his preoccupation was with the abstract individual *in* himself not with the outside world. Such a view '... had to be replaced by the science of real men and their historical development' (Engels, in Marx and Engels, 1968, p. 607). The most telling refutation in Engels's estimation of this 'crotchety' philosophical legacy is *practice* making an end of the ungraspable 'thing-in-itself' of Kant. Images of real things are then comprehended materialistically in our heads – the conscious reflex of the dialectical motion of the real world. On Marx's part the first and last marker put down for the supersession of Feuerbach is contained in these words: 'The materialist doctrine that men are products of circumstances and upbringing, and that, therefore, changed men are products of other circumstances and changed upbringing, forgets that it is men that change circumstances and that the educator himself needs educating' (Marx, in Marx and Engels, 1968, p. 28). This is effected through revolutionary practice without which there is just the contemplation of single individuals in, and it should be said determined by, civil society. This analysis comes not from the later Marx but from an old notebook of 1845 not intended for publication found by Engels and appended to his own (1888) reanimated critique of Hegel and Feuerbach.

It is significant that Engels, without any particular resolution, uses both senses of the word 'reflection': an image seemingly taking on the properties of the object which is then cast back *and* to consider meditatively. The fact that these two usages are potentially in opposition is left largely unexplored. However, not only is the role of consciousness crucial in both senses but Marx builds into it a dimension of 'distance' from which to contemplate objective activity with which man, he says, does not directly merge: 'It is therefore in his fashioning of the objective that man really proves himself to be a *species-being*. Such production is his active species-life. Through it nature appears as *his* work and his reality. The object of labour is therefore the *objectification of the species-life of man*: for man reproduces himself not only intellectually, in his consciousness, but actively and actually, and he can therefore contemplate himself in a world he himself has created' (Marx, 1992, p. 329). Whereas the animal is not distinct from and is immediately one with its life activity (i.e., it *is* that activity): 'Man makes life activity itself an object of his will and consciousness. He has conscious life activity. It is not a determination with which he directly merges. Conscious life activity directly distinguishes man from animal life activity. Only because of that is he a species-being. Or rather, he is a conscious being, i.e. his own life is an object for him, only because he is a species-being. Only because of that is his activity free activity' (Marx, 1992, p. 328). In his later work Marx makes the point that the difference between mankind and the best of bees is that man's 'hive' of activity and its end product are held in mind pre-emptively; a world, of whatever magnitude, is constructed initially by the 'architect imagination'.

Marx's conceptualisation of consciousness, then, was generated initially in his critique of Hegelian idealism and the materialism of Feuerbach. In fact: 'Marx wanted to assert his conviction that consciousness is not independent of material conditions, against idealism, and that consciousness is not a passive reflection of external reality, against the old materialism' (Larrain, 1983, p. 18). Whilst originally taken with the materialist inversion of Hegel evident in Feuerbach, by the mid 1840s Marx had made the decisive step to outstrip both philosophies. Life was not, then, to be derived from thought typical of Hegel and thought was not to be generated by life in the fashion of Feuerbach (or, for that matter, Locke). Instead, the 'thinking creature' typical of both directions of interpretation was to be supplanted by active human beings, in as much a philosophy of praxis. By this time, thought and activity are not separated in Marx's mind; thought *is* activity. Through activity thought encounters the world. Consciousness, then, was not to be separated off into some rarified realm divorced from life which it somehow determines as had been the case for idealism. However, it should be remembered that declining to detach thinking from life had also occurred to Hegel who often seemed to stress the *deed* and *activity* above all else. Indeed, Marx wanted to replace the *activity* of idealism, for him developed abstractly minus real, sensuous activity as such, with the 'practical–critical' activity of social life; the starting point of socialism for Marx being the theoretically *and* practically sensuous consciousness of the essential being of man in nature. But what was Marx taking man in nature to be?

MARX'S CONCEPT OF MAN

Hobbes's naturalistic view of human nature contemplated a war of everyone against everyone in an epic power struggle whilst Rousseau saw reason as subordinated to the rule of the heart and emotions with man innately good until corrupted by society and its institutions. Adam Smith at one point rendered man innately egoistic and selfish but at another considered man naturally altruistic and aware of social obligations. Hegel, as has been seen, viewed man as being estranged from his essence. Marx, in contrast, it is most often concluded, rejected any fixed ahistorical notion of human nature as found in a romantic, economic or idealist 'man'[1]. He contended that it is membership of society – together with achievements of culture and technology – that confers humanity upon men and women who are, nevertheless, estranged from the creation of humanity because of the divisiveness of the division of labour in capitalism. Classically, Marx viewed man as a teleological being developing through labour, although as man becomes human only in society, the socioeconomic system of that society will determine the nature of humanity. Under capitalism man's potential is constrained and if all their senses and faculties are not geared to conscious self production, then they are not in a position to realise their nature as fully 'human'. Marx was persuaded that humankind is impelled to realise its species-being in universally externalising its powers; objectivising for all the species. Yet, how can this be achieved under a system of expropriation with an ascendance of things at the expense of human life; the product over the producer? Not only does Marx refer in his early work to consciousness as man's 'inner life' but also to alienated labour being the alienation of consciousness. In the alienation of his essential powers, man's essential nature is bespoiled and he is lost to himself. Marx is in no doubt that (capitalist) production produces man both mentally and physically as the self-conscious and self-acting 'human' commodity and because man feels his suffering he is a passionate being – an essential power used in attaining his object. Individual and species-life, then, are not two distinct things: 'It is true that thought and being are *distinct*, but at the same time they are in *unity* with one another' (Marx, 1992, p. 351). The abstract hostility between intellect and sensuous existence is inevitable whilst man's own labour is not his own.

Marx appears not to subscribe to a static view of human nature, as does Rousseau, nor to the mere 'placing' of man at the centre of things, as does Feuerbach in his reaction against Hegel. Idealists had abstracted consciousness from material life, whereas Marx saw consciousness as contingent upon maintaining ourselves in the natural world as embodied beings where consciousness presupposes a material, physical existence. Indeed, in so doing, Marx asserted the priority of human labour in the creation of material life and, with it, the creation and re-creation of a social and historical human nature.[2] Marx's image of the world is one in which self realisation of human potentiality, comes with the creation of material life. In this view, skill, for example, is ideally plied in the work situation, but capitalist expropriation removes the social object from the worker. In the resulting situation of expropriation men are *per se* alienated. Marx had taken from Hegel an emphasis upon labour as the self-confirming essence of man but rejected the idea of consciousness as that in which and through which alienation was to be resolved. Sometimes Marx separates off social being from consciousness to demonstrate that, in contradistinction to Hegel, the former determines the latter. In consequence, Marx's early work on human nature culminating in the

Theses on Feurbach, despite the emphasis on the social and historical, had already introduced without apparent resolution the 'tendencies', 'abilities' and 'capacities' of human beings.[3]

Marx criticised bourgeois society because within it universal human nature could not express itself. The Romantic tradition (Rousseau, for example) had suggested that we get in tune with our inner voice, itself expressing our relation with nature. This might be encompassed by the more modern expression of 'getting in touch with our feelings'. The inner impulse is the tempo of truth and that 'heart beat' is nature within us. The legacy of disengagement from Descartes means we are estranged from hearing the harmony of ourselves with nature. The problem then becomes – for each in their own way – how to express and fulfil nature by sounding the accordant pulse? Reason and sensibility can be thus reconciled. Rosen connects this interpretation of the expressionist turn in social thought characteristic of Taylor (1975; 1992), with the early work of Marx. In alienated labour the individual is not able to express their true nature to become what they should ideally be – fully realised in their species-being in self actualization through labour. Such expression is a revelation leaving oneself open to an understanding of self, others and social situation. Rosen sees the failure to express oneself in this way as constituting, in as much, a loss of identity. He says that :

> Hegel, in a famous phase, describes freedom as remaining '*in seinem Anderen bei sich selbst*' (roughly, 'with oneself in otherness'). On this view, the autonomous self is one that neither withholds itself from nor loses itself in its actions : its expressions remain truly its own. Correspondingly, the unfree self, in becoming separated from otherness, can be said to have suffered a 'loss of identity'.
>
> (Rosen, 1996, p. 40)

But the question remains are we referring to individual identity here? This question mark lies at the heart of the work of the early Marx and might be seen as indicating the 'failure on Marx's part to carry through his own programme – to complete the purge of Hegelianism from his social thought and to replace its overarching collective subject with properly individualistic micro-foundations' (Rosen, 1996,

p. 270). Certainly it is far from clear that we can identify in Marx either a disengaged or unsubstantive self on which he intended to build.

Nevertheless, Marx does describe how he sees the necessity in avoiding establishing ' "society" as an abstraction over against the individual. The individual *is* the *social being*. His vital expression – even when it does not appear in the direct form of a *communal* expression, conceived in association with other men – is therefore an expression and confirmation of *social life*' (Marx, 1992, p. 350). Marx says society produces man as man and is produced by him. He refers to the human essence of nature existing only for social man bound by a bond with other men – the vital element of human reality of his existence for others and their existence for him. Social character, social activity and social consumption is everything here. Man has natural powers of a corporeal, living, real, sensuous, objective being with real, sensuous objects as the object of his being in which is embodied the vital expression of his life. In Marx's view a natural being playing its part in the system of nature is a being which has its nature *outside itself*, which raises the stakes of the significance of the symbolic world of language and communication as well as the world worked on transforming nature *and* human nature. Certainly there are echoes of Hegel's self–Other dialectic in Marx. In referring to man having an objective nature engaged in objective relationships he says: 'A being which does not have its nature outside itself is not a natural being and plays no part in the system of nature. A being which has no object outside itself is not an objective being. A being which is not itself an object for a third being has no being for its *object*, i.e. it has no objective relationships and its existence is not objective ... To be *sensuous*, i.e. to be real, is to be an object of sense, a *sensuous* object, and thus to have sensuous objects outside oneself, objects of one's sense perception. To be sensuous is to *suffer* (to be subjected to the actions of another)' (Marx, 1992, p. 390). How much is this an echo of Hegel in the past and the work of Sartre yet to come?

CONSCIOUSNESS AS PRAXIS

Marx maintains that consciousness is immanent in history rather than lying – other worldly – outside of the real processes of history. Likewise, consciousness is not merely something appertaining to the material world but, in fact, is constituted in practical–critical activity charged with the task of changing the world – an injunction Marx had been developing since his early writings. In holding that man is both a natural *and* a social being, Marx breaks down the opposition of a subjective consciousness and an objective world. If the starting point is seen to be man's active contact with nature in the creation of material life it is praxis that overcomes the opposition of subject and object. Marx ultimately rejects the subject–object opposition, seen as inherently conservative, to be superseded by praxis – practical–critical activity. Human social life is a creative product of this encounter with nature; a fundamentally historical process. With this collapse of the dualism of subject and object also comes the demise of subjectivity as disinterested presence with, and perception of, the world. There is no room for passive contemplation of the world if there is active engagement and productive interaction *in* the world through which consciousness is fashioned in the incessant struggle. Indeed it would seem that consciousness for Marx most often did not connote a withdrawn mentalistic reflection but, rather, represented the quality of active engagement with the world. Though for Marx this consciousness is human not *Absolute,* he still owes Hegel a debt for the seminal interpretation of man's relation to the world; it is social relations that either make or break man as a 'human being'.

If Marx's position is examined the partial, passive and personalised nature of *experience* discussed in Chapter Two contrasts sharply with a truly practical acquaintance of knowing or proving by use: practice – actually doing. In practice, knowledge comes from actively creating and recreating the material world not from undergoing exposure to accomplished reality. The implications for consciousness, of practice as opposed to *experience,* are profound. Marx concludes that: '[S]ocial life is essentially *practical.* All mysteries which mislead theory to mysticism find their rational solution in human practice and in the comprehension of this practice' not in 'the contemplation of single individuals in "civil society"' (Marx, in Marx and Engels 1968, p. 30). After establishing in *Theses on Feuerbach* the primacy of the 'ensemble' of social relations over human essence as an abstraction in each single individual, the pre-eminence of an active role for men in changing their circumstances, Marx asserts the significance of 'revolutionary', 'practical–critical' activity. Consciousness is created in the totality of human practice, and it is by practically producing and transforming reality that human beings come to know it – representing it as they construct it. Practice is the process of social reality being produced and reproduced by the sensuous activity of men in an unceasing recreation of their material life and the social relations within which they live. Petrovič contends that man for Marx is not merely a rational, a political or a tool-making animal but is embodied in his whole way of being – which Petrovič asserts Marx designated by the word 'practice'. For Petrovič, Marx's emphasis upon work on the objective world is the key to man's species-being with man constantly creating the world and himself. Man is thus an integral being defined by practice; not outside of history and unchanging but a general humanity and its conscious life's activity: universal – creative, self-creative of the world and humanity: 'Man is man if he realises his historically created human possibilities' (Petrovič, 1967, p. 80).

As a legacy of reaction against Hegel and the transformation of materialism Marx's work seems to lend itself to at least two rival interpretations as it pertains to consciousness. The first of these sees consciousness as determined by the material world, i.e., by social being. Here, life and consciousness appear as separate spatio-temporally. The second denies such a division by indicating that consciousness and life are totally fused in the act, the subject being totally one with the object in inextricable union, i.e., consciousness *in* activity. The first emphasis tends to invoke the theory of reflection (i.e., consciousness reflects social being), whilst the second seizes upon praxis. In holding to the distinction between inner and outer, apparent and real, Marx is indicating that the reflection is of the manifest forms not the underlying structure and, in arguing that capitalism cannot be understood from its appearances, he is demonstrating the existence of an underlying real world. The imminent risk with the prioritisation of praxis has been seen to be the prospect of a spilling over into a discredited idealism and empiricism preoccupied with consciousness as creative and proactive. It has been argued (Hoffman, 1975) that an inordinate emphasis on praxis has had the effect of portraying the chaos of fortuitous events of the objective world as only awaiting their ordering by the mind of man. Praxis becomes the solution to the conundrum of determinism; there is free creativity rather than the reflection of reality. It is a reintroduction of the empiricist subject–object divide where the "world" can be made and unmade seemingly at will. This, for Hoffman, amounts to a rejection of an objective dialectics in the social and natural world and a conflation of appearance and reality. Praxis, too, it should be added, can anyway be as disordered as thought and as various, and Marx never doubted that the medium of estrangement (alienation) was a practical one. Perhaps the determination/praxis distinction really amounts to a different way of looking at the same phenomenon or a different level of abstraction (much in the fashion associated with Spinoza).

In direct historical terms, Marx and Engels indicated that a crucial stage in the development of consciousness was the division between mental and manual labour. Formerly, thought and practice characterised the activity of all human beings, but then with the separation of mental labour from its manual counterpart, consciousness became divorced from practical activity. The loss by the ruling class and intellectuals of a direct connection with the creation of material life in manual activity and knowledge results in the generation of disengaged consciousness promulgated by control of the means of mental production. This forms the horizon of working-class 'limited material practice' and a crucial step, intrinsic to the division of labour, in the creation of classes. Inevitably, according to Marx, individuals are born into social relations independent of their will and as a consequence material conditions are produced by human practice which acquires an independence over and above individuals as an objective power which dominates them. Revolutionary practice becomes the struggle against this dominance, but the real character of practice itself is concealed by appearances: 'Appearances are reproduced in consciousness, not as an unavoidable result, but as an outcome of a "limited material mode of activity" .... Yet by conceiving the possibility of a revolutionary practice, Marx asserts that those appearances can be overcome' (Larrain, 1983, p. 34). But this prospect is inevitably informed and mediated by specific historical ideologies to the extent that 'sometimes Marx and Engels treated the phenomenon of ideology in conjunction with the principle of the social determination of consciousness, without explicitly examining the differences. Even more, they shifted from one to the other without adequately signalling the distinct levels of generality ... One can easily conclude from this that "consciousness" and "ideology" are coextensive and interchangeable' (Larrain, 1983, pp. 48–49).

What, then, did Marx mean by ideology which so clearly attends on consciousness?

CONSCIOUSNESS AS IDEOLOGY (ENGELS)

One reading of Marx and Engels is that they viewed ideology not as an epistemological category entailing a cognitive defect, but as an objective social phenomenon of class struggle.[4] In such a perspective, ideology does not constitute an individual's blindness to that which underlies their thinking – a condition itself which might be rectified, as it were, on the road to Damascus. What is definitive of ideology, it appears, is its role in the class struggle and Marx is concerned with specific ideologies which serve class interests by forming evaluative elements embodied in those interests. McCarney (1980) indicates that although there are intimations in Marx of men becoming conscious of the real nature of ideology (*The Preface*), of ideology forming a barrier to such consciousness (*Class Struggles in France*), and other instances of consciousness being ideology or ideologically constituted *(The German Ideology)*, the critical meaning of ideology for Marx emphasises the role of ideas in the class struggle as a medium for its expression, i.e., ideology is linked to the consciousness relevant to the class struggle. In effect, class interests have an inevitable bearing upon the social arrangements in capitalist society; though ideology is not engendered sufficiently by class interests it necessarily serves as the medium in which they are articulated. A contrasting interpretation (Larrain, 1983) of ideology across the whole range of Marx's work suggests that he referred to the 'inverted consciousness' of the world corresponding to an 'inverted world', which later in his critique of capitalism was given actual economic content. As regards ideology, Larrain adduces the dichotomy of the 'positive' – political ideas of class and the totality of forms of social consciousness – and the 'negative' – distorted thought and the masking of contradictions. He sees the emphasis on the solving of contradictions in practice as characteristic of the early Marx and as such, in fact, prior to Marx's critique of capitalism. Larrain indicated that Marx's re-reading of Hegel, leading up to the *Grundrisse* and *Capital*, introduced the tension of appearance and the underlying reality which had inevitable implications for ideology in Marxist thought. This was the recognition that complex capitalist relations are not revealed in their totality, i.e., capitalist practices are hidden by appearances or concealed by phenomenal forms, which not only conceal but are a manifestation of the underlying contradiction. Ideology, which denies the existence of such contradictions, was grounded by Marx in his analysis of production and circulation and exchange in capitalism, in itself a recognition that the capitalist 'inversion' of past labour dominating living labour creates corresponding inverted conceptions of a transposed consciousness.

In *Grundrisse*, Marx's (1973) more typical usage of ideology is as unexamined categories and assumptions inhibiting scientific investigation. Hence, distortion is not a result of mendacity but as a result of the play of dominant social relations, with capitalism being portrayed as harmonious and domination and subordination hidden. Ideology typically provides a distorted or inadequate representation of contradictions. By that token, ideology is not illusory because it is generated by those contradictions which it in turn misrepresents in the interests of the ruling class; ideology performs the role of hiding and concealing the contradictions of capitalism by denying their existence. Even without the intervention of ruling ideas the working class are not in a position to self-evidently come to know the real nature of capitalist social relations. Social being, as material practice, is the source of ideas about the world according to Marx. But, quite crucially, he recognised that men do not create the world just as they please but as inherited from the past and that working-class social being constitutes a limited material practice, which is itself generative of ideology. Larrain summarises ideology as referring 'to a limited practice which generates ideas that misrepresent social contradictions in the interest of the ruling class' (Larrain, 1983, p. 27). As Larrain indicates: 'Ideology is to do with those ideas which express practice inadequately' (p. 23). The reason for this is the limitations of practice itself, where, through the alienated division of labour in capitalism, the worker is beset by the hidden nature of the contradictions of social relations and the reproduction of the objective power of capital over labour. From Marx's viewpoint

> if the conscious expression of the real relations of these individuals is illusory, if in their imagination they turn reality upside-down, then this in its turn is the result of their limited

material mode of activity and their limited relations arising from it.
                              (Marx and Engels, 1976, vol. V, p. 36)

Ideology will only disappear when the contradictions that give rise to it are themselves removed, as Marx and Engels say: 'The removal of these notions from the consciousness of men, will . . . be effected by altered circumstances, not by theoretical deductions' (Marx and Engels, 1976, vol. V, p. 52).

Engels in a famous letter to Mehring referred specifically to the process of ideology (in the *Grundrisse* tradition) but simultaneously opened the door to the idea of false consciousness. He remarked that:

> Ideology is a process accomplished by the so-called thinker con-
> sciously, it is true, but with a false consciousness. The real
> motive forces impelling him remain unknown to him; otherwise
> it simply would not be an ideological process. Hence he imagi-
> nes false or seeming motive forces.
>   (Engels, in Marx and Engels, 1968, p. 690)

Although Engels indicated, by an attack on the popular forms of idealism, how ideology obscures the material source of its existence, the question is raised at this point as to whether or not an individual proletarian can become aware of the presence of ideology which develops a dynamic of its own – feeding on itself independently of its material base – remaining unknown to those subject to it. He says: 'That the material life conditions of the persons inside whose heads this thought process goes on in the last resort determine the course of this process remains of necessity unknown to these persons, for otherwise there would be an end to all ideology' (p. 618). This, for Engels, is definitive of ideology and such an interpretation is not confined to this isolated passage which links ideology with false consciousness. Perhaps most characteristic even in this instance is not false consciousness *per se* but that real, economic forces remain unknown to those subject to them. Engels also maintains that ideology is the medium of the inversion of economic relations, which forms a further critical aspect of ideology as the medium of contradictory social relations, contradictory consciousness and a limited practice. Ideologies do not exist to 'cover-up' reality but are generated systematically by the system of social relationships. Social struggle is then conducted ideologically without reference to their generative material conditions, with particular (vested) interests being presented as general interests.

Engels remarks that in the history of society ' . . . the actors are all endowed with consciousness, are men acting with deliberation or passion, working towards definite goals; nothing happens without a conscious purpose, without an intended aim' (Engels, in Marx and Engels, 1968, p. 612). But the *consciously* desired aims of individuals that reign on the surface have consequences other than actually intended; what is willed happens rarely and numerous intentions clash with each other – cross each other out. On the surface accident holds sway whilst history comprises hidden laws to be discovered. The many individual desires that impel movement constitute history but the real question is: 'What are the historical causes which transform themselves into these motives in the brains of the actors?' (p. 613). It is inner general laws that govern the course of history and move (in) the minds of men. History in Engels's view is constituted by the unintended consequences of the consciously desired ends of each person; manifold effects in the outer world being produced by many wills operating in different directions. Driving forces lie, very often unconsciously, behind the motives of men acting in history. Without giving in to full blown irrationalism he asks the question what driving forces stand behind these motives and which driving forces lie behind them, as it were, carrying the investigation further and further back. Engels is not interested in single individuals but rather in classes and masses resulting in historical transformation. Though he says everything which sets men in motion goes through their mind, the form it takes depends on historical circumstance.

Similarly, in *The Preface* of 1859, Marx concludes that a distinction should be made between the material transformation of the economic conditions of production ('the real foundation') which may be determined by the precision of natural science and 'the legal, political, religious, aesthetic or philosophic – in short, ideological forms in which men become conscious of this conflict and fight it out. Just as our opinion of an individual is not based on what he thinks of himself, so can we not judge of such a period of transformation by its own consciousness; on the contrary, this consciousness must be explained rather from the contradictions of material life, from the existing conflict between the social productive forces and the relations of production' (Marx, in Marx and Engels, 1968, p. 182). If men have become conscious of this conflict in ideological forms and fight it out, such consciousness, however, is not the means to judge the real nature of the transformation. Elsewhere, in the Preface of the first German edition of *Capital*, Marx confides that 'here individuals are dealt with only in so far as they are the personifications of economic categories, embodiments of class-relations and class interests'. His standpoint, Marx claims, 'can less than any other make the individual responsible for relations whose creature he socially remains, however much he may subjectively raise himself above them' (p. 230). According to Marx 'we do not set out from what men say, imagine, conceive, nor from men as narrated, thought of, imagined, conceived, in order to arrive at men in the flesh. We set out from real, active men, and on the basis of their real life process we demonstrate the development of the ideological reflexes and echoes of this life-process . . . Life is not determined by consciousness, but consciousness by life' (Marx and Engels, 1976, vol. V, p. 47). Upon these very social conditions of existence an entire class creates and forms its consciousness

> out of its material foundations and out of the corresponding social relations. The single individual, who derives them through tradition and upbringing, may imagine that they form the real motives and starting point of his activity . . . [a]nd as in private life one differentiates between what a man thinks and says of himself and what he really is and does, so in historical struggles one must distinguish still more the phrases and fancies of parties from their real organism and their real interests, their conception of themselves, from their reality.
>
> (Marx, in Marx and Engels, 1968, pp. 117–118)

Not only, then, is there a distinction drawn here between what a man (sic) says and does, which is not really Marx's primary concern, but also the impression given that the superstructure of consciousness generated by the creation of material life, to individuals who imbibe and enact it, is an imaginary relation to the underlying reality.

For Hegel, and Marx drew on this idea, it is only when spirit has reached a certain point in its supra-personal development – its completion – that the individual can know itself in terms of Spirit. This envisaged scenario raises some difficult questions. If a certain stage has to be reached before the individual plays a self-conscious part, has the movement of *Geist* hithertofore been purely providential without need of human intervention? If so, why should this supra-personal dynamism abate once individuals recognise themselves in the reality of which they are part? Such a prospect is grist to the mill of anti-humanist, structuralist Marxism. There are, however, copious examples of Marx and Engels referring, quite advisedly, to individuals (Forbes, 1990). If on the one hand to refer to mind or ego as an abstract entity divorced from the real world is for Marx patent nonsense, the individual human personality is for him, on the other hand, a psychosomatic unity firmly rooted in the natural *and* social-historical world. Nevertheless, the status of the human subject in the thought of Marx has remained problematical and it is a question to which this discussion will return in Chapter Six.

CLASS CONSCIOUSNESS (LENIN)

Notwithstanding cases made by Hobbes and Hegel, we have in Marx a very explicit usage of consciousness in a collective sense. The fundamental ontological dualism in Marxism is that of the bourgeoisie and proletariat – owners of the means of production and sellers of labour power and, whilst a class is formed objectively in relation to capital, awareness of that relation remains contingent on the emergence of class consciousness. Marx's most characteristic position is the class 'in itself'/'for itself' dichotomy as a transition from an objective before to an objective and subjective after (Marx and Engels, 1976, vol. VI, p. 211). A class 'for itself' has come to a profound understanding of its objective and inherently conflictual connection with another class, recognising the need to defend itself and its common interests against the exploitative class. At this point there is a conjunction of objective and subjective components; to *be* in that position within the forces and relations of production and to achieve consciousness of it. Class consciousness, contradictory in structure and dialectical in development, is created through struggle. Following Marx, Lenin's emphasis tended to be on a before/after consciousness with the enterprise being to get from one to the other – a class 'in itself' to 'for itself'. The dichotomy of consciousness posited by Lenin (1960) is that of trade-union consciousness as opposed to proletarian scientific ideology, with ideology forming the expression of the interests of a class, i.e., there is proletarian ideology as there is bourgeois ideology. Therefore, ideology is not necessarily negative or false consciousness: bourgeois ideology is wrong because it is bourgeois, and ideology loses its pejorative, negative connotation characteristic of Marx. Here ideologies are being seen as contending knowledge frames about society, where sets of ideas – as ideology – bring values to bear on the class struggle with socialism being the ideology of the class struggle of the proletariat. It would be instructive at this stage to project forward a review of just a few of the classic contributions on this issue, with consciousness being seen to possess not only social and historical content but ideological content at that – though the terms of reference change.

LUKÁCS AND REIFICATION

For Marx, ideology was, at least, distorted knowledge working in the interests of the dominant class, yet the emphasis from Lenin onwards has seen a dissolution of this initial 'negative' usage. There is exemplified in Lukács (1971) the tension noted above between practice and thought and the necessity of overcoming the mystification of capitalism and existential dichotomies of consciousness. Lukács saw class relations, in providing different vantage points, as determining consciousness, with thought a product of place in the world of production. Whereas the working class can attain a true picture of capitalism, the bourgeoisie is inevitably trapped in false consciousness because of its structural position – an idea in itself testimony to the influence of Hegel on Lukács's thinking. To Lukács, true consciousness is to be obtained by the proletariat and ideology for him, as for Lenin, is tied to different class interests and the role of ideas in the class struggle. Lukács tended to view ideology as a class *weltanschaung* (world view) which is largely a substitute for the concrete practices of the class itself. From his point of view the proletariat had the ability to see the social totality as a concrete historical phenomenon; but ironically enough, that in itself was not sufficient: the inevitable struggle was against the consequences of the totality of capitalist ideology. Lukács follows Hegel and Marx in envisaging on

the part of the human subject a crucial identification with and assimi-
lation to the external world, abolishing the object as mere datum and
the focus of contemplation. Here, Lukács is intent on steering a
middle course between the abstract, autonomous 'consciousness' of
Hegel and the legacy of Engels with its repudiation of an active role
for subjects to be replaced by the working out of determinist laws.
Whilst, simultaneously, avoiding succumbing to the isolated, egoistic
individual subject of bourgeois myth, Lukács holds on to the potentiality of a creative role for human activity and consciousness, but,
ironically, in the process tends to elevate the proletariat to the
abstract status of Hegel's *Absolute Idea*. Lukács indicated how Hegel
sought to overcome the antitheses of rationalism by redrawing the
inheritance of the dialectical method to facilitate the *aufhebung*-
supersession-of antitheses in reason. Pointing out how Hegel's system
consumed itself without establishing the real identical subject–object
of history, Lukács turned to the proletariat to fulfill that destiny, but,
in doing so, however, introduced the source of the frustration of that
destiny–reification.

In a situation of reification, social forces and objects appear mutually independent and are only 'unified' in the rationalisation of formal laws masking the partial autonomous functioning of society:
only the immediate structure of capitalism is revealed. The way in
which social being is experienced is through consciousness built up in
the world that appears natural and self-evidently real. The alternative
suggests not experience, but , rather, knowledge of history, causality,
structure and action in all their complexity. Consciousness implies
knowledge but also practical–critical activity: thought and practice is
practical thought, though there is inevitably comprehension, meaning and capacity before consciousness. Reification is thus undermined
and overcome only labouriously and piecemeal – from centre to
periphery and periphery to centre. Yet, Lukács contended that it is
not possible to be human in bourgeois society and man's double
bind is a world of things to overcome that are the objects of his
desire; commodities that have the magic of creation in the shaping
of the world in man's own image. The immediate ways in which
this encloses cultural horizons was not explored by Lukács and, in
effect, the reified world of consumption beyond the work situation –
where commodity production impacts on consciousness – is left
on one side. The various forms of reification in advanced capitalism

are not theorised at all by Lukács who refused to engage set social and historical instances. He himself never seemed to resolve the contradiction between the contention that the working class had the 'right' class *weltanschaung* and his assertion of its inevitable suffusion by reification – even of its own making. This, coupled with his initial blindness to the nature of the wage relationship and its concomitant effect on culture, means that the dialectic remains unresolved. Lukács is concerned to explicate '[t]he dialectical cleavage in the consciousness of the proletariat' (1971, p. 73). But is this 'dialectical cleavage' ever resolved in the thought of Lukács himself? In criticism, it has been remarked that:

> The main problem with Lenin's and Lukács's conceptions of ideology was that they could not resolve dialectically the opposition between spontaneous consciousness and socialist ideology, between psychological consciousness and ascribed consciousness, between philosophy and common sense. So these pairs become dichotomies which separated the perfect and fully lucid world of science from the distorted and in coherent world of spontaneous consciousness.
>
> (Larrain, 1983, p. 86)

According to Lenin spontaneous class consciousness, including trade union consciousness, is a resource of the bourgeoisie. To counter this, revolutionary consciousness had to be ushered in by the party. Lukács, too, at one stage, insisted that imputed consciousness had to be implanted from 'outside'. He tends to talk in terms of 'closing the gap' and healing 'the cleavage' between psychological and imputed consciousness. This would be achieved not, as it were, via a 'breakthrough' from one to the other, but in sloughing-off alien ideologies contaminating working-class consciousness. McCarney (1980) insists, that there is no room for impure ideologies in either Lenin or Lukács. Revolutionary ideology is, for them, simply the ideology of the working class and could only possibly be masked by bourgeois ideology.

GRAMSCI AND HEGEMONY

Lenin – spontaneous trade-union consciousness and proletarian scientific ideology – Lukács – 'actual' or 'psychological' and 'ascribed' or 'imputed' consciousness – and Gramsci – 'two theoretical consciousness (or one contradictory consciousness)' (Gramsci, 1971, p. 333) – have each developed alternative compartments to consciousness. Larrain indicates that Lenin, Lukács and Gramsci were not familiar with the 'negative' view presented in, the then unpublished, *The German Ideology* which, in itself, Larrain adduces as one contributory factor in the transition from the 'negative' to the 'positive' conception of ideology. Larrain contends that Gramsci, too, developed the 'positive' dimension whilst recognising, unlike Lenin and Lukács, that proletarian ideology can express working-class interests imperfectly and that bourgeois ideology could win the support of the masses. Gramsci's position, whilst not diverging from Marx or Lenin in terms of the overall political project, problematised the potential inherent in consciousness by highlighting a coexistent, symbiotic, contradictory consciousness that inevitably poses a problem for the before/after project of a class 'in itself' transformed into one 'for itself'. For Gramsci, the working class has two theoretical consciousnesses or one contradictory consciousness: one consciousness implicit in their practical activity unifying them with the other members of their class, the other superficially explicit or verbally accepted unquestioningly from the past creating a contradiction between intellectual beliefs and conduct and a contrast between thought and action. Here we have the coexistence of two conceptions of the world, with the one couched in words and the other displayed in action. The submission and intellectual subordination of the working class to the bourgeoisie and bourgeois conceptions of the world means that it is this conception of the world that the working class verbally affirms and believes itself to be following. Passive consent to the dominant class emerges not because the bourgeois world view reflects the practical activity and aspirations of the working class, but because they do not have the conceptual tools with which they would be able to comprehend effectively and act upon their predicament. Being subject to and lacking the purchase of a network of dominant cultural institutions, the working class cannot develop the theoretical framework within which to formulate any radical alternative which might accrue from their activity.

Gramsci's analysis provides a distinction between 'common sense', which is seen as 'good' sense, and 'folklore'.[5] Yet, he saw the working class being weaned away from seeing the world in folkloristic terms and being initiated into traditional, mainstream culture by the transmission of the universal, humanistic culture. At his most Leninist, Gramsci pointed out how the working class would come to appropriate human culture through education, though, at his most prescient, he described the mechanism whereby the cultural emancipation of the working class is held in check. Not only does this comprise the hold that middle class has on education, with their culture being conducive to success within it, but the very operation of hegemony – an undoubtedly critical concept in the analysis of consciousness. Though the usage of the concept hegemony in the thought of Lenin and Lukács should not be ignored it is a crucial dimension of Gramsci's rendition of hegemony that one class directs whilst the other appears to consent – both pulling together. Discussing the phenomenon, Gramsci stated that 'this consent is "historically" caused by the prestige (and consequent confidence) which the dominant group enjoys because of its position and function in the world of production' (1971, p. 12). Through the institutions of civil society and the structured influence of the occupational order the ruling class's view of the world comes to be accepted. The obverse of hegemony is that it allows the so-called subordinate class to pursue its own ends within the framework of capitalism, facilitating the integration and cooperation of the working class rather than their imminent emancipation. As a consequence the working class developed marked contrasts between thought and action, itself an expression of the contradiction of the social historical order as experienced by the great social masses. Flashes of organic group action informed by its own (if embryonic) conception of the world, rest uneasily with a preponderant affirmation of the normalcy of working class submission and subordination. This view, according to Gramsci, is not so much generated from working-class social being in capitalism, but is, instead, 'borrowed' from the dominant class itself.

CONCLUSION

Anderson has shown that accounting for the actual or alleged philosophical influences on Marx and marxism can reveal a complex, if inconclusive, picture. Certainly, Marx does not engage directly with the nature of consciousness and self *per se* inherited from rationalism, empiricism and idealism. Ultimately, it is not his problem. The change in the philosophy of consciousness charted here is not just one of a shift from idealism to dialectical materialism, in the transition from Hegel to Marx, but a change in the very constitution of consciousness. Marx says that consciousness is from the very beginning a social product and remains so as long as men exist, i.e., it is a secondary and derivative phenomenon to be changed by changed circumstance. In Marx and the classical Marxists consciousness appears as socially determined – but *not* as a mere reversal of the direction of influence of subject and object generally or that indicated specifically by Kant. Rather, consciousness is determined in social and historical specificity by the mode of production and its concomitant political and ideological forms. Consciousness is formed and informed by set historical locations and has, as such, 'content'. The extent to which this 'content' is self-evident or illusive has preoccupied the classical Marxists discussed here as has the question of whether a collective, class-consciousness can be achieved, whilst most often begging the question of whether such consciousness was ever a defining moment in the life of any one individual.

The difference between all rationalist and idealist philosophers and Marx is that the former, after Kant, speculated on appearance as opposed to the thing in itself (its inherent properties, supposed, in the main unknowable) whilst the latter sought to reveal underlying social relations by unmasking the 'thing' without which abstract essence remains inevitably unknowable. It is undoubtedly the case that Marx conceived of an underlying reality of *real* economic and political forces which remain unknown to those subject to them. If appearance and reality always coincided, Marx informs us, there would be no need for science; the tool, fashioned in his hand, to cut through the delusive appearance of everyday life in capitalism. Ideally, truth and knowledge realise one another in practice, as for Marx truth involves not only practice but also, inevitably, its comprehension. Unfortunately, in a situation of a pre-determined, unconscious practice, seemingly imposed by an external, objective power, truth appears as independent of knowledge of it. Truth and knowledge are not viewed as either side of an essential process of practice but as divorced and, at best, unrelated and relativistic judgements about the social world. Unlike positivism which posits truth as residing in reality awaiting subsequent verification – a pre-packaged truth which a certain kind of knowledge will eventually avail – truth for Marx does not pre-date the creation of material reality but is immanent in the process: 'For Marx there is no absolute truth waiting to be unveiled, but there is an objective historical truth which deploys itself in the historical process as men and women practically construct their social world. However, this does not mean that Marx adopts a pragmatic conception whereby truth becomes that which is useful or adaptive for the individual nor does it mean that men and women can arbitrarily produce reality as they wish' (Larrain, 1983, pp. 214–215).

In Marx's view man is ultimately purposive and it is this that distinguishes humankind from other species: men make society and society makes men, incurring the philosophical dilemma of how one thing can be both determining and determined simultaneously. Intent on laying bare the inner dynamics of capitalism, Marx subsequently set himself the seemingly intractable problem of 'voluntarism' versus 'determinism' as the back cloth to his philosophy of history. One of these views of man is of an active agent in the world who by making/ changing that world, makes/changes her/his own nature. The other, is of a being conditioned by capitalism and contingent upon its inner dynamics; a bearer of an objective, structural instance. If thought is totally identified with praxis what then is the status of reflection as contemplative meditation? Marx seems to berate this prospect at every opportunity. Between Hegel's fantastical, omniscient consciousness and Marx's consciousness instantiated in practice, there appears to be no room for a pared down faculty of human beings to recognise which way to turn. Why agonise over what people say *or* do when, in fact, individuals remain agents and bearers of objective structures? It is the objective system of regular connections that matter and the alternative derives from a problematic of the subject where 'agents of a social formation "men", are not seen as the "bearers" of objective instances (as they are for Marx), but as the genetic principle of the levels of the social whole. This is a problematic of "*social actors*", of individuals as the origin of "social action": sociological research thus leads finally, not to the study of the objective co-ordinates that determine the distribution of agents into social classes and the contradictions between these classes, but to the search for *finalist* explanations founded on the *motivations of conduct* of the individual actors' (Poulantzas, in Urry and Wakeford, 1973, p. 295).

Consciousness in the period of classical Marxism, becomes something other than the sum or the average of the thought and feelings of given individuals; it does not constitute the mere psychology of the individual or of the moment in time. Nor is consciousness merely the idea which men form about their situation in life and their concomitant needs and wants – the mutual self-awareness of a group – which itself perhaps reflects an earlier usage of the word consciousness as 'shared knowledge'. The meaning of consciousness as it has evolved and featured characteristically in the Marxist literature generally, suggests that consciousness is a social and historical product *but* that it exists also as a shared system of symbols and meanings, i.e., language. Consciousness exists for individual human beings because it is a social product inscribed in social practices, connecting consciousness with materiality through the means of physical communication and apprehension, i.e., the 'practical consciousness' of language. Nevertheless, it will be language and communication as concerns that will endure in isolation from consciousness, although it is not clear that is what Marx intended. Though Marx himself came to be preoccupied with the deep structures of capitalism (*not* of language) where no one speaks for themselves, later Marxist thought, as will be seen, has held fast to a Marxism of language as a substitute for the political economy of consciousness. The impetus for this began before the end of the nineteenth century as consciousness came under attack from a wide range of philosophers largely indifferent to the revolutionary ideas and ideals that had fired Marxism.

4

THE OVERCOMING OF CONSCIOUSNESS IN PHILOSOPHY

Consciousness is the last and latest development of the organic and consequently also the most unfinished and weakest part of it.

(Nietzsche, 1977, p. 158)

IRRATIONALISM - SCHOPENHAUER AND NIETZSCHE

Contemporaneously with developments in Marxism and in stark contrast, philosophical thought embarked upon a radical reorientation of the legacy inherited from Hume to Hegel. Russell has remarked that:

German philosophers, from Kant to Hegel, had not assimilated Hume's arguments. I say this deliberately, in spite of the belief which many philosophers share with Kant, that his *Critique of Pure Reason* answered Hume. In fact, these philosophers – at least Kant and Hegel – represent a pre-Humean type of rationalism, and can be refuted by Humean arguments. The philosophers who cannot be refuted in this way are those who do not pretend to be rational, such as Rousseau, Schopenhauer, and Nietzsche. The growth of unreason throughout the nineteenth century and what has passed of the twentieth is a natural sequel to Hume's destruction of empiricism.

(Russell, 1961, p. 646)

The similarities of Hume, Schopenhauer and Nietzsche on the primacy of instinct over logic, reason and consciousness is pronounced
and indicates the extent to which, whilst suggesting the opposite,
human beings are driven back from a world based upon reason and
rational cooperation. Additionally, by raising the issue of instinct and
giving the impression that this is a property of all human beings, i.e.,
shared collectively, the real drift to a super individualism where it
remains ultimately *my* judgement, *my* imagination, etc., is effectively
concealed: 'For Hume, instinct and custom must be the guides in life;
we must, of necessity, act on principles we cannot possibly justify.
Human reason, for him, is limited, weak, and best employed as a
"slave of the passions". Pursued for its own sake, it can lead only to
the destruction of "all assurance and conviction"' (Aune, 1970, p.
71). Not only for Hume does consciousness have recourse to habit,
but reason alone cannot be a motive for action of the will with will,
itself, being viewed as the spring of action. Although the problem of
will had been considered by the ancient Greeks and St Augustine and
in the early modern period will was regarded an act of thought and
identified with judgement in Descartes and Spinoza and as the last
'appetite' or 'inclination' in deliberating by Hobbes, it is really with
Schopenhauer that will is (un)covered systematically. In Taylor's
view: 'Kant's debt to Augustine is as obvious as Rousseau's. Everything depends on a transformation of the will' (Taylor, 1992a, p. 365)
but whilst for Rousseau will stems from our feelings, for Kant it is our
rational nature that constitutes the inner impulse. Even whilst recast-
ing him, Schopenhauer feels he is the real heir of the Kantian tradition
and Fichte, Schelling and Hegel, in particular, are loathed and vilified.
    Schopenhauer likens himself to one who measures the height of a
tower by directly applying the measuring rod to the tower itself
whereas Kant, he says, is comparable to the person who measures the
tower from the shadow it casts: 'Philosophy, therefore, is for him a
science *of* concepts, but for me a science *in* concepts' (Schopenhauer,
1969, p. 453). Schopenhauer insisted that concepts were the medium
of philosophy not its subject matter, as that, itself, was reserved for
deepening our understanding of reality; it is the proper connection of
inner *and* outer experience that provides the only possible solution to
the riddle of the world (p. 428). He holds it is perception that is the
only source of all evidence and it is this world of perception which
surrounds us that Kant skips over; to extend the figure of speech, this

world is insufficiently defined and differentiated in the shadow that reproduces only the external outline. Schopenhauer says he himself starts from direct, intuitive knowledge whilst Kant starts from indirect, reflected knowledge which leads to a lack of discrimination between intuitive knowledge and abstract, discursive knowledge. To circumvent the problematic legacy of Kant with the noumenal realm being the cause of our experience but with causality itself only having meaning as it adheres to the phenomenal world, Schopenhauer suggested a double-aspect theory of reality. He argued that the phenomenal and noumenal are the same thing understood differently rather than the noumenal being the cause of the phenomenal. The world *is* our representation. What exists, exists only for the subject. This is the extent of the existence of reality and with the maxim 'no object without subject' (p. 29) materialism and dogmatism (realism) are confounded. In effect: 'The world is entirely representation and as such requires the knowing subject as the supporter of its existence' (p. 30). Schopenhauer says that '[b]esides the will and the representation, there is absolutely nothing known or conceivable for us' (p. 105). For him we can never get at the inner nature of things from without, for however much we investigate we obtain nothing but images and names as a combination of representations – social enquiry, by implication, is left to sketch the ramparts and forbidden entry to the keep. Schopenhauer argues that the world as representation, as appearance, is an illusion and reality is hidden behind the 'veil of Maya'. The will (and the realm of ideas) is one, whereas there can only be multiplicity in the phenomenal world of representations. Looking inward what is observed is not anyone's individual will but, rather, *the* universal will.

Consciousness is the starting point of Schopenhauer's philosophy but is rendered the mere surface of the mind. Like the earth we do not know the inside just the crust. He agrees with Kant about the *a priori* capacities of consciousness and proceeds to divide consciousness, of the psyche, into intellect and will – of which the latter, as will be seen, is the more important. Consciousness is concerned with knowledge; will, in contrast, is not. The will is pre-eminent over the intellect which is secondary, subordinate and conditioned: 'My philosophy' he says 'is the first which has come to place the essence of man, not in consciousness, but in the will, which is not necessarily linked with consciousness' (Schopenhauer, quoted in Larrain, 1994, p. 35).

Whilst Schopenhauer is prepared to countenance that consciousness has to do with the choice of means in any activity and that it can be filled up with only one thing at a time, reason is downgraded and a subordinated intellect remains at the behest of the will. Acts of will, in themselves, are in no way under our control; blind impulse rules as motives are rationalised. Will is eternal becoming, an endless flux, with an absence of all aims and limits. Although there may be knowledge of what is willed here and now, that does not extend to what is willed in general. Willing as a whole has no end in view, despite each individual act having an end or purpose, and our inevitable fate is a fluctuation between desire and boredom. No sooner has the present given way to a much anticipated future than it loses its allure, as promised happiness fails to materialise, though we remain convinced that the emptiness of today is only a stepping-stone to a fulfilled tomorrow. Sexual desire, the classic instance for Schopenhauer, is both the expression of the body – the will objectified – and an alien impulse within us. Individualism is illusory and a source of evil when it comes to be felt that 'we' and our desires actually matter. The solution is to give up desire and be released by will – for will to be denied, i.e., asceticism. In the full light of consciousness, will, the in-itself of everything as endless striving, is seen for what it is – endless suffering. Only rarely, and then by genius, is consciousness emancipated from the will in contemplation of the aesthetic. However, as Larrain (1994) points out there is a manifest contradiction here for how can reason – even in exceptional circumstances – be released sufficiently to come to recognise its own servitude. Ordinary mortals are trapped by will in the mundane, though it is will that forces reason to hide the fact. Pain is dressed up as hope and the desired object is provided, at least, as a consoling image.

In Schopenhauer the feeling that there is more at work in the human condition than 'reason' and the 'rational' connects his philosophy to the preoccupations of Hindu and Buddhist philosophy which informed his own work and to which he compared its achievements and to the ideas of Kierkegaard and Nietzsche to come in the west.[1] Anticipated, here, in Schopenhauer is the work of Freud on the unconscious and the ideas of Bergson on *élan vital* (life force), as well as the obvious echo of Hobbes's view of human nature. Schopenhauer has provided rich pickings for subsequent philosophical thought though not always acknowledged. His work also provides a seminal discussion of the body which has also been picked up – though inconsistently. Russell has remarked that ' Schopenhauer retained the thing-in-itself, but identified it with will. He held that what appears to perception as my body is really my will. . . . The phenomenon corresponding to a volition is a body movement; that is why, according to Schopenhauer, the body is the appearance of which will is the reality' (Russell, 1961, pp. 723–724). But it is Nietzsche that inherits Schopenhauer's mantle wherein he turns the vice of will into an incipient virtue. Indeed, Schopenhauer's description of a dissembling and dilatory consciousness enfeebled by reason is remarkably similar to that plied later by Nietzsche. The ultimate challenge to the emphasis in western social thought on reason and rationality and conscious control over the self, indeed, does come with Nietzsche though there are, in fact, precedents.

Montaigne (1958), for example, tells us at one point that he cannot keep his subject (himself) still as with a 'natural drunkenness' it staggers on befuddled – a condition he takes it in at the moment he turns his attention to it. Although Montaigne's method was based on this kind of shrewd self-scrutiny and introspection fed on irony, where self-understanding is contingent upon a grasp of one's corporeality and is an intuitive means to the understanding of others, for him human action is affected as much by chance as by design, with vice figuring as much as virtue in private and public affairs. Montaigne himself was well aware of the insights of Machiavelli and recognised that human beings invest in their world an unwarranted natural status regarding what is, in fact, mere convention. His is the recognition of the range and recreancy of belief. The corollary of Montaigne's philosophy is a thorough-going relativism and scepticism born out of the contention that in human social life nothing can be construed as immutable. Human life is ultimately dynamic in a situation in which there are no absolutes and courses of action have to be adopted in that knowledge. Nietzsche in his early work, already much taken by Schopenhauer, was, in turn, attracted to Montaigne's 'cheerfulness' and opposition to systematic thought and dogma. Whilst Schopenhauer argued that the phenomenal and the noumenal are the same thing understood differently, Nietzsche conflates appearance and reality. Being and the thing-in-itself, for Nietzsche, whilst appearing to be so much, if not everything, are actually empty of meaning; conversely the will-o'-the-wisp, flickering dance of spirits of appearance – a feeling it achieves in its self-mockery – is active, living itself and not a cover which can be, finally, blown away.

Nietzsche points out, in his early essays, that it should not be a question of delving deeply down the shaft of your being seeking after the 'real' you with all its attendant dangers, but , rather, your authentic self lying high and dry uplifted on the revered objects of your life that form a 'stepladder on which until now you have climbed up to yourself; for your true being does not lie deeply hidden within you, but rather immeasurably high above you, or at least above what you commonly take to be your ego' (Nietzsche, 1995, p. 174). He describes a mistaken search for a higher self supposedly lying hidden somewhere so that the spatial dimension of Nietzsche's thought here is quite tangible. His rejection of 'inwardness' in the form of consciousness was to become emphatic: 'From consciousness there proceed countless errors which cause an animal, a man, to perish earlier than necessary. . . . If the preservative combination of the instincts were not incomparably stronger, if it did not in general act as regulator, mankind must have perished through its perverse judgements and waking fantasies, its superficiality and credulity, in short through its consciousness' (Nietzsche, 1977, p. 158). Nietzsche, although implacably opposed to the idea of consciousness, provides, as is his way, a uniquely insightful interpretation. He, too, recognises that a great deal of human thought and activity goes on without the need of the 'reflection' of consciousness. Man, he says, thinks continually but does not know it. He rehearses the maxim that a thought comes when 'it' will, not when 'I' will. Consciousness, according to Nietzsche, owes its origins to the human capacity and need for communication; it is, in effect, a connecting network between man and man compelled by their own individual frailty and vulnerability to make known their need for help. The need for man to 'know' what he lacks, how he feels and what he is thinking thus becomes the raison d'être of consciousness. For Nietzsche the evolution of language and consciousness go hand in hand, conscious thinking taking place in words and communication-signs. The 'sign inventing' man, he remarks, is the man ever more sharply conscious of himself but, paradoxically, his attempt to understand and know himself in an individual way only brings to mind (to consciousness) not what is individual in him but the perspective of the community (or 'herd' Nietzsche says disparagingly). Actions that are personal, unique and individual no longer seem to be so when translated into consciousness. Nietzsche, his vituperation never undermining his assiduous grasp of detail, inveighs presciently that 'the world of which we can become conscious is only a surface-and-sign world, a world made universal and common – that everything which becomes conscious thereby *becomes* shallow, thin, relatively stupid, general, sign, characteristic of the herd, that with all becoming conscious there is united a great fundamental corruption, falsification, superficialising and generalisation' (p. 67). Increasing consciousness, he divines as one who should know, is in danger of becoming an illness. He was unconvinced that the claim from Kant to Schopenhauer of the knowing subject's reflection on itself could be in any way indemnified. Even the virtuoso of self-reflection denied himself: for Nietzsche no analysing himself, no 'knowing' himself, no self-observation – all a sign of degeneration. He rejects emphatically self-reflection and its inevitable generation of a false consciousness.

In Nietzsche, instincts are elevated above reason and are not to be denied and his pragmatic theory of truth seems to hang on just how successful instincts will be. But instincts can drag us down if they are not life-enhancing; torrents of the soul have to be channelled, not allowed to dry up. He says: 'The world seen from within, the world described and defined according to its "intelligible character" – it would be "will to power" and nothing else. –' (p. 229). Nietzsche attests that thinking is the relationship of drives one to another; it is the only 'reality' there is. The idea of nothing mysterious connecting the parts but their relation forms a pronounced echo of Hume. Nietzsche develops the curious idea of a tyrannical, demanding 'something' in the soul leading to a 'defiance of oneself'. Our body, for Nietzsche, is only a social structure composed of many 'souls' commanding and obeying as the very embodiment of will: 'And life itself told me this secret: "Behold", it said, "I am that *which must overcome itself again and again*". To be sure, you call it will to procreate or impulse towards a goal, towards the higher, more distant, more manifold: but all this is one and one secret' (p. 225). The idea of man 'overcoming' himself is one that Nietzsche uses often. He later implores: ' "*Will a self*" – Active, successful natures act, not according to the dictum "know thyself", but as if there hovered before them the commandant: *will* a self and thou shalt *become* a self' (p. 232). How much is this an ironic parody of the rational system of Hegel? Here, Nietzsche is describing those who create themselves as new, unique and incomparable and a law unto themselves.[2] Perhaps one of the reasons for Nietzsche's antipathy to consciousness is that it is the dissuader as its 'Voice' is heard. Yet whereas the self (and the 'subject' and the 'ego') for Nietzsche is an illusion, individual identity exists as the vehicle of original and creative instinct – free to make its way in the world.

In relation to knowledge and truth, Nietzsche was persuaded in his later work that there are different alternative systems of thought which interpret the external world and no independent, authoritative criterion for determining that one system is more valued than another. The prospect of a single reality independent of our interpretations is abandoned as is the centrality of the human subject. Knowledge and truth is what is useful and works in practice; not true or false but effective or ineffective, with truth paying dividends in the ultimate test of experience. Nietzsche assumed that it was mistaken to believe in an order of things other than, and superior to, that which is experienced directly. In this view, knowledge and truth do not exist above or outside of the social world; they are placed in the world pragmatically. Nietzsche claims that truth issues from an ascendant will, giving those who hold that belief a feeling of strength and power. For him all reasoning is a rationalisation and language, from this standpoint, falsifies and distorts reality in simplifying experience, in effect producing a fatal incommensurability between language and the world. That world, in a constant state of flux, cannot be grasped by language. However, another interpretation of Nietzsche's view of language is that there can be no private 'communication':

> Or perhaps better, the "privacy" of certain experiences cannot be a matter of knowledge, strictly so called. That is, either there are shared terms for shared experiences, or there are no experiences (nothing identifiable as an experience, much less as an experience of *mine* or of *Nietzsche's*). The ability to communicate, Nietzsche says, is a condition of any awareness of what is to be communicated. We do not first become aware of what we are going to say, and then figure out a way to express it to others.
>
> If, then, there were an experience for which one did not yet have a common language, by Nietzsche's lights this would not – not *yet* anyway – *be* an experience in the strict sense of the word.
>
> (Havas, in Dreyfus and Hall, 1992, p. 242)

We are unable to escape the constraints of language and we have no option but to operate within its confines. Should we wish to cut through those chains which bind us we are unable to do anything but rattle further the chains themselves. If we could express the ineffable we would not be trapped, but every such 'idea', we find, needs must coat itself in the *concept* regardless. This interpretation of Nietzsche's position on language obviously anticipates Wittgenstein as will be seen in Chapter Six. Nietzsche (like Heidegger, as, too, will be seen) contends that human convention is contingent and groundless, yet there *are* only human truths not deep metaphysical ones and it is not possible to stand outside the world with which we are present. Life then, is the source of its own significance. Nietzsche's thoughts on these issues anticipate Mach and the philosophical school of pragmatism each of which, in their own way, provides a more unbounded denouement to the story of consciousness thus far than that even provided by Nietzsche himself.

MACH, JAMES AND THE PRAGMATISTS AND BERGSON

The work of the physicist and philosopher Ernst Mach, drawing on both Comte and Hume, amounts to an elimination of all metaphysical questions and results in perhaps *the* most complete disavowal of the self and ego. The 'I', self or ego is no unitary phenomenon in this view with the religious consequence of no survival of the soul after death. It is clear to see, as Mach came to, how this viewpoint coincides with the Buddhist world view. In fact Mach saw ethical virtue in not overvaluing the self. If the self as such did not exist there could be no question of isolation of it in the universe – no solipsism. This was a charge levelled at Mach's approach of sensationalism and phenomenalism where sensations ('relative' to each other and logically prior to objects) are the ultimately only real components of the world through which anything knowable can be discovered and where material objects become permanent possibilities of sensation. Mach's view of the self has been captured wonderfully well by Pannekoek: 'What we denote by "I myself" is a complex of recollections and feelings, former and present sensations and thoughts connected by continuity of memory, bound to a special body, but only partly permanent' (Pannekoek, 1975, p. 47). Mach adduces that sensations are the true elements of the world forming the simplest constituents of phenomena. For him the world is comprised of our sensations, in effect the only means we have of knowing that world including our 'selves' which consist in sensations alone. Not only is 'I, myself' a complex of sensations, but elements are mutually connected up in many 'myselfs' as their nodal points which continuously change – arising and disappearing – producing differing arrangements of the physical *and* psychical worlds which both consist of like elements only ordered in a different way. In Mach's view every object is both physical and psychical simultaneously in the sensual realm of consciousness. This disposes of dualisms of body and mind and sets the scene for an 'inter-subjective world' of all such subjects. Pannekoek indicates that Mach is at very least equivocal on the question of the existence of an outer world independent of man, perhaps revealing his penchant – more obvious in his later work – for subjectivism and idealism. But it is really with empiricism that Mach should be associated and, like Hume, he sees value in an unsophisticated 'naive realism' for its utility in the life-world of mankind. On this count a telling polemic against Mach and his pupil Avenarius and his theory of empiriocriticism can be found in Lenin (1960). Avenarius believes that by focussing upon then replacing 'introjection' he, like Mach, has done away with all dualisms. The 'in-me' of introjection is replaced by a 'before-me' and what is 'imagined' transformed into what is 'found present'. For Avenarius thinking is no 'other side'; thinking for him, is not even produced by the brain. He dispenses entirely with the mind as a 'special something' yet the world consists only of my experience of it. Both Avenarius and Mach start from, and dissolve the entire world into, personal experience. Habermas remarks that in Mach: 'The only reflection admissible serves the self-abolition of reflecting on the knowing subject . . . [where] The levelling out of subjectivity has its counterpart in the effacement of the distinction between essence and appearance. Facts are all there is' (Habermas, 1978, p. 85).

In the work of Peirce, too, in setting the scene for the pragmatists, states of consciousness, as singular events, lack cognitive status. A thought is an inexplicable fact with Peirce holding that 'no present actual thought (which is a mere feeling) has any meaning, any intellectual value; for this lies not in what is actually thought, but in what this thought may be connected with in representation by subsequent thoughts; so that the meaning of a thought is altogether something virtual' (quoted in Habermas, 1978, p. 105). In his critique of Descartes, Peirce makes clear that for him the self is not inborn but develops, that it is fallible and that self consciousness is inferential not intuitive. We cannot suppose we have a power of introspection. In fact, the direction of influence goes in the opposite direction, 'out' to inference from external facts. Imagination and emotions, for example, have an external object, i.e., they are not susceptible to introspection as internal mental states. He holds that the person is not absolutely an individual as their thoughts are that which they share with – 'say to' – that other self coming into being in the flow of time. All thought, for Peirce, is a sign, largely of the order of language, but it is also the 'persuasive' medium of mutable selfhood. Thought is seen to be embodied in signs connected to other signs, self referentially, in an interdependent system. We have, here, a whole web of relations comprising an external objectivity. He has recourse to the logic of language as constitutive of reality together with emphasis on the universal relations as only meaningfully conceived in relation to a community of all intelligible beings and their possible true interpretations. As Habermas observes: 'Peirce arrives at the conviction that what reality is coincides with what we can truly state about it. A Kantian "phenomenalism", omitting the thing-in-itself, seemed to him to accord with the principles of realism' (Habermas, 1978, p. 108). Reality, then, for Peirce, is construed in terms of a model of language, a symbolic, universal relation existing independently of states of consciousness. He proposes that such a theory of reality is 'instantly fatal to the idea of a thing in itself – a thing existing independent of all relation to the mind's conception of it. Yet it would by no means forbid, but rather encourage us, to regard the appearances of sense as only signs of the realities' (Peirce, quoted in Habermas, 1978, p. 109). An inter-subjective world without the need of introspection is envisaged which, if language underlying experience is introduced, anticipates Wittgenstein somewhat as will be seen.

We can discern by the end of the nineteenth century the connecting up of themes in which the contribution of empiriocriticism and the pragmatists feature pivotally. William James, who refers to Mach favourably, is associated with pragmatism and the early definition of psychology as the description and explanation of states of consciousness. Initially James was an introspectionist unimpressed by Hume's isolated building-block view of experience, though it is he who inherits the legacy of David Hume. James substitutes the image of a continuous 'stream of consciousness' for the Lockean–Humean legacy of discrete sensations, impressions and ideas and, in consequence, *relations* in the field of consciousness come to feature alongside *qualities*. This early work is remarkably insightful as it is there that James indicated how the trick of consciousness is turned:

> For how would it be if the Thought, the present judging Thought, instead of being in any way substantially or transcendentally identical with the former owner of the past self, merely inherited his title . . . It would then, if its birth coincided exactly with the death of another owner, *find* the past self already its own as soon as it found it at all, and thus the past self would thus never be wild, but always owned, by a title that never lapsed . . . Each pulse of consciousness, each Thought, dies away and is replaced by another. The other, among the things it knows, knows its own predecessor, and finding it 'warm', greets it, saying: 'Thou art *mine*, and part of the same self with me' . . . Each Thought is thus born an owner, and dies owned, transmitting whatever it realizes as its Self to its own later proprietor.
> (James, 1950, pp. 339–340)

Successive thoughts in the stream of consciousness are referred to by James as 'successive thinkers'. He says that we do not have to suppose a ceaseless thinker with a 'substantial' identity – an abiding principle of absolutely oneness with itself. Consciousness of self is a stream of thought, at any one moment the 'I', which remembers and embraces its own past and appropriates its contents as 'mine'. James contended that the 'I', or pure ego, is that which is conscious at any given moment whilst the 'Me' is just one of the things of which it is conscious. The 'I' is the thinker but this is the passing state of consciousness itself. Though each of us considers the 'I' to be substantive and enduring it is, in fact, borne along by the successive states of the stream of consciousness, i.e., it is a changeling not a soul or a transcendental ego. There is no *substantial* identity between 'today's' and 'yesterday's' states of consciousness; the one is past forever, the other ever present: 'Successive thinkers, numerically distinct, but all aware of the same past in the same way, form an adequate vehicle for all the experience of personal unity and sameness which we actually have. And just such a train of successive thinkers is the stream of mental states' (James, 1961, pp. 69–70). Following James's maxim that 'the thoughts themselves are the thinkers' it has been remarked that '[i]t is sufficient to think of the thinking "I" as a thought thickened with an appropriation of a model of the self . . . [that] draws on or appropriates the relevant information about what kind of person I am, what I care about, and so on' (Flanagan, 1992, p. 179). In other words: 'Each of us is an agent. Each of us has an identity. But there is no small, more-powerful agent inside each of us. There is no need to posit a " 'sanctuary within the citadel' of our personal life" (James)' (Flanagan, 1992, p. 182).

According to James, providing grist to the mill of phenomenology, as will be seen: 'Thought is always emphasizing something . . . It contrasts a *here* with a *there* . . . a *now* with a *then*: of a pair of things it calls one *this* the other *that*. *I and thou, I and it*, are distinctions exactly on a par with these – distinctions possible within an exclusively *objective* field of knowledge, the "I" meaning for the Thought nothing but the bodily life which it momentarily feels . . . All appropriations *may* be made *to* it by a Thought not immediately cognised by itself' (James, 1950, p. 341). James maintained that the mind is a theatre of simultaneous possibilities at every stage and consciousness consists in the comparing and selecting of some options and the suppressing of others through the reinforcing and inhibiting capacity of attention. Data is successively sifted and filtered as we 'sculpt' our world from all that may be conceivably possible. Attention both selects and suppresses and has the capacity to both reinforce and inhibit. As one way forward is chosen others are rejected and what was momentarily a possibility sinks back into the preconscious mind to be recovered later or never to resurface at all. Similarly, what appears spontaneously in consciousness is the result of thinking not the process of thinking itself. Consciousness is filled with relations; we see things as relative to other things and judge them in accordance. But as we cannot think of everything at once, consciousness is necessarily selective. Consciousness, for James, is that which works in a practical orientation to the world. Mentality is identified with the relating of means to achieve ends; teleology is viewed as the only essential 'weapon' in mind. Intelligence, thus defined, is in evidence in seeking out more profitable or effective future relations with the objective world. Not only is James associated with a pragmatic conception of truth but also with a pragmatic conception of consciousness – both being judged by their efficacy in contriving future relations. If ideas become true in helping us into satisfactory relations with the parts of our experience, consciousness has the same ontological property and predilection. The truth is created through action in this view and thought is purposive as shaped by practical interests.

Mind, for James, 'engenders' truth upon reality and thought is there to change the world but it is only through the activities of the body that the world *can* be changed. James sees consciousness as totally embodied and to which egoistic interests are directed. The body is the centre of vision, action and interests. In addition our feeling of bodily changes following on from perception of an exciting fact *is* emotion. The equation of feelings and bodily symptoms is the sum of emotion and on reflection should bodily feelings be subtracted there is no 'mind-stuff' left behind out of which the emotion could be constituted. Indeed, in an essay of 1904 entitled 'Does "Consciousness" Exist?', which denied the significance of the dualistic subject–object relation, i.e., the subject or knower becoming aware of the object the known, consciousness became, for James, a 'nonentity'. He had always believed that consciousness goes away from where it is not needed and now he was prepared to take that maxim to its logical, if ironic, conclusion. Late in his career, then, James concluded: 'For twenty years past I have mistrusted "consciousness" as an entity; for seven or eight years past I have suggested its non-existence to my students, and tried to give them its pragmatic equivalent in realities of experience. It seems to me that the hour is ripe for it to be openly and universally discarded' (James, 1971, p. 4). He did not deny that thoughts were the medium of knowing and that that medium constituted 'being conscious', but he rejected the idea of consciousness as a thing in itself. The primal material, for James, was 'pure experience' – the immediate flux of life furnishing the material for subsequent reflection. In James, thought and the stream of experience are totally identified – we meet experience thinking – and the self emerges through the accruing of experience. For James the relations between things are matters of particular experience just as much as the things themselves. In fact, relations of experience *is* reality (the

directly apprehended universe) and requires no other connective support. This would appear to be the macro-level equivalent to James's
contention that thoughts themselves are the thinkers; at one, both
relationist and minimalist. Concentrating upon the 'pragmatic
equivalent' to consciousness 'in realities of experience' James pro-
ceeded to articulate a theory of 'instrumentalism' or 'pragmatism'
that involved a new definition of truth.[3]

Although James, like Nietzsche, was sceptical of language in the
'flux of life', the pragmatists would maintain that whether a statement about objects in the world is 'true' or 'false' can be answered
only with reference to a system of other statements which have, by
trial and error, worked in the past. The idea of an inseparable connection of rational cognition and rational purpose is confirmed in the
thought of Peirce, James and Dewey. But in the interim states of
success, doubt or failure are ongoing inherent properties of the
experience or situation and are thus *objective*; they do not refer to
interior personal states of *subjectivity*. Dewey, above all, makes this
quite clear. We are doubtful because the outcome of the situation is
inherently doubtful. Dewey talks of distinctions being drawn in the
world and differences being made not by 'mind' or by 'consciousness'
but by the organism as an active centre of a system of activities judged
by the measure of practical value. He stresses the mind as a verb
denoting modes of action – of doing and undergoing – which,
unfortunately, has been rendered an underlying, independent property which attends, purposes, cares, notices and remembers, i.e., an
entity or substance from which actions then proceed. In as much as
consciousness has 'existence' for Dewey it is the *action* of consciousness in organic releases of behaviour as the condition of awareness
which, in turn, modifies its content.

If we turn to Bergson (1991), in contrast, we can see that actualised
consciousness becomes a synthesised 'outtake' from all that is potentially available. The rest of the world is the condition of possibility of
consciousness and the *phenomenology* of consciousness only makes
sense in that engagement in Bergson's view. The material with the
potentiality of consciousness wells up inside us but much of it dries
up before it reaches a state of consciousness or runs off into an arte-
sian reservoir for the future but we are also in the process of screening
out from the world what is not significant for us. We are awash on the
inside with rival claimants to the status of consciousness and beset on

the outside by possible captives for attention – though the process, experientially is, most often, smooth and seamless. In Bergsonist philosophy the operation of consciousness involves a selecting out from the world of what is of interest. There is an actualisation of consciousness in the process of 'latching onto' a particular aspect of the available world. In Bergson's imagery, a light is shed on a side of things that is of interest to us. The rest is cast in the shadow of disinterest. This process of negation, inhibition, of factoring out is itself at issue. There is not only a process of 'homing in' on something but also one of filtering out of other things that, to all intents and purposes, do not matter. The idea of connecting with an aspect of the world forms an echo of the pragmatists and is similar in many respects to the phenomenologist's idea of *intentionality* as we shall see, but the sifting and the selection processes in Bergson engages within *and* without. Yet as regards pure perception in Bergsonian philosophy we engage in an immediate intuition and touch the reality of the object as we are actually placed outside ourselves. This process of perception is so closely identified with its object that Bergson seems to find it hard to refer to it as mental at all. Pure perception's characteristic feature is that it is *activity*. Indeed, for Bergson the body which is forever turned towards action has, with a view to that action, the essential function of limiting the life of the spirit. Thought is the means of action which, in turn, constitutes being according to Bergson. The past we are informed is that which acts no longer. Action is identified with everything positive whilst contemplative insight is seen as 'dreaming' and about action lies the life force pushing us blindly onwards from behind. Bergson's adoption of the idea of a basic life force (*élan vital*) is the underlying principle of his philosophy and echoes Schopenhauer in its totality.

Whilst, for Bergson, the intellect seems to be characterised by a natural inability to understand life, intuition is instinct that has arrived at disinterestedness and self-consciousness so that it can reflect on its object and enlarge it indefinitely. Intellect is concerned with space, as intuition is concerned with time. The intellect is capable of imagining the shapes that things will fall into but consciousness and the phenomena of life can only be apprehended in immediate intuition. Quite crucially, Bergson sees memory as the intersection of mind and matter where the past must be imagined by mind and acted by matter. His theory of *duration* connects with his theory of memory in which things remembered survive in memory and interfuse concern with present things, i.e., past and present become mingled in the unity of consciousness. There is, in Bergson, a continuing free self that is present throughout the flow of time and which is revealed by introspection. Reviewing what he describes as 'the New Bergsonism', Watson says that in this view '[w]e don't *have* memories, we *are* memories; or at least we *are* duration, and memory is a function of duration' (Watson, 1998, p. 13), i.e., it is built into what we are; the organism *is* duration. We are not programmed to receive, we *are* the programme to receive. Bergson construes this inner experience as an interpenetration of 'before' and 'after' comprising the changing reality itself. *Durée* (duration), as he describes it, the experience of 'time' from within, is very different from external clock-time which is spatialised time measured by the hands of a clock or how long it takes to do something or to get from one place to another. He refers to *intuition* as capturing the nature of the state of mind which is aware of the flow of inner consciousness – a feeling state rather than one primarily conceptually based, though it may be based on previous intellectual groundwork. Most philosophical positions emanating from Bergson place a great deal of emphasis on memory. Bergson's contention that the following moment, over and above the one which preceded it, always holds the *memory* the latter has bequeathed it, is, in effect, Hume and James in other words. Indeed, Bergson's idea of experience as a stream rather than a succession of states is complementary to James's position on consciousness. Whatever image or metaphor utilised, experience is an indivisible continuum not a series of demarcated stations of consciousness, and Bergson's entire philosophy is a rejection of frozen and cut-up spatialised structure resulting in subject–object, or inner–outer dimensions.

DILTHEY AND THE *GEISTESWISSENSCHAFTEN* TRADITION

What is now most often described as the *Geisteswissenschaften* debate amongst German philosophers and historians at the end of the nineteenth century, which sought to distinguish the approach and method appropriate to the understanding of the meaning-infused social world as distinct from the techniques utilised in generating the 'laws' of the natural world, itself reintroduced consciousness – subjective *and* inter-subjective – onto the agenda of social thought. An attempt to overcome the stark duality of subject and object, thought and extension, found in a tradition reaching back to Spinoza, appears again at this time in the work of Dilthey. According to Spinoza, thinking substance and extended substance are one and the same, comprehended under one attribute then the other. They are not, then, a somehow coordinated, parallel alignment of the mental and the physical. Instead, the mind and the body are closely identified, with mental and physical ability being the substantially same ability – a single order of nature – conceived under two different attributes. Dilthey, over two hundred years later, remarked on the need to think of the mental and physical spheres of experience as different aspects of the same thing. He says at one point: 'Experiencing and experience are not separate; they are merely different terms for the same thing' (Dilthey, 1979, p. 234). In this view inner and outer worlds of mind and matter should not be considered as separate parts of reality. The distinction is a product of looking at reality using different methods and with different interests. In fact, mind and body are counterparts with the human–social–historical world consisting of such psycho-physical persons. He says: 'Every mental action reveals its relationship to a change in our body through the nervous system and a physical change is accompanied by a change in our mental state only via the nervous system' (p. 165). 'Mind' and 'matter' are, for Dilthey, merely convenient conceptual abstractions from experience.

Dilthey refers to three linked parts of mental life comprising the structure of the mind: intelligence, emotional life and acts of will. A human being is an imagining, feeling and willing creature in Dilthey's view. The inner relationship of mental processes within a person is described as *life*, knowledge of which is growing awareness and reflection on life. The emphasis in Dilthey on the mind understanding a mind-created objective world in an echo of Vico (1982) and the concern with the way in which this objective world aids or hinders human activity mirrors the priorities of pragmatism. In Dilthey's view, rather than real blood it is only the diluted juice of reason, a mere process of thought, that flows in the veins of the knowing subject of Locke, Hume and Kant. What is needed for knowledge of ourselves, the external world and culture is a view of human nature that takes thinking alongside feeling, willing and imagining as complementary aspects of the real life process. Man is a psycho-physical unit who knows himself through the mutual relationship of experience and understanding. Man may become aware of himself in the present, recognise himself in memory as someone who once was and then try to hold on to his states of mind by turning attention on himself, but, Dilthey claims, this shows up the narrow limits of such an introspective method of self-knowledge. What teaches man about himself in Dilthey's view are his creations and actions and the effect they have on others. To this whole human being external reality is as immediately given and certain as his own self and something independently part of life – not the mere idea, the phenomenon, of the perceiving mind. Once this is appreciated we are in a position to *understand* mental life, not primarily in its interiority, but, through knowledge of the objectifications of the human mind in history and culture, i.e., through understanding lived experience. Indeed it is a precept of Kant's that the subject be rediscovered in the object.

To Dilthey *experience* is the well-spring of human action and constitutes the subjective, mental life of individuals – comprised of a fusion of thought, desire and will – from which actions flow into *life:* 'Experience, in short, is man's subjectivity through which his ordinary, unreflectively lived existence is realised and mediated. It is in the nature of experience never to remain merely subjective, however, but to exteriorise itself in actions and in the permanent artefacts that actions leave behind: buildings, monuments, works of art, and written documents' (Collin, 1997, p. 106). Human experience is crystallised in such artefacts and it is this 'outside' world which ultimately concerns Dilthey. Understanding, for him, is to replicate, to recreate, to re-engage that original experience of agents in their production of the objective world. In fact, experience of this sort is life itself for Dilthey when it is engaged with understanding: 'Understanding presupposes experience and experience only becomes knowledge of life if understanding leads us from the narrowness and subjectivity of experience to the whole and the general' (Dilthey, 1979, pp. 187–188). This is how the mind-constructed world is disclosed. Dilthey seems to suggest that the external world remains only a phenomenon to the perceiving mind, whilst this external reality is no mere idea to the imagining, feeling, willing 'whole' human being but something immediately given and an independent part of life and as certain as his own self. Though Dilthey refers to life as the engaged activity of experience, action has to be accompanied by an account of the context of life, circumstances, means and purposes in order to reveal the inner life from which it arose.

Dilthey declares decisively that experience suggests not a psychologistic analysis of mankind but an account of the expression of the social and historical life-world. Experience is organised by symbolic structures, which means that, as Habermas expresses it: 'An experience is not a subjective process of becoming conscious of fundamental organic states. Instead it is relative *intentions* and is always mediated by an act of *understanding meaning*. Dilthey comprehends historical life as a permanent self-objectivation of mind. . . . The life of the mind consists in externalising itself in objectivation and at the same time returning to itself in the reflection of its externalisations' (Habermas, 1978, p. 147). Here, we have mind in a self-formative process engaged in a reflective relation with its own objectivations in the social and historical life-world. In any one individual, significance constitutes the structure and unity of experience. It is the relation of the whole to its parts, grasped by ego identity, that invokes significance. Dilthey graphically portrays the vertical dimension of the life history intersecting the horizontal level of a communication community. Habermas adduces that: 'Self-consciousness constitutes itself at the point of intersection of the horizontal level of inter-subjective mutual understanding with others *and* the vertical dimension of intra subjective "mutual" understanding with oneself' (p. 158). The ego communicates with itself as its Other in the retrospective interpretation of the course of its life. Though in Dilthey there is emphasis on the pervasive effect of community that informs consciousness, on language as the objective distillation of interior life and on inter-subjectivity, he still clings on to a role for empathic understanding. Whilst the specific achievement of hermeneutics can be explained according to Habermas by the model of participation in communication learned via interaction, Dilthey never abandoned the contrary emphasis on empathy even in his later writings in Habermas's view. There, the emphasis is still placed on the transference of oneself into a situation, a transposition, a reproduction or a re-experiencing. Despite the emphasis on

biography the relation of observing subject and object stubbornly
resists that of the participant subject and partner of hermeneutics
where understanding is a communicative experience. The observer–
re-experiencer of Dilthey is left desiccated and bereft of their own
identity when they should, in fact, according to hermeneutics be
enacting the role of the reflected partner in a communication
structure.

A meeting described by Heinemann (1958, p. 52) between Dilthey
and Husserl in 1905 led the last named to be confirmed in his conviction that his turn in the direction of the subject was a way well worth
going. Indeed, Husserl was deeply impressed to discover Dilthey
holding a seminar on his philosophy; Husserl's work on the subject
and inner-experience being seen by Dilthey as a fundamental new
departure in philosophy. 'Contents' of intentional experiences were
very much in inverted commas in the theories of both men. For
Dilthey's part he had already established a precedent for discussing
life as life: 'Erlebnis constitutes the fundamental content of consciousness, which Dilthey sometimes refers to as "immediate lived
experience"; it is prior to any act of reflection' (Giddens in Bottomore
and Nisbet, 1979, p. 278). In turn, Habermas says of Husserl that
he defends pure consciousness against the 'intermediate domain of
linguistic communication' (Habermas, 1990, p. 167). In Husserl's
philosophy intuiting the essence of phenomena and their essential
relations to one another is the programme of transcendental phenomenology, which entertains the possibility of a radical experience
where the intuition of essences recasts the relationship of subject and
object. From this point of view such immediate experience is not
linked to sense perception (as in Humean empiricism) and, in that,
Husserl, like James, of whom he was well aware, is a radical empiricist who ultimately seeks to transcend the limits of sense perception
data. Nevertheless, Husserl would still seem to be located in a tradition of idealistic rationalism, wrestling alone with the meanings
intended by consciousness. Ultimately, Husserl is contending that
there is no distinction between what is perceived and the perception
of it and that the essence of objects is to be correlative to states of
mind; the object only has significance in so far as consciousness is
directed upon it.[4] However, for Husserl, in order for the transcendental phenomenological 'reduction' to take place ordinary encultured experience and expectations had to be 'bracketed'. Yet,

paradoxically, it is just such a 'natural attitude' generated in the 'lived in world' that pre-occupies the later Husserl but without ever fully rejecting the earlier premise.

CONCLUSION

Quite clearly, then, well before the end of the nineteenth century the issues being taken forward are that there is no enduring, substantive self, that thoughts themselves *are* the thinker and that reason is the slave of the passions – *will* in the case of Schopenhauer and Nietzsche. Nietzsche not only abandons a body and soul dualism but also questions the idea of an enduring substance-self which he associates with the belief in the eternal 'Soul-Survivor' of Christianity. In his eyes the focus on the isolated individual in philosophy is mistaken – an albeit reluctant recapitulation of Hegel. The self is illusory and the subject a fiction according to Nietzsche. But the catch-22 that this position introduces – which chimes well with the irrationalist project overall – is that it is conceded that no one ever believes any of this! The legacy of the Cartesian Theatre and *res cogitans* – an immaterial thinking being having consciousness of its own thought – is that somehow people tend to believe a 'folk psychology'–Cartesianism as an account of their own inner workings. People actually work on the assumption that they have a self or soul, that there is someone on the inside in charge of operations and that we are in control of ourselves. Nietzsche, like Hume, indicates that whilst such inferences are groundless they have practical value. The enduring or permanent substantive-self is a practical product of the inference of the human intellect, producing a useful and necessary fiction though not so in the case of individual identity. He believes the whole of life is possible without regarding itself in a mirror, with the greater part of life passing, anyway, without the benefit of such reflection. Clearly, though, Nietzsche did not have in mind, here, individuals becoming bewitched by their own reflection as the end of identity as he still feels able to refer to 'a superior, critical consciousness that attains a certain ironic perspective on his own necessary inner nature' (Nietzsche, 1995, p. 138). What puzzled Nietzsche was not just that we have thoughts at all but we are *aware* of having them which introduced for him the prospect of self-consciousness as distinct from consciousness. Self-awareness and reflection are, for him, essentially social and consciousness – as much as it is anathema for him – is forged in the crucible of collective life. Individuality and self-consciousness are late-comers as they are finally shaped in that exchange of heat.

As well as observing the scene being set for language to supersede the classical opposition of subject and object, what is genuinely surprising in an overview of this nature is the extent to which *activity* replaces passivity in the terms of reference of philosophical discourse. Looking forward, and anticipating James, Nietzsche thought he saw a 'popular superstition' at work in separating off subject and agency where no such subjective agent existed as a 'being' behind the *doing* – the doer having been added to the *deed* by the imagination. This view of *doing* and the *deed* being everything, which can be located originally in Hegel, is carried forward by the pragmatists who are concerned with practical activity, as is Bergson in his own terms. In order to capture action, a net of relationality is cast by these same philosophers: relationality of drives is for Nietzsche the only reality there is and the relations of experience is the sole reality for James. In the same arched movement any contrived distance between appearance and reality is collapsed. In a sense this facilitates the flattened plane of experience, which has moved on from its role in empiricism as how things appear to the subject – regardless of the merits of the case for an objective, external, real world – to a kind of shorthand for what the world is like for us. It is the flux of life of James or the stream of life of Bergson. One of the sources of confusion in the literature on consciousness is that theorists are not always working at the same level of abstraction – even when they enter together into dialogue. One classic example is the difference between those who hold on to a social and historical consciousness as a first-order principle as opposed to those who would wish to review a 'contentless', constitutive process of life itself. Whilst the first position would argue that there can be no analysis of life without historical specificity, without the life-course, without child development and language the only possible recourse with the alternative is to assert the primacy of a transcendent life process itself – which is the case with Schopenhauer, Nietzsche, Dilthey and Husserl for example. Moreover, there is undoubtedly cross-fertilisation and reinforcement of the 'life as life' position.

Initially, it is in Nietzsche that the opposition between appearance and reality is collapsed and truth is relegated from the status of absolute to something relative and perspectival. On that basis, there is only the apparent world and a supposed 'real world' it is deduced has been added as a lie. Appearance, then, *is* life with 'truth' becoming that which is life affirming. For him the thing–in–itself is empty of meaning. There is no other 'reality' to which we can rise or sink than that of our drives, desires or passions and such a world contains, in itself, infinite interpretations. The problem with this kind of thinking is that a thing-in-itself – or at least an absolute – is reintroduced by the back door. The essential truth of the world has been revealed at last by negation: truth is what you want it to be as you skate across the surface of a community of meaning. Nietzsche's contention, is that history is without direction or control and is not the triumph of reason culminating in the Absolute Spirit of Hegel. Nietzsche's 'highest specimens' are the only proper goal for humanity not something that lies idly at the end of time. There is no journey from darkness into light, only the reflex of strength overcoming weakness. This preoccupation with irrationality and power beginning in the late nineteenth century culminated in a triumphant conclusive rejection of consciousness.

Pragmatism, Bergsonism and the legacy of Mach and empiriocriticism inform the philosophical climate of the times of the early twentieth century. Although exhibiting different priorities they have certain key features in common: a reaction against Cartesian body and soul dualism and the substitution of an embodied mutable self as a stream in the flow of time; an emphasis on objective properties not interior personal states or subjectivity, and; a concern with action and a practical orientation to the world, itself, a relational reality of experience. They share a concern with how experience is grasped (or is not) by the intellect, yet, with the exception of Bergson, there is a ubiquitous rejection of metaphysics and all abstraction and with it, finally, consciousness. Though in Dilthey we understand the subjective by grasping the objective, cultural world that is its product it appears to be a fundamental precept and tenet of the *Geisteswissenschaften* tradition that the agent has inner thoughts that lie behind and inform the meaningfulness of any ongoing action. It is the inner plan and its monitoring that confers on action its status *as* action. A putative 'inside' of mental process is indispensable to the inference of motive in this view. In fact, the reaction to this particular thesis defined the entire direction of twentieth century sociology. Their course set, the first generation of 'sociologists of mind' – buffeted by the swell of Hegel and Nietzsche and already drawn by the undertow of Kant – found themselves navigating the open water of society and history.

PART II

5

THE SOCIOLOGY OF CONSCIOUSNESS

That form in which all psychic reality comes to consciousness, which emerges as the history of every ego, is itself a product of the creative ego. Mind becomes aware of itself in the stream of becoming, but mind has already marked out the banks and currents of that stream and thereby made it into 'history'.

(Simmel, 1971, p. 5)

THE INTERVENTION OF THE SOCIOLOGICAL PERSPECTIVE

There are several strands in the sociological analysis of consciousness originating in the early years of the twentieth century, none of them entirely pure nor always mutually exclusive, which form a considerable legacy and which may be cross-cut, in theory, in any number of different ways. The analysis attempted here will consider just five main strands taken over three generations: the first is exemplified by the work of Durkheim and Pareto which develops a case for structuralism and, indirectly, irrationalism. The second strand is itself multi-textured and leads on from Weber, to Schütz, to Mannheim, to the sociology of knowledge and the social construction of reality perspective. Here, both the individual and consciousness feature in high profile as does, eventually, a determinist view of society. The third begins with the work of Simmel, on the cusp between sociology and philosophy, which has a place for consciousness *and* the 'non social' and whose prioritisation of the individual bridged over the Atlantic in the form of the Chicago School. This was already itself, by this time, the location for the coming together of other relevant lines of enquiry which culminated in the work of George Herbert Mead and symbolic interactionism where the problem of consciousness is superseded – the fourth strand considered here. The fifth strand, theoretically connected by the work of C. Wright Mills, is ethnomethodology and witnesses the outright repudiation of consciousness. In each case, the coverage of contributions to the creation of a sociology of consciousness will be selective and will concentrate on those aspects relevant to this discussion.

DURKHEIM AND PARETO

In general terms, for philosophers of the eighteenth century the individual had been the source of experience and knowledge, but '[s]tarting with Hegel, and continuing through Comte, Marx and Durkheim, society becomes the medium in which ideas originate and which is also the source of standards for the truth of ideas' (Piepe, 1971, p. 33). In the positivism of Auguste Comte subjective experience had been regarded as a figment of metaphysics and the self-reflexive subject was ignored. From that point on a, somewhat variegated, strain of thought emerges in early sociology which actually looks askance at individuals' own explanations of experience. The classic instance of the latter tendency was Durkheim who remarked that 'social life should be explained, not by the notions of those who participate in it, but by more profound causes which are unperceived by consciousness . . . causes . . . to be sought mainly in the manner according to which the associated individuals are grouped' (quoted in Winch, 1958, p. 23). Much like Marx, it is Durkheim's view that 'the members of society – though subject to or bearers of 'social facts' – more often than not are deluded about the nature of social reality. They are more likely to substitute the 'representations' of 'social facts' for the real thing. These '*notiones vulgares*' or '*idola*' are illusions which distort the perception of real social processes and are entirely the products of the mind "like a veil drawn between the thing and ourselves"' (Hughes, 1990, p. 26). In Durkheim is found an expression of the constitutional duality of the individual; a duplex existence rooted both in the properties of the individual organism *and* the individual as an embodied extension of society. He indicates at various junctures the duality that exists between the mentality resulting from individual experience and that consequential upon collective experience – with the latter having ascribed to it a higher *dignity*. Nevertheless, the word *dignity* is used by Durkheim in relation to how the enduring soul has been popularly viewed; for him, in contrast, the sacred soul is essentially social. In as much, the personality is constructed out of social elements and our behaviour is shaped by our common beliefs and attitudes not our consciousness. To take poetic licence with the Durkheimian position it would seem that consciousness is a bridgehead to a world held by the force of society.

Undoubtedly Durkheim *is* well prepared to consider what might lie at the heart of our 'inner life' and in attempting to draw a boundary between sociology and psychology Durkheim does not suggest the former perspective must reject all reference to states of consciousness: 'The point is that social phenomena cannot be studied either by the concepts or with the methods of individual psychology, which looks at the individual as an isolated subject . . . In saying that social facts are "external" to individuals, Durkheim states, he does not wish to make the "absurd" assertion that society has some sort of separate physical existence to the individuals who compose it. A combination of units yields new properties which cannot be derived from the study of any one of these units considered in isolation' (Giddens, 1972, pp. 33–34). Concepts appropriate to psychology which refer to individual consciousness, are not, in consequence, amenable to an understanding of 'external' reality in Durkheim's view. Yet, 'external', here, should not be equated directly with the 'physically observable' as, in fact, states of consciousness are not excluded. Indeed, Durkheim says: 'Undoubtedly social life is composed of values and values are properties added to reality by human consciousness; they are wholly the product of psychic mechanisms. But these mechanisms are natural facts, which can be studied scientifically; these evaluations which human judgement makes of things depend upon causes and conditions which can be discovered inductively' (Durkheim, quoted in Giddens, 1972, p. 31). But the social world, for Durkheim, is not a mere creation of the will of the observer as it exists, like physical objects, independently of observation. Its characteristics cannot be discovered by introspective examination of the observer's consciousness, nor by *a priori* reasoning. As well as seeing *emergence* as a vital dimension of the philosophy of science Durkheim had learned to recognise a distinction between different levels of reality or of being as a basic discontinuity – ranging from the material to the thought world – which cannot be reduced one to the other or be explicable in their respective terms.

The tension over what might constitute consciousness evident in the divergence of Hegel from Kant is reflected in Durkheim – though he chooses selectively from both. For Durkheim religion and ritual are the main agencies for endowing mankind with reason. In trying to round off that which remains unfinished in Kant's thought 'Durkheim's theory of concept formation amounts to the claim that they arise by controlled and collective social imposition. This theory is meant to explain why *all* men are rational: why all men think in severely circumscribed, shared and demanding concepts, rather than in terms of privately assembled and perhaps wildly diverging associations' (Gellner, 1992, p. 41). Durkheim rejected the prospect of interpreting social phenomena by reference to the 'inside' of the minds of individuals, which itself is reflected in his sharp separation of the individual and collective mind. The latter, in Durkheim's later work, becomes so residually infused with Hegelianism that collective consciousness obeys quite independent laws of its own in mutations unconnected to underlying reality; collective consciousness, then, is no mere epiphenomenon of its morphological basis. Ironically enough Durkheim is still prepared to contend that *'thought has as its aim not the reproduction of a given reality but the construction of a future reality'* (Durkheim, in Giddens, 1972, p. 251). But how we could conceivably attain sufficient levels of disinterest from that of which we are made to actively construct the future is an unresolved conundrum in Durkheim.

Elsewhere, in the work of Pareto there is a confluence of structuralism and irrationalism where consciousness becomes both shallow and inconstant. Pareto drew a distinction between 'logical' and 'non-logical' action and between 'residues' and 'derivations'. Logical action is the conscious relating of means to ends that are attainable, when what is envisaged and realised at some point coincide. In the meantime good grounds for this belief are to be assumed that, ultimately, the end state is empirically identifiable. 'Non-logical' action, conversely, exhibits a systematic disjunction between subjective intentions and their social consequences – action, intended result and actual result do not, or only contingently, ever coincide. 'Residues' are the constant, recurring elements in a society, whilst, 'derivations', much more variable, are the explanations that people adduce for their behaviour and represent the work of the mind (i.e., what remains after the variable element is discarded in taking account of the 'residues'). In fact, derivations amount to rationalisations. Pareto observed that there is a propensity for individuals to make connections between elements, even when they remain unaware of any observed or logical links between them. Structural features of social situations, then, are not self-evident and may be largely unknown to the actor and non-rational values and behaviour intervene to modify the relationship between means and ends. Cultural life is largely non-rational as it grows up around spontaneous action divorced from rational thought processes, but once established it has a binding force on members. Non-rational ideas, therefore, result from social and cultural experience. In one direction, then, such prognoses of the situation lead on to various kinds of structuralism; in another direction they lead to a preoccupation with consciousness as the source of actual (self) deception. In the words of Pareto, the arch-proponent of this view, 'human beings have a very conspicuous tendency to paint a varnish of logic over their conduct' (Pareto, 1963, § 154), whilst the theories and ideas to which people do hold, have very little actual effect on their behaviour. For him, behaviour is prior to attitudes which embody a *post hoc* veneer of rationality where without the slightest scruple to their logic the individual may successively assert contradictory things. The preservation of inconsistency is a simple achievement and forms the pragmatism of a shifting series of contradictions. Indeed for Pareto inconsistencies come to appear natural in the equivocation of positive and negative 'reasonableness'.

It is notions such as these that lead Winch to conclude that there is a 'powerful stream of thought which maintains that the ideas of participants must be discounted as more likely than not to be misguided and confusing' (Winch, 1958, p. 95) and H. Stuart Hughes in *Consciousness and Society* to suggest that the intellectual innovators of the 1890s were preoccupied with the issue of irrational motivation in human conduct. There is, here, undoubtedly an echo of Schopenhauer and Nietzsche in the identifying of an inverse relation between the problem of consciousness and the rule of the unconscious.

WEBER

In certain quarters it might now be convenient to ignore that the subjective meaning of an action, the prospect of underlying motivations, the utilisation of empathy and a reliving of the experience to be analysed were ever part of the sociological repertoire of Max Weber, but such selective amnesia is unhelpful. Following Dilthey there is in the work of Weber an emphasis on an inner experience of consciousness distilling meanings in human life. In Weber, *Verstehen* (understanding), although used in several different ways, tends to have been taken to mean an empathic understanding of meanings; access to, and interpretation of, the meaning of others via introspection, memory and imagination. Weber assumes that to understand meaning is to understand intentions, with the researcher possessing a capacity to 'feel himself' empathically into a mode of thought. By 'motive' Weber understands 'a complex of . . . meaning which seems to the actor himself or to the observer an adequate (or meaningful) ground for the conduct in question'(Weber, 1968, p. 5). What is to be read into the 'which seems to the actor himself' aspect of this? It would appear to be something along the lines of the actor asking of himself (sic) certain questions – i.e., 'talking' to himself. Indeed, the definition of 'action' for Weber does seem to include 'inner' activity. In Weber's estimation every level and possible range of communication 'counts on' producing in those to whom it is addressed certain effects in the 'psyche' (see Löwith, 1982, p. 44). Generally speaking, 'action' for Weber is to be analysed and explained through the analysis of subjective meanings which orient conduct. Parkin indicates that *Verstehen* as used by Weber seems to suggest that individuals are aware of their subjective states in general and typically aware of their motives for action in particular. Actors' own definitions are inevitably important in the explanation of action as their own view of reality is what motivates their conduct. Weber's notion of *Verstehen* can be attributed to Dilthey though it is the case that for Weber it was the first step towards a more causal analysis. What Weber did do, however, according to Parkin, was to largely ignore this implication of his theory and contend, instead, that individuals' ability to grasp subjective meaning and the significance of their own action was severely limited. For Weber:

In the great majority of cases actual action goes on in a state of inarticulate half consciousness or actual unconsciousness of its subjective meaning. The actor is more likely to 'be aware' of it in a vague sense than he is to 'know' what he is doing or be explicitly self-conscious about it . . . Only occasionally . . . is the subjective meaning of the action, whether rational or irrational, brought clearly into consciousness. The ideal type of meaningful action where the meaning is fully conscious and explicit is a marginal case.

(Weber, 1968, pp. 21–22)

Parkin's commentary on this is that '[i]f the actors themselves are not, after all, especially well equipped to know their own motives and to understand their own meanings, what exactly is the use of Weber's method? How could we even begin to make sense of social action through the eyes of the participants if, on Weber's reckoning, the participants themselves have such a myopic view of everything? Weber's not very helpful piece of advice is that the sociologist should proceed 'as if' actors behaved in a fully meaningful way' (Parkin, 1982, p. 27).

So, Weber as the apparent last bastion of the account of the rational actor appears less than secure. Yet, Weber viewed unpredictable, irrational action as more probably the hallmark of the insane rather than the inner drive of the free personality. The idea of careering about irresponsibly on impulse is derided by Weber as is acting on conviction without considering the consequences. The model of the individual actor he prefers is where a feeling of freedom stems from actions we know we accomplish rationally when a clearly conscious purpose is pursued by the most adequate means. In this teleological orientation we display a projection in purpose involving deliberation, calculation and a weighing up of possible outcomes. However, once means become exclusively ends in themselves to totally dominate life, Weber registered his fear for the fragmentation of the human soul. Not only was Weber alive to the irrational in history, then, but his underlying assumption was that the human mind cannot objectively grasp reality as a meaningful whole. Reality for Weber, is an infinite stream of events in a chaotic flux of experience (an echo of Hericlitus, of neo-Kantianism generally and Nietzsche in particular). Both 'within' and 'without' ourselves we are presented with a multiplicity of occurrence in succession and coexistence which appears and disappears as soon as we chance reflection on it. Weber was convinced that an external reality existed independently of the human mind and that human beings acquired knowledge of it by relating it to their values, i.e., we attribute a cultural significance to reality. This external reality is devoid of intrinsic meaning; categories and concepts of mind, in no way part of the external reality itself, 'factor in' meaning. Therefore, value orientation and cognitive interest attribute a *cultural* significance to reality; we make of it what is important to us. Indeed, it is a Kantian precept that consciousness finds in things only what it has put into them. In our attempt to come to terms with the level of non-cultural reality we create, as completely distinct from it, a further layer – a 'finite segment' – of cultural life to make sense of the meaningless infinity. The cultural 'hold' on reality is one that is, of necessity, partial. There is no absolute or overall grasp of events but, instead, a series of value positions from which the world is beheld. No standpoint can be conceived as being separate from the individual who holds it and there is no transcendent order of things. We have, here, from Weber, emphasis on the world instantiated in particular points of view (a premise of Nietzsche's) but also a concern with what is to be found in the *minds* of human beings. The points of view are, in fact, totally engaged positions and it is as such that they are encountered. Nevertheless, Weber was in no doubt that *Verstehen* and social action opened out onto a real, experiential world of power and conflict. For him classes, status groups and parties actually *are* phenomena of the distribution of power and social interaction *is* conflict. It is not experience then power and conflict at a remove (with which we can deal later) but power and conflict instantiated *in* and *as* experience.

SCHÜTZ

The most meticulous connecting up of the diffuse and problematic legacy of Dilthey, Husserl and Weber is undoubtedly contained in the work of Alfred Schütz, which, itself gives added momentum to the sociological analysis of consciousness. Of several lines of enquiry pursued by Schütz in criticism of Weber's thinking, one of the more far reaching is his contention that Weber does not really clarify the difference between the meaning which the action has for an actor and what appears to them to be their motive. Weber confuses 'meaningful' with 'motivated' actions according to Schütz, for whom the motive of an action cannot be understood unless the meaning of that action is already known. From Schütz's recognition of the importance of a fine distinction between meaning and motive comes his own contrast between 'because' and 'in order to' motives – the purpose or project which the actor was seeking to obtain. Yet the particular problem that Schütz finds with Weber's observational and motivational understanding is that subjective meaning ultimately has no place in either. Schütz contends that he has proved the impossibility of motivational understanding based on observation alone. A person's motives cannot be 'sized up' from their actions by 'taking stock' of the context but requires, instead, knowledge of the actors past and future in a whole structure of 'intended meaning'. Observational or direct understanding is that which is exercised in daily life in direct relations with others where people understand ('read') events 'in the mode of actuality'. It is the corollary of a shared present in which people participate experientially. It is for this reason Schütz claims that inference from overt behaviour to intended meaning lying behind it is far from clear cut. Conversely, motivational understanding is not tied to the world of direct experience, as it can take as its object any action past, present or future (the worlds of predecessors, contemporaries or successors). It is concerned with the accomplished act unlike the ongoing act of observational, direct understanding.[1] In Schütz's view, following Husserl, what is seen as meaningful has already been constituted as such by a previous 'intentional' act of consciousness. When the world is taken for granted the intentional operations of consciousness within which meanings have already been constituted is left out of awareness. Conversely, it becomes a world, an emergent world, when the 'intentional' operations of consciousness which originally conferred the meanings are reviewed. But this is not merely the revelation of the world as constantly being constituted, but also the awareness of the ongoing passage of internal time-consciousness. Schütz remarks that 'history takes place in objective time, whereas consciousness takes place within the inner duration-flow of the individual' (Schütz, 1967, p. 213).

Meaning, then, is a certain way of directing one's gaze at an item of one's own experience and for Schütz concerns only that which is already over and done and is a property of the reflective glance, i.e., only a past experience is *meaningful*. Meaning does not lie *in* the experience but in the reflective grasping; experiences are not meaningful just by virtue of having been lived through. Moreover, experience implies consciousness for Schütz and he contends that 'we are *conscious* of an action only if we contemplate it as already over and done with, in short, as an act' (p. 64). He also refers to *finite provinces of meaning* to indicate different tensions of consciousness (in Bergson's sense) comprising a range of ways of attending to reality. He is referring, here, to the accent placed on reality not separate states of mental life. *Finite provinces of meaning* are the domain of our intentional lives and are experiences in the inner–time of our stream of consciousness. It is the meaning of these experiences that is at issue not the ontological structure of the objects that constitute reality. Yet, Schütz suspects that the true foundation of the empirical social sciences will lie not in transcendental phenomenology but, rather, in the constitutive phenomenology of the 'natural attitude'. He suggests that Husserl's enduring contribution lies in elucidating the nature of the *Lebenswelt* (Life-world) so both men end up perpetuating a contradiction: a detailed analysis of consciousness is to no avail as 'the world is from the outset not the private world of the single individual but an intersubjective world, common to all of us, in which we have not a theoretical but an eminently practical interest' (Schütz, 1982, p. 208). This is all the more perplexing in the case of Schütz as his theory of meaning, as has been seen, is predicated on consciousness.

Schütz appears to want to insist that there is the context–bound world of pragmatic considerations whose rules we all work but, also, an inner-world of meaning, decision making and action in its own right. He says that when someone is speaking he is aware of their voice as well as their words but his gaze goes right through any outward symptoms to the inner man of the person speaking: 'Whatever context of meaning I light upon when I am experiencing these outward indications draws its validity from a corresponding context of meaning in the mind of the other person' (Schütz, 1967, p. 104). The meeting of minds of meaning here is undoubted but so, too, is a spatial sequence tapping into subjective depth with Schütz making a great deal of spatial allusion in his work: consciousness in layers. Schütz says that he knows that 'every sign has it author and that every author has his own thoughts and subjective experiences as he expresses himself through signs' (p. 209) and at one point remarks that '[w]e interpret those external events which we call "another's act" as indications of a stream of consciousness lying outside our own' (p. 30). Yet elsewhere he says that meaning, interpretation in the social world is, in fact, 'pragmatically determined'; in ordinary life we only pursue other people's meanings until our ongoing practical questions are answered. In fact, though, the tension between 'my world' and 'outer world' and how to get from one to the other remains unresolved. Nevertheless he still returns to the idea of a world taken for granted as his measure of 'everyday life'. In effect previously produced 'objective meaning', ultimately represents for Schütz 'commonsensical' or 'taken for granted' reality. In Schütz, the emphasis is placed upon taken for granted, habituated knowledge of typical common sense constructs which routinise and render intelligible everyday experience. According to this view, the individual translates such routines into 'cookery-book knowledge' – a recipe that produces unreflective and immediate knowledge of how to carry off certain performances, with the inevitable implication of maintaining the social structure as stable and legitimate. Thereby, social order is linked with common sense in a largely unproblematic way. Whereas Husserl in the Cartesian tradition had *doubted*, in Schütz *doubt* is suspended – things are what they seem. Additionally, whilst inter-subjectivity is being courted by Schütz it is still ultimately a question of the individual and their unique world, i.e., ego and subjectivity.

Whilst William James intentionally restricted his inquiry on 'multiple realities' to the psychological aspect of the problem without further investigation of its implications, Schütz associates *the* paramount reality of the world of daily life with the world of work (which seems to mean 'work' as effort directed towards an end). This is the world of 'purpose and project' with its fundamental anxiety (death) and hopes and fears that arise from it. Schütz, nevertheless, seems to have introduced a dilemma by grafting on to the idea of 'multiple realities' one of 'paramount reality'. By drawing here on James and Bergson – with the latter's idea of tensions of consciousness, the highest being the 'full awakeness' and 'full attention' of the world of work – Schütz does not consider actual multiple realities competing for attention one against another in themselves, and, because he holds on to multiple realities as experiential options for the self alone accompanied by inevitable transitional 'shocks', there is a limited social dimension. Schütz is in a tradition tracing back through Husserl to Descartes which holds that whilst knowledge of others' consciousness is always open to doubt, knowledge of our own consciousness is indubitable and, in Schütz's case, that we know other minds by analogy with our own. He stands at an interesting crossroads of social thought which points forward to the concerns of ethnomethodology and an enduring concern with pragmatism in philosophy, whilst simultaneously holding on to the ideas of both Weber and Husserlian phenomenology. Schütz also triangulates between Husserlian phenomenology, Heidegger's thoughts on Being and Time and the philosophy of Bergson. This is rather more than Schütz making 'his due obeisance to the transcendental ego' (Giddens, 1976, p. 27) that Giddens has remarked upon. Nevertheless, it is the raising of such an agenda that has bridged over from phenomenology to the sociology of knowledge, which itself became a medium for the articulation of 'consciousness'.

THE SOCIOLOGY OF KNOWLEDGE

The thought of Karl Mannheim in *Ideology and Utopia*, influenced as it is by James and Nietzsche, provides an interesting point of juxtaposition with the present discussion. His analysis of consciousness involved not only an operationalisation of that concept saying what, throughout, he was taking it to mean – but also an elaborate definition of the concept of ideology and articulation of a concomitant epistemology. In practical terms this provided a bridge between thought and action to be crossed by sociological theory. In modern times the key names associated with the sociological analysis of consciousness, thought and meaning are according to Mannheim Marx, Dilthey, Nietzsche, Pareto and Lukács. Against this backdrop Mannheim charted in some detail the role of German idealist philosophy in the conception of consciousness and the evolution towards a 'total' conception of ideology as he described it. He proposed that it is through the application of the precepts of German idealism that social thought had moved away from a conception of consciousness as a timeless, unchanging, fictional unity to one of consciousness that varies with epochs, classes and states whose various elements cannot be understood in isolation. What is essential, he

contended, is the interrelation and interdependence of meaning recognised as forming a process of constant change. The 'speculative
manner' characteristic of German idealism and Hegel in particular
would, however, be translated into 'empirical research' according to
Mannheim, who set himself the agenda, in the first instance, concerning the nature of thought, thinking and consciousness. His views
form a seminal, modern discussion of these issues in indicating the
significance of the emergence of 'those fundamentally new modes of
thought and investigation, the epistemological, the psychological,
and the sociological, without which today we could not even formulate our problem' (Mannheim, 1960, p. 11). That problem, the analysis of modes of thought and experience, had not been solved entirely
by philosophy and psychology in his view – being, in turn, critical of
both. In mapping out the territory of the sociology of knowledge,
Mannheim, sought to emphasise the relationship between knowledge
and existence and the interrelations between thought and action – the
active social conditioning of knowledge – 'a research interest which
leads to the raising of the question when and where social structures
come to express themselves in the structure of assertions, and in what
sense the former concretely determine the latter' (p. 239). This concern with the social and existential determination of actual thinking
forms the common ground for the pursuit of the sociology of
knowledge.

Laying down the ground rules for the sociology of knowledge,
Mannheim was also preoccupied in establishing a modern theory of
knowledge which took account of the relational as distinct from the
relative character of knowledge. This would start from the assumption that it is impossible to conceive of truth in thought existing
independently of the position and values of the subject and their
social context – an historically determined and continuously developing structure. He argues that it is men in groups engaged in collective
activity who create knowledge and that truth emerges through the
synthesis into a unified whole of all different perspectives, with a
crucial role reserved for a free-floating intelligentsia harnessing
interest-free knowledge. Mannheim describes a situation as regards
human knowledge 'where men, while thinking, are also acting, and
finally, that in certain fields knowledge arises only when and in so far
as it itself is action, i.e., when action is permeated by the intention of
the mind, in the sense that the concepts and the total apparatus of

thought are dominated by and reflect this activist orientation. Not purpose *in addition* to perception but purpose *in* perception itself reveals the qualitative richness of the world in certain fields' (p. 265). This view seems to closely approximate that associated with Merleau-Ponty, as will be seen, as a statement on the phenomenology of perception. But we cannot confine our observations to individual mental processes as the loci of ideology, or 'we shall never grasp in its totality the structure of the intellectual world belonging to a social group in a given historical situation. Although this mental world as a whole could never come into existence without the experiences and productive responses of the different individuals, its inner structure is not to be found in mere integration of these individual experiences' (pp. 52–53).

Individual members of the working class do not experience all the elements of the class *Weltanschaung* (world outlook), but rather participate in certain fragments of this thought system whose totality is not the mere sum of such fragmentary individual experiences. The thought system is no mere 'casual jumble' of the fragments of experience of given individuals but is integrated systematically. For him, novel forms of knowledge grow from conditions of collective life and do not rely for their emergence on the prior demonstration of their theoretical possibility. Likewise an important idea to take from Mannheim is that of various historical 'thought styles' embodied in the social structure as a whole – 'the web of interacting social forces from which have arisen the various modes of observing and thinking through the existing realities that presented themselves at different times' (pp. 45–46). He continuously stressed the significance of a *Weltanschaung* and style of thought of a group in a given social and historical situation, with meaning being crystallised from experience. However, he remarked: 'If we examine the many types of ontological judgements with which different groups confront us, we begin to suspect that each group seems to move in a separate and distinct world of ideas and that these different systems of thought, which are often in conflict with one another, may in the last analysis be reduced to different modes of experiencing the "same" reality' (pp. 88–89). Even though Mannheim came to question his view that there were no true beliefs and no socially independent criteria of truth, and abandoned his assumption that social origins determined truth, as incorrect, the issues of 'different thought – "same" reality' raised in the above two quotations had already come to shape the subsequent agenda of sociology.

THE SOCIAL CONSTRUCTION OF REALITY

Though over a generation ago now Berger and Pullberg concluded that 'the critique of consciousness has been the province of philosophy, while on the other hand, the empirical analysis of the social location of consciousness has been the province of sociology and other social sciences' (Berger and Pullberg, 1966, p. 70). The comprehensive perspective they were advocating at this time demanded cooperation between sociology and philosophy with consciousness, as we shall see, being closely aligned with reification, i.e., the world apprehended as thing like facts of life with human authorship of the world having been forgotten. Berger and Pullberg proceed to distinguish three levels of consciousness: 'First, there is direct and pre-reflective presence to the world. Secondly, founded on the latter, there is reflective awareness of the world and one's presence to it. Thirdly, out of this second level of consciousness there may in turn arise various theoretical formulations of the situation' (p. 65). Reification, they claim, occurs on the last two levels, though the foundations of theoretical reification lie in pre-theoretical reification of oneself and the world. Subsequently, Berger and Luckmann were to claim that reification is a modality of consciousness in which typically the real relationship between man and his world is reversed. Not only is consciousness closely identified with reification in this analysis but guesses are hazarded at social and historical locations. Reification, they say, exists in the consciousness of 'the man in the street' and that, far from a fall from grace in an originally non-reified state, the original apprehension of the world is highly reified. Indeed 'an apprehension of reification *as* a modality of consciousness is dependent upon an at least relative *de*-reification of consciousness, which is a comparatively late development in history and in any individual biography' (Berger and Luckmann, 1967, p. 107). Coming together, here, is the union of philosophy and sociology as providing the critique and empirical analysis of the social location of consciousness respectively (though Hegel is the only philosopher covered in any detail); the linking of consciousness with reification and other related dimensions associated with the thought of Marx; the fact that consciousness can be divided up dimensionally (three, in this case) to reveal states or levels or presence with the world, and consciousness, in these terms, viewed as socially and historically specific, i.e., consciousness is dynamic and subject to change. This programmatic statement on the analysis of consciousness was never seriously courted by sociology – for reasons that will become evident in the course of what follows – and these authors' own concerns became more narrowly defined within the epistemic analysis of the sociology of knowledge. Ironically, though, Peter Berger's work is now often quoted favourably by authors on all sides.

In *The Social Construction of Reality*, Berger and Luckmann concluded that sociology had inherited the philosopher's mantle of a concern with the nature of the constitution of reality. They claimed that this brief had been abrogated by philosophy, but they themselves were reluctant to take on board within the sociology of knowledge all of the epistemological issues raised. Following Mannheim their priority was to establish the relationship between human thought and the social context in which it arises, despite the fact that Berger and Pullberg had made clear that man is a world-producing being and that human subjectivity is always intentionality in movement continuously objectivating itself rather than being a closed sphere of interiority. Berger and Luckmann state quite succinctly what they take consciousness to mean:

> Consciousness is always intentional; it always intends or is directed towards objects. We can never apprehend some putative substratum of consciousness as such, only consciousness of something or other. This is so regardless of whether the object of consciousness is experienced as belonging to an external physical world or apprehended as an element of inward subjective reality.
>
> (Berger and Luckmann, 1967, p. 34)

In this view experiences are retained (sedimented) in consciousness, one upon another, as recognisable memories for recollection. Unless, such a process took place individuals could not make sense of their lives, though they claim only a small part of the totality of experiences is actually retained in consciousness. The socially constructed world is internalised in consciousness in terms of 'the self'; to be rehearsed now and in the future. In this sense, consciousness is reflective and is capable of moving through different spheres of reality with different constituent objects to which it is attentive in quite different ways. The shift in attentiveness attendant on the transition causes the experience of shock. Thus, they are positing 'multiple realities' – originally James's idea according to Schütz – pre-eminent amongst which is the reality of 'everyday life' which makes greatest demands on the attentiveness of consciousness. Though Berger and Luckmann, like Schütz, view everyday life as just one of many 'multiple realities' it is variously described as 'reality par excellence', 'paramount reality' and as having a 'privileged position' and an 'imperative presence'.

As a result, they concluded that '[s]ince everyday life is dominated by the pragmatic motive, recipe knowledge, that is, knowledge limited to pragmatic competence in routine performances, occupies a prominent place in the social stock of knowledge' (p. 56). In consequence : 'The validity of my knowledge of everyday life is taken for granted by myself and by others until further notice, that is, until a problem arises that cannot be solved in terms of it. As long as my knowledge works satisfactorily, I am generally ready to suspend doubts about it' (p. 58). There is, then, the idea of immediate, pragmatic, relevant stocks of knowledge, as opposed to unfamiliar, remoter, 'sketchy' areas which if known at all are not easily typified. To Berger and Luckmann this represents a zone of illumination, against a background of darkness. However, taken against this they stressed the objectivated meanings of institutional activity as knowledge, viewed as the 'collective sedimentation' of inherited shared meanings, i.e., a class *Weltanschauung* view notwithstanding primary socialisation leading on to modificatory secondary socialisation. Though these authors developed a dichotomy between objective and subjective reality, as a dialectical relationship through which the world is mediated by significant others in the creation of individual identity, they nevertheless stated that: 'An institutional world, then, is experienced as an objective reality. It has a history that antedates the individual's birth and is not accessible to his biographical recollection. It was there before he [sic] was born, and it will be there after his death' (p. 77). In summary, in Durkheimian fashion society always appears *a priori* in this approach. Emphasis was placed upon (primary) socialisation, habitualised activity, roles and attitudes and on a stable, institutionalised environment any deviance from which, in itself, appearing as a departure from reality. These social phenomena perform certain functions in the perpetuation of the social order, though elsewhere Berger and Luckmann imply that social reality is precarious and reified. Although Berger and Luckmann undoubtedly problematise 'reification', such phenomenologically inspired sociology deals with action only as meaning rather than praxis, fails to recognise power in social life and does not acknowledge that social norms are interpreted differently according to divisions of interest. In effect phenomenology can manage 'social interaction' but not 'society' nor certainly 'mode of production' despite a recognition on the part of Berger *et al.* of the enduring legacy of Marx.

THE INFLUENCE OF SIMMEL

Perhaps the most influential contribution to the lambent sociological debate on consciousness is that of Simmel, who inherits the mantle of Heraclitus with reality conceived of as eternal flux. Simmel's fundamental starting point is the legacy of Kant's unknowable thing-in-itself and Schopenhauer's 'will' as thing-in-itself in a dualism with the world as representation, and like Durkheim (Pareto) and Weber, of whom he is a contemporary, the debt Simmel owes to German idealist philosophy is quite obvious: 'The imprisonment of our empirical existence by nature has, since Kant, been counteracted by the autonomy of mind: the picture of nature in our consciousness, the conceptualization of her forces and of what she can be for the soul, is the achievement of the soul itself' (Simmel, 1971, p. 4). In Simmel, there is both an individual (subject) opposed to a social world (object) and life itself opposed to the cultural forms into which it is inevitably, but reluctantly, forced. He poses a restless but limited and time-bound subjective life over and against its cultural contents which are timelessly valid once created with the prospect of an alien objective cultural world gaining omnipotence over the subjective culture which created it, in as much *reification*. This 'otherness' of cultural objects links up more and more as a self-contained world independently of the individual psyche. The connection here with Marx and what was to come after, beginning with Lukács, is obvious. This opposition of the subjective and objective is reflected in Simmel's later work, influenced by Nietzsche and Bergson, where the vital flow of energy of life struggles against the cultural form into which it is compressed as a river overflows the banks it, itself, has created. A constantly developing and fluctuating life-process is objectified into external forms which, in time, become a fetter on the life-process itself whose constraint life seeks to rend asunder before throwing up yet more new forms: 'Our inner life, which we perceive as a stream, as an incessant process, as an up and down of thoughts and moods, becomes crystallized, even for ourselves, in formulas and fixed directions often merely by the fact that we verbalize this life . . . there still remains the fundamental, formal contrast between the essential flux and movement of the subjective psychic life and the limitations of its forms. These forms, after all, do not express or shape an ideal, a contrast with life's reality, but this life itself' (p. 352).

Simmel is persuaded that both Schopenhauer and Nietzsche, in their different ways, were not after the *contents* of life (for example, deep-seated ideas) but, instead, stressed life as the sole substance of its contents, as the determination of itself, as the meaning and value of life *as* life. He says: 'One can only inquire into knowledge and morality, self and reason, art and God, happiness and suffering, once this first puzzle has been solved. Its solution decides everything else. It is only the original fact of life which provides meaning and measure, positive or negative value' (p. 380). Nevertheless, he is concerned with 'sociation' (*Vergesellschaftung*), which is the consciousness of forming a unity with others. Simmel maintains that consciousness of sociation is sociation's immediate agent and inner significance and that consciousness of constituting a unity with others is actually all there is to such unity. Society exists by virtue of the consciousness shared by its members which reflects the influence of Kant on Simmel's thought. By this token, a collectivity is contingent on consciousness as the yoke of its existence. There will be any number of actual different *forms* of 'sociation', which are to be studied detached from any particular content. For him society is realised directly by its own elements which are conscious and synthesising units themselves. People are in a position to 'play' society through consciousness of sociation, wherein its inner significance is worked out and thought experiments are tried, i.e., re-cognising the (rules of the) game whilst it is in play. In order to be able to survive this achievement Simmel's individual has to be inwardly resourceful. He refers to the 'freedom of the human spirit' which he equates with 'form-giving creativity' and describes a situation where 'individuals . . . feel themselves to be egos whose behaviour grows out of autonomous, self-determined personalities. The objective totality yields to the individuals that confront it from without, as it were; it offers a place to their subjectively determined life-processes, which thereby, in their very individuality, become necessary links in the life of the whole' (p. 22). Simmel drew on both Kant and Rousseau to demonstrate what he recognised as the individual striving to be a whole against the one-sidedness that society demands of its members. According to Simmel the individual of social life is simultaneously within and without society; a product of society and yet embodying life from an autonomous centre: 'The a priori of empirical social life consists of the fact that life is not entirely social' (p. 14). As he remarks on the dilemma of simultaneously knowing and not knowing about the consequences of our actions: 'The slightest consideration shows how every single step of our life is determined and rendered possible by the fact that we perceive its consequences, and likewise because we perceive them only up to a certain point, beyond which they become confused and finally escape our vision altogether' (p. 354). Like Plato's philosopher, man in general for Simmel stands between knowing and not knowing and just as we straddle a border of knowledge and ignorance we straddle a border of an inner life and a social life.[2]

It is worth noting that the balance of Simmel's metaphysics of the non-social was left behind by the first generation of American sociologists whose emphasis upon the importance of everyday life and on a pragmatic theory of truth (of which Simmel was not persuaded) can be seen as typifying the thought of the Chicago School. Pragmatism had emphasised the role of experience – which obviously invokes the idea of the 'subjective viewpoint' and the particular perspective. The Chicago School's approach was to emphasise concrete experience embedded in problem solving and this preoccupation with individuals and practical spheres of activity echoes the concern of pragmatism. But, this is not the 'isolated' individual but individuals engaged in self-knowledge, identity and social interaction. Following the neo-Kantianism of their forbears the stress from the Chicago school is on particulars rather than abstractions, assuming only phenomenal forms can be perceived (i.e., the surface). Nothing else constitutes 'truth' or can be 'known' from such a standpoint. The legacy of Simmel to the Chicago School was mediated through particular individuals such as Small and Park. It is interesting to observe that the Chicago School did not view certain positions as mutually exclusive or necessarily contradictory. Certainly there is an emphasis on consciousness and interiority (to a large extent a reaction against developments in behaviourist psychology) drawing on Cooley's emphasis that the solid 'facts' of social life are the facts of the imagination. Park, for instance, refers to 'our inner lives' and conceives of us living out a 'dual existence' of a private and public life. For him there is something at work behind the masks we don for the roles of our social lives, where we find ourselves in constant conflict with ourselves. Rather than adopting a primarily hermeneutic method, Park holds that in the analysis of documents, human actions are interpreted and made intelligible when light is thrown on motives and subjective aspects of events. But human subjectivity for Park is a product of collective life and mental life has come into being out of the effort to act collectively. In fact, an additional dimension in the Chicago School's armoury comes into play at this point. Park concluded that what impressed upon human nature and human society their most distinctive traits was 'the conscious participation in a common purpose and a common life, rendered possible by the fact of speech and by the existence of a fund of common symbols and meanings' (Park, 1927, p. 737). We have here the invocation of a symbolic world of gestures and intentions – though conflictual – as the currency of experience. This is an emphasis on the world of primary groups and on inter-subjectivity anticipating symbolic interactionism and exemplified by Mead's influence on Ellsworth Faris. With the Chicago School we are presented with a pronounced tension between objective constraints of a situation and subjective definitions of that self-same situation. But despite what might be argued by certain commentators (Plummer, 1983) the Chicagoans held on to motives as primarily subjective and to the idea of human nature and imagination.

In functionalism, the paradigm which superseded the Chicago School in American sociology after the Second World War, the individual actor and their personality and what they might think and say is taken against a shared value system, i.e., the individual's orientations and actions are judged against an abstract value system. What had been the relation of subjective consciousness (attitude) to object (value) in the Kantian tradition of the Chicago School becomes transformed. In general terms Talcott Parsons, the leading light of functionalism, was concerned with the problem of order dating back to Hobbes. Why *did* societies cohere? In answer to this question Parsons saw himself developing an all-encompassing theory which would juxtapose an action frame of reference, which viewed social action as voluntaristic and incorporated the needs of the personality, and the social system, i.e., any ongoing set of interrelated social actions. For Parsons social action is oriented by and towards norms and values. In functionalism, values, which are internalised through socialisation, are associated with a normative dimension prescribing conduct – 'a standard is not a value unless internalized' (Kluckhohn, in Parsons and Shils, 1951, p. 400). Weber seemed to suggest that inquiry begins with the question: 'What motives determine and lead the individual members and participants in [a given] community to behave in such a way that the community comes into being in the first place and that it continues to exist?' (Weber, 1964, p. 107). Although it is undoubtedly the case that a motivated psychic state is imputed here, in functionalism what comes to feature is means related to ends in ultimately value (the end) orientated behaviour. In a tautological twist the spring of action *is* the orientation to the end – an outcome, it is to be suspected, Weber, too, always intended.

Parsons and Shils confirm that '[m]otivation (or motives) . . . may be conceived as denoting certain more or less innate systems of *orientations* involving cognition of and cathectic attachment to certain more or less implicit and unconscious "plans" of action aimed at the acquisition of cathected relationships to goal objects' (Parsons and Shils, 1951, p. 111). This describes a situation of subject orientated to objects (social and non-social) of its desire (cathect) and such *motivational orientation* is described elsewhere in Parsons and Shils as being to do with the gratification (or deprivation) of the actor's *need* – dispositions. But it is also linked with cognition and is, therefore, apparently *un*conscious and conscious at the same time. On balance, motivation is considered in the same breath as 'drives' and 'needs' and is seen to have a primarily biological point of reference. In fact motivation is canalised by values. Action choices are selected on the bases of values; actors are, in fact, oriented to values. Values organise a system of approved action though the actor is always beset by possible choice. Belief, says Kluckhohn, refers to 'true' and 'false', 'correct' or 'incorrect' whilst *values* imports the ideas of 'good' and 'bad' or 'right' and 'wrong'. Values are to do with conduct not behaviour and refer to an enduring standard transcending selfish motivation.[3] According to the Cornell Value-Study group quoted by Kluckhohn values are constitutive of a person's sense of identity, i.e., they are involved in the individual's existence as a self. Indeed, a great deal of the thrust of functionalism is concerned with the creation of an integrated personality. This concept of personality, inherited from Weber, has moved away from a Romantic–naturalistic interpretation which locates its true sanctum in an irrational inner core, towards an 'essence' based in the constancy of an inner relation to certain ultimate meanings and values, which in the course of action are turned into goals translatable into purposive-rational action. It is difficult to know the extent to which functionalism took stock of the unsubstantive self inherited from Hume but their emphasis on stabilising the adult personality has certainly an ironic ring to it when taken in comparison. In fact, in its reaction against the mono-causal explanation of self-interested 'economic man', functionalism had produced the 'over-socialized' individual with social norms totally constitutive of human agency (Wrong, 1961). It was a rôle model already being emulated elsewhere.

SYMBOLIC INTERACTIONISM

The school of thought that seems to obviate the need for consciousness whilst simultaneously holding on to a role for individuals and the self is symbolic interactionism, developing its concerns at a tangent to those preoccupying the Chicago School and functionalism. Symbolic interactionism owes a great deal to C. H. Cooley (see Coser, 1971) and his idea of the *looking glass self*, to W. I. Thomas and his emphasis on individual's *definition of the situation* and to the early work of William James. It is, nevertheless, primarily associated with the synthesising work of George Herbert Mead. Cooley emphasised the role of primary socialisation and saw the development of the child going through set stages of social development. Additionally, the prospect of secondary socialisation stretches out through the life-course. The child knows other selves before they know themselves; knowledge upon which the self's emergence depends. Children learn that their reactions and responses affect others and as a consequence children develop a sense of immediate power over persons and it is only subsequently that increasingly complex identities come to be taken on, which are tried and tested when social assignment and self-appropriation coincide, i.e., the individual is placed or situated as a social object by others in congruence with the way the individual sees themself. The individual's perception of themself will change over time as a consequence of exposure to this kind of scrutiny; identity is never a once-and-for-all achievement, though it may be imagined in constancy in the eye of the beholder. In effect, individuals engage in symbolic ordering of their life's events as they actively make sense of the past. For Cooley, society is the interplay of mental selves engaged in the inner–imaging of the working of other minds. Society is a uniquely mental phenomenon whose 'social facts' lie in the imaginations people exercise in relating to one another. This interchange of impressions and evaluations is then a resource for motivation in Cooley's view. Imagination and sympathy are harnessed to share in states of mind and to project the motives of others.

Although inspired by James, Cooley's work was too concerned with the inner – mental – realm for Mead's liking. Nevertheless, Mead is at one with Cooley that the effect of the social world of Others and our calling upon them is prior to introspective consciousness and calling on ourselves. The problem, then, seems to be not that the self becomes an Other to them, an object, as they hear themself talk and reply in the symbolism of social intercourse, but the precise status of the inner conversation comprising the mechanism of thought. Precisely with whom or between whom is the inner conversation taking place? For Mead the mechanism of introspection is given in the social attitude which an individual necessarily assumes towards themself, but when emphasis falls upon inner speech as forum and workshop of thought what exactly is the balance between the social and the personal and its imputed 'parts'? What Mead calls the 'generalized other' is the social group or organised community which gives to the individual their unity of self. Attitudes of others are taken on board as are their goals in order to develop a 'complete self' and the extent to which Mead develops this theme is reminiscent of Durkheim. The 'generalized other' is the social control of the community entering into an individual's thinking and only by this eventuality can the individual think at all. Only through the taking of the attitudes of the 'generalized other' towards themselves is the existence of a universe of discourse – a system of common, social meanings which thinking presupposes – rendered at all possible for individuals. Once generated, this self can respond to itself, and treat with itself, as it would with another – one talks to one's self as one talks to another person. In other words, individuals carry on conversations of gestures with themselves. Consciousness in Mead's analysis becomes a response or reaction to the objective world and the process of thought itself is a 'play of gesture between selves, even when those selves are part of our inner self-consciousness' (Mead, in Thayer, 1982, p. 350).

Thinking for Mead is an 'inner conversation' and reflective intelligence is preparatory to social action; what one thinks is then addressed and expressed to an audience. Individuals separate the significance of what they are saying to others from the actual speech – getting it ready before saying it, i.e., it is thought out first. In this process one addresses oneself *and* the other simultaneously; the development of this is in response to the 'monitoring' self *and* the other. For Mead individuals are not a self in a reflexive sense (responding to themselves) unless they become an object to themselves which comes about through the use of language. The community of communicative interaction is the most inclusive and extensive of all abstract classifications of individuals. They are united in a universe of discourse and a system of universally significant symbols. Because people share symbolic meanings and react to them in a similar way, an individual can predict how others will respond by judging how they would behave in such a situation. But not only in this view are individuals able to empathically take on the role of the other but they are also able to imagine how they are viewed by the other, i.e., they regard themselves from the others' perspective with the self being able to reflect on action as if it were the act of another. According to Goffman (1971) people try to stage-manage the impression they give of themselves to others, so that they will be viewed in a favourable light. But our conception of ourselves is always vulnerable – will our identity pass muster on the parade–ground of the unremitting world in which we find ourselves? In this view the self is seen as constantly changing and precarious rather than being fixed and immutable – although, over time, a more enduring residual core will develop. In this view, the mind, as a filter of reflexive intelligence, works on the present selectively and from out of the infinite range of the possible the significance and meaning of present objects and events is selected out.

Mead attested that becoming aware of the self as an object was predicated upon a differentiation within the self of two separate elements or phases. For him the 'I' and the 'me' are both selves. The 'me' the 'I' addresses is the 'me' similarly affected by the conduct of others and he addresses himself by the means of social stimulation which affect those around him. Mead refers to the social 'me', as the self which arises through the taking on of the attitudes of others and to which we react as an 'I'. The 'me' is constituted as the organised set of attitudes of others which one assumes, and is associated by Mead with social control and setting of limits, whilst the 'I' is the response to the attitudes of others. The 'me' is a product of the laying down of memories of the social evaluation of others; memories whose traces then form the basis of subsequent judgements to be made by the 'I' – itself the moment by moment, active (sometimes) calculating consciousness which may, nevertheless, be impulsive. Schopenhauer's 'no object without a subject' is echoed by Mead's 'an object involves a subject' – a 'me', therefore, is inconceivable without an 'I'. But Mead describes this 'I' as a *presupposition* bound never to be a presentation of conscious experience as the 'I' passes into the objective case (the 'me') the moment it is presented. The 'I' is disclosed only by ceasing to be that very subject for whom the object 'me' exists. It is only in retrospect, in the exercise of memory, where subject and object, the 'I' and the 'me', observer and observed are remembered experience, that a reintegrated self appears to us. Mead, incidentally, here, draws a great deal on James's emphasis on subsequent reflection revealing an intrinsically whole self. In other set-piece descriptions of the 'I' and the 'me', Mead's figures of speech are reminiscent of James's 'stream of consciousness' idea. Mead says that '[t]he self appearing as "I" is the memory image of the self who acted toward himself and is the same self who acts toward other selves' (Mead, in Thayer, 1982, p. 352). On the other hand, the 'me' is induced by the 'I' as it is observed and addressed – if the 'I' speaks the 'me' hears says Mead. He says that '[t]he "I" does not get into the limelight; we talk to ourselves, but do not see ourselves' and that 'I cannot turn around quick enough to catch myself' (Mead, in Strauss, 1956, p. 252) – a remarkably similar turn of phrase to that used by Hume to capture the ever-elusive substantive quality of apperception. For Mead it is the combination of the remembered self which exists and acts over against other selves *and* the inner response to action that, taken together, are essential to the self-conscious ego – though neither aspect of self-consciousness is a *subject* when appearing as objects of our experience.

It is largely unclear whether the 'I' and the 'me' exist side by side, one or other to be elicited by circumstance, or whether they exist layered one upon the other. Perhaps this itself is an indication of the ultimately unresolved nature of this dualistic formulation in the work of Mead. Mead makes several allusions which suggest that he is thinking in terms of depth such as 'besides', 'inner' and 'at the back of our heads' and also uses the kind of words which suggest a plurality of presence as in 'we', 'our' and 'accompany' to further describe extension in mental process. (Ironically, Descartes saw thinking substance as having no spatial dimensions.) There is something, then, 'behind' and responding to what 'we' may be doing, saying or thinking; 'we' are clearly conscious of 'our own' responses, remarks and reflections. He says: 'The actual situations is this: The self acts with reference to others and is immediately conscious of the objects about it. In memory it also re–integrates the self acting as well as the others acted upon. But besides these contents, the action with reference to the others calls out responses in the individual himself – there is then another "me" criticizing, approving, and suggesting, and consciously planning, i.e., the reflective self' (Mead, in Thayer, 1982, p. 354). In addition, Mead draws attention to that constant feature of consciousness of a running current of 'awareness' of what we do, distinguishable from the consciousness of the field of stimulation whether that field is without or within. Such 'accompanying awareness' disappears, according to Mead, when we are intensely preoccupied with the objective world. This it is to be construed is a kind of 'practical consciousness', where we have to recollect the experience to become aware that we were at all involved as selves.

In criticism of the work of Mead it is undoubtedly the case that the 'generalized other' appears as a monolith and excludes the possibility that individuals may be exposed to different influences at varying levels of generality. Additionally, the development of the self from Mead's point of view tends to be a primarily cognitive affair and the part played by affective elements in personal relationships, in particular emotions and sentiments, is underplayed. Mead's is an analytical scheme with process, but which lacks content – there is social behaviour but not social structure and social institutions. Symbolic interaction does not deal with large scale, macro-level social structure, such as the capitalist mode of production for example. Indeed, do interactions occur as a consequence of such systems of power or do they actually create them? The construction of social reality is not just people's creative interpretation of social life; there are levels of reality, and alternative realities, of which participants are largely unaware. It is here that the power relations of social structure both forge and finish social and historical individuals – a dimension largely lacking in symbolic interactionism. Yet, if symbolic interactionism conveniently manoeuvres around consciousness it is systematically malleated out of existence in the hands of ethnomethodology.

THE TRADITION OF ETHNOMETHODOLOGY

An organic connection between symbolic interactionism and ethnomethodology can be found in the work of C. Wright Mills who was introduced to philosophy at university in Texas coming across the pragmatists (in particular Peirce), Mead, James and Veblen – of whom the latter two were held in particularly high regard. A precocious talent might be a fitting epithet to describe Mills; the American sociological establishment often used much less flattering terms. His three journal articles prior to the Second World War drew on insights from the above which he harnessed with confidence and clarity whilst still in his early twenties. In *Language, Logic and Culture* (1939) Mills obviously connects with the pragmatists, Mead, Marx, Mannheim and even, surprisingly for this date in American sociology, Weber. In that article Mills sees human mental life as pivotally symbolic and mind as the interplay of human beings with symbolically mediated social situations. Although Eldridge (1983) says little about the subsequent *Situated Actions and Vocabularies of Motive* (1940), other than remarking on its anti–reductionist view of motivation, it is, in fact, both a seminal and prescient piece remarkable in several respects. Mills states unequivocally that language is not to be understood as expressing something prior 'in' the person, as it were designating the private state of the individual (the legacy of Wundtian psychology for Mills – see Chapter Seven), but serves rather a social function with language being taken by others as an indicator of future action. By the same token, subjective motives are not to be construed as fixed elements 'within' individuals, constituting 'springs' of action, but, instead, are to be thought of as the imputation and vocalisation of motives by actors to themselves and others – 'motives are the terms with which interpretation of conduct *by social actors* proceeds' (Mills, in Horowitz, 1967, p. 440). As individuals live out immediate acts of experience with attention directed outside themselves it is only when acts are frustrated that awareness of self and motive occur. In this view motives are, in fact, words which 'stand for anticipated situational consequences of questioned conduct' (p. 441). In 'question' situations motives are what is accepted justification for any past, present and future act and course of action. Motives are intrinsically social in character and according to Mills have no value without attendant social and historical specificity.

This constitutes the second part of Mills's thesis. For him, there will be different vocabularies of motive corresponding to institutionally different situations which will turn out to be appropriate to their respective patterns of behaviour. Institutionally and historically, then, motives are always embedded in a context out of which they cannot be considered to scan. Additionally, Mills sees motives as verbalised promotion of favoured outcomes; as indicating preferences in a range of options and as recommending courses of action. He suggests that the sociological quasi-metaphysical quest after real 'motives' is accompanied by a 'view held by many sociologists that language is an external manifestation or concomitant of something prior, more genuine, and "deep" in the individual. "Real attitudes" versus "mere verbalization" or "opinion" implies that at best we only infer from his language what "really" is the individual's attitude or motive . . . The only social items that can "lie deeper" are other lingual forms. The "Real Attitude of Motive" is not something different in kind from the verbalization of the "opinion" They turn out to be only relatively and temporally different' (p. 446).

And again: 'When we ask for the "real attitude" rather than the "opinion", for the "real motive" rather than the "rationalization", all we can meaningfully be asking for is the controlling speech form which was incipiently or overtly presented in the performed act or series of acts. There is no way to plumb behind verbalization into an individual and directly check our motive–mongering' (p. 447). The verbalised motive, then, is not an index of something inside individuals but a basis of inferring a typal vocabulary of motive of a situated action. It is this prescient position that informs the subsequent sociology, if they would accept that designation, of ethnomethodology and later of Coulter who very much typifies the legacy.

Ethnomethodology is undoubtedly in the tradition of phenomenology with an emphasis on the practical world of common-sense as a repository of ideas, i.e., the study of the world of the layman and not that of the scientist. Garfinkel (1967), who draws particularly upon Schütz but also stresses his indebtedness to Parsons, sees the separation of scientific rationality and that of the 'natural attitude' (the former exemplified by Weber's approach; the latter by Schütz) as leading to a situation whereby the observer's criteria – means/ends schema – marks off what is rational whilst all else is deemed irrational. He claims that this should no longer be a residual category and lists a considerable number of these 'rationalities'. The lay actor is seen as a practical social theorist and Garfinkel reiterates Schütz's suspension of doubt notion, though moving away from phenomenology – with its Cartesian emphasis upon the primacy of subjective experience – towards the study of situated actions as 'publicly interpreted linguistic forms'. As will be seen in the next chapter this is a movement toward Austin and the later Wittgenstein. However ethnomethodology does not use their terminology and introduces the notion of 'indexicality' instead. In essence, a semantic token may have different meanings in different contexts and semantic tokens (components) may be expressed differently according to context. According to Garfinkel these form an obstruction to social-scientific observers in their description of social activity. This is an attempt to ignore reflexivity which according to Garfinkel social actors utilise to 'bring off' any piece of social conduct. He is in agreement with ordinary language philosophers and Wittgenstein, in that the significance of language lies not as a mere symbol but as a contextual utterance – the performance of the speech act. However, unlike these philosophers Garfinkel wishes to stress temporally situationed conversations (i.e., in situ), and not just the utterances of abstract individuals. The natural attitude and common sense are stressed and a preoccupation with language emerges in quite a technical sense (witness the emphasis on 'indexicality').[4]

To ethnomethodology action is to be treated as 'rational' only in so far as it is 'accountable' – the activities that produce the settings of everyday life are identical with the actor's procedures for making these settings intelligible; identifying 'rationality' with 'accountability' thus cuts off the description of acts of communication from any analysis of purposive or motivated conduct. Indeed 'Garfinkel has no interest in developing the kind of motive–analysis favoured by [Schütz], but it is concerned with how the "natural attitude" is *realised* as a phenomenon by actors in day to day life' (Giddens, 1976, p. 36). From this point of view activities which produce the contexts of day to day life are coterminous with member's procedures for rendering these contexts intelligible. Thus, as Giddens remarks 'identifying rationality with "accountability" cuts off the description of acts and communications from any analysis of purposive or motivated conduct, the strivings of actors to realise definite interests' (Giddens, 1976, p. 40). 'Situated actions' of publicly interpreted linguistic forms, then, become the focus of attention for Garfinkel not the primacy of subjective experience. Garfinkel remarks that 'meaningful events are entirely and exclusively events in a person's behavioural environment . . . Hence there is no reason to look under the skull since nothing of interest is to be found there but brains' (quoted in Bruce and Wallis, 1983, p. 64). There have been sharp exchanges between critics and proponents of this position. As an instructive instance of this, Bruce and Wallis initiated a debate with the legacy of Mills's seminal 'insights' concerning 'vocabularies of motive' which they located within the pre–suppositions and topics of analysis of ethnomethodology. They contend that the motivational stories being told by actors are being denied explanatory status in such approaches and that the conflation of talk and motives means that the one cannot be used to understand the other. In the approach they are criticising, accounts are not an expression of reasons leading to decisions, but, instead, *post hoc* justifications and rationalisations. This begins, they contend, with Mills's suggestion that 'motives be viewed as rhetorical devices, not as things in the personal consciousness of actors' (Bruce and Wallis, 1983, p. 63). Conversely, Bruce and Wallis assume that there are 'real' motives and reasons for action that can be accessed, in theory, in an explanatory connection with behaviour. In their rejoinder, Sharrock and Watson concluded that there is no general problem of motives and that identifying motives is problematical for sociologists and other members of society; when this is problematical it is not 'because of the epistemological or ontological status of motives but because of the relationship of action to the contexts in which they occur' (Sharrock and Watson, 1984, p. 449). They contend that members of society cite motives as explanation of action: some of which are accepted, some of which depending upon circumstance are not. Ethnomethodology does not reject or accept what actors have to say about their motives but suspends judgement on their adequacy on both whether ascriptions of motive identify motive correctly and whether motives proffered in explanation are in fact explanatory, thus seeing whether members of society treat sceptically or, conversely, endorse, specific motive attributions, i.e., are they 'bought into'. For them what has been argued by ethnomethodology and conversational analysis is that talk is a kind of action between which there is no 'disjunction'; action cannot be discriminated from the account of that action.

Despite a great deal of talking past each other in this debate, a fundamental question remains: *are* human beings inwardly impelled to do things and, if so, how is this to be distinguished from *post hoc* reason giving? If 'motive' applies to the latter (following Mills) what sense do we make of the former? Is this inaccessible and inconsequential for us until it is verbalised and becomes something else (a motive!). By this token does it exist at all? Discerning the ontological and epistemological status of motives does, then, seem to matter. Drawing on Mills and others in sociology and the work of Wittgenstein on language, Coulter seeks to explore reason-giving as a complex achievement of practical action. Investigation of such socially constructed, communication he argues does not entail the uncritical acceptance of reasons proffered for what a person does, nor need that inquiry problematise competing reasons for action, i.e., his approach differs from the 'psychologistic' propensity to treat the lone person as possessor of abstracted mental properties. Moreover, in questioning the way in which agents' reasons for action have been analysed, often as correct or incorrect, right or wrong, Coulter proposes that agents' reason-giving practices are themselves kinds of contextualised social action. He discusses in what sense sociologists can explain the beliefs and claims to knowledge of respondents in the research situation. The questions raised are: do sociologists accept at face–value elicited explanations, even after establishing reasons for belief? Or, do sociologists look beyond and behind the stated case to social circumstances, causes and underlying conditions, which begs the question of how individuals come to hold beliefs the conditions for which remain unknown to them? In fact Coulter believes sociolo-

gists should really be looking for 'the *logic* of agents' actual conceptual, communicative, relational and instrumental conduct as
they constitute their objective-universes' (Coulter, 1989, p. 36). The
overriding interest of the kind of approach he is exemplifying is
concerned with: 'Exploring the connections and ramifications of
concept-use for any domains of human interest within social contexts, practices and institutional arrangements – the grammars of
cognition' (p. 50). This is defended as being more than a 'logical'
inquiry by invoking its sociological brief to explore the occasions of
use and context and the basic 'data' derived from social events
and processes. He is persuaded of Mills's line that the arch-fallacy
is seeking after inner, deeper, 'real' reasons in the member's mind
that somehow lies behind an utterance. For if reason-giving is
deemed insufficient why should the putative contents of minds be
privileged as a source of greater veracity? This, as we have seen,
is the dilemma bequeathed by Weber and apparently 'solved' by
Mills. Ironically enough, it is far from clear whether the early Mills
referred to so reverentially by this approach should be the major
point of reference for consciousness-critique. It is, at least, worth
considering.

Horowitz has referred to Mills's 'life long contempt for all forms of
metaphysics' (Horowitz, in Mills, 1966, p. 13). Yet, in his later work
this does not appear so clear-cut. Gerth and Mills employ the term
'*psychic structure*, to refer to man conceived as an integration of
perception, emotion, and impulse. Of course there are other psychic
functions, memory and imagination, for example; but we shall limit
our term at this point. For our purpose, "psychic structure" will refer
to when, how, and why man feels, perceives, and wills' (Gerth and
Mills, 1970, p. 20). They do, in addition, consider the 'feeling-state'
of mood which at times we cannot control. But a major reference
point in their analysis, unsurprisingly, is Mead whose work is seen as
a daring effort to anchor personal consciousness in the social process.
But working through the dialectic of inner narration and outer utterance, as a precursor of subject and object, Gerth and Mills begin to
posit a private person. They say 'inner speech may be very important
in the person's self-understanding. To communicate our inner
speech to others we have to translate it into discursive, outer speech,
and it is this explaining to others which gives rise to "objectivity"'.
(pp. 126–127). What appears to be going on here, quite remarkably

coming from Mills, is that '[t]he subjective is what the person presents only to himself. When he communicates it to another it is no longer subjective, but objective, no longer private but socialized. We may communicate such private feelings, moods, and motives in intimate relations, or even sometimes among perfect strangers' (p. 128). Given an urbane character structure, 'private' motives will only be given away in 'public' by the yokel or the fool. Topics which are excluded in public conversations by a strongly enforced taboo will more likely remain part of 'the private world of the individual' and will tend to become unconscious. Not only will the person be unable to discuss them with intimates he will not be able to discuss them with himself. The 'unconscious', here, means that which is unverbalised or even unverbalisable, but there is definitely a portrayal of a person who may or may not verbalise feelings internally – depending on whether they are conventionally tabooed – even 'when alone'! They also refer to gestures hiding 'inner feelings', yet even when the vocabularies of motive are situated – Mills's most characteristic stance – the private person does not seem to want to go away. Nevertheless, there is still a return to the concerns of Mills's early work, but one that seems, curiously, much more troubled: 'Back of the motive–mongering and the self-doubts of persons as to their own motives is the fact that in modern life there is often no stable or unquestioned vocabulary of motives available. And back of this is the fact that the institutional arrangements of roles demand that we rapidly give up and take on roles and along with them, their socially appropriate motives' (p. 123). Here is a situation that is far from stable not only inter-subjectively but intra-subjectively too. In fact, it is this very C. Wright Mills (1959) who refers in his later work to the human mind as a 'social fact' and to 'self-reflective' habits that serve to keep the 'inner-world' awake.

CONCLUSION

To a large degree, as has been seen, the era from the 1890s onwards, if anything, leaned towards a rejection of consciousness; by some (James, for example) because it was mistrusted and for others (Nietzsche) because it was not sufficiently elemental. In effect, the extent to which an undefinable human nature lay behind human consciousness had come to form one crucial parameter of the debate on consciousness. With structuralism – exemplified classically by Durkheim – it is not just that structures (societies) overarch and subsume individuals but also that individual consciousness is merely a repository and reflection of a collective consciousness; this is the individual level of the superficial, surface and appearance taken against a real world of deep-structure comprised of the *ideas* of religion, culture and society which inform the every move of the individual captive creature. Thus began a trend towards what more recent sociology would term the 'decentring' of the individual, where the individual is removed from centre stage to be replaced by structure. The individual, then, in this view is determined by social structure and in the process a level of reality is created that is neither native to the individual nor to the institutional arrangement *per se*. For Durkheim a combination of units yields fresh properties not present in any of them taken in isolation. Such a level of reality is not self-evident to participants according to both Durkheim and Pareto. Nevertheless, the 'social', in this view, tends to have a monolithic quality in determining consciousness. The emphasis in Pareto on – albeit non-rational – psychological forces is reflected in the English title of his major sociological work – *Mind and Society*. Yet, a great deal of subsequent commentary has failed to recognise a crucial connection between the two dimensions (this is certainly true of Winch, 1958), that the non-rational impetus creates subsequently overarching social structure. What price then rule following?

It is with Weber that the individual social actor and their inner motives comes into play though this situation may be far from unequivocal or self-evident in the work of Weber himself. As will be seen in the next chapter, Wittgenstein's contention that intentions are imbedded in their situation, in human institutions and custom is a remarkable echo of Weber. Following Wittgenstein, Winch delivers such a tendentious reading of Weber that he does not seem to recognise that in, at least, one respect the corollary of that author's position is so similar to his own. For Weber the logic seems to go: individuals create rule-governed institutional reality through social action and from that point on subsequent action is oriented to that social system. Hence, it might be seen to be the role of the sociologist to provide ideal typical models of action of that social system rather than being primarily preoccupied with individual meaning. There are, in fact, two theories of action as the legacy of nineteenth-century social thought: one develops the sequence as consciousness then action whilst the other holds that action leads on to consciousness or, more accurately, consciousness *is* action. The reason that a motivating or intentional consciousness of individuals (re Weber) does not figure in this alternative theory of action is that individuals are mere conduits through which flows a much stronger stream of life force. Experience is the stream or flow in question, never static but always in flux with social structures, such as they exist, being viewed as seamless webs of interrelations through which individual biographies come to pass and pass away. This amounts to the contention that the nature of human kind lies outside itself. In the sociology and philosophy of inter-action, experience and flowing encounter there is no recourse for participants or social scientific practitioners to the nether reaches of social structure or system on the one hand or interiority and mentality on the other. There can be no prospect of a disengaged taking of stock where the ultimately macro *or* micro dimensions can themselves come into play. They are in play in this view or they have merely a virtual or notional 'existence' of latency or potentiality. They are of the moment of life as it is lived or they are nothing of immediate consequence and immediate consequence is everything. The subject–object dualism of western philosophy becomes fused or, more correctly, interfused in this view.

The sheer weight of numbers pushing 'experience' into centre stage of social thought is very nearly overshadowed by their inordinate variety. Dilthey, perhaps the perpetuator of the preoccupation; Nietzsche; William James, emphasising 'pure experience' as we saw in Chapter Four; Mannheim emphasising 'collective experience' and different modes of experiencing the same reality; phenomenologists such as Schütz and Berger and Luckmann pointing up the significance of 'everyday experience', and ethnomethodology, invariably using experience as the ultimate point of reference. Phenomenology was originally an approach which stressed description of experiences above causal explanations, where to return to 'things in themselves' is to return to a world which precedes knowledge. The world is 'already there' for phenomenology, though this 'facticity' carries with it little historical and material content. The neo-Kantian heritage, evident in different ways in thought ranging from Husserl to Mannheim, means that reality remains reclusive and man can have only imperfect knowledge of it. It is then but a very short step to see social reality not in a natural or material form but, rather, as a meaning – structure formed out of the meaningful *experiences* of individual actors. In this process, it would seem, there can be no transcendental or universalistic conception of *truth*, *as truth* can only ever be located in particular societal contexts. In sum, social reality exists only in so far as it has *meaning* for its participants and knowledge cannot be separated from the human interaction by which it is produced. If what 'transcendental phenomenology' was trying to achieve is summarised it is possible to detect the supersession of the original agenda. This had emphasised the intuitive act of the phenomenological reduction, intentionality itself including emphasis on the 'style' of what consciousness intends (fearing, hoping, desiring, for example, i.e., including emotionality), and a concern with experiencing in memory, involving inner time and projections into the future. The 'phenomenological reduction' sought to 'bracket' our encultured view of the world – to lift 'the veil of culture', i.e., to question the way we have been taught to look at the world. It is concerned with the essential meaning of objects as constituted by the activities of our minds not the objects themselves. But, whilst a 'disturbance' of the taken-for-granted was an essential starting point for 'transcendental phenomenology', common sense and the inter-subjective has been introduced by subsequent theorists drawing inspiration from the later works of Husserl. In effect, what for 'transcendental phenomenology' formed the problem, for phenomenologically influenced sociology comprised the solution. Such phenomenology has become identified with the subjective approach of ethnography, of symbolic interactionism, of ethnomethodology and the various sociologies of 'Everyday Life', where individuals create and shape their own worlds. The inherent paradox of Dilthey, Husserl and Schütz is that whilst each expends a great deal of energy establishing the analytic credentials of consciousness and subjectivity they all turn ultimately to the objectivity of the historical world and the *Lebenswelt* of everyday life.

A range of theorists have tended to prioritise certain consistent dimensions which indicate the legacy from the nineteenth-century philosophy of consciousness: the objectifying capacity of consciousness and the creation of an objective world; the paramount significance of *acting* in the world and being totally engaged; a practical concern with the world and how we make our way in it; and a recognition of the collective life of a public world. Certainly we would encounter, here, Simmel, Schütz, Mannheim and Berger and Luckmann. These theorists, however reluctantly on occasion, are loath to abandon consciousness as thought, memory and imagination going on, as it were, on the 'inside'. Simmel, much like Dilthey, has bequeathed an ambiguous legacy. In both there is life as life *and* subjectivity. At one point Simmel prioritises life as life over contents but elsewhere refers to the form-giving creativity of subjectivity. Although commonalities have been seen in Simmel's *forms* and Weber's *ideal types*, equivalence might be imputed between Simmel's *forms* as life itself and Weber's insistence on the ubiquitous presence of power and conflict – into which shape everything is forced. If conflict cannot be excluded from social life it cannot be excluded from experience of it. What is remarkable about Simmel, however, is his stress on the non–social and that the individual exists both within and without society. As has been seen Mead's view can accommodate the carrying on of an inner (secret) conversation in individual self-narration and the presentation of different selves to different people. Despite the emphasis to be found in Mead on language mediating the self he also stresses the self as inner, covert and mental concerning itself with intentions, motives and attitudes mediated through symbolic processes located, in part, in consciousness. The symbolic-interactionist, according to this manifesto, should be feeling their way 'into' this experience of subjectivity. In fact, one of the major stumbling blocks to the progress of post metaphysical philosophy, as we shall encounter it in the next chapter, is the introduction by the pragmatists, Mead and Schütz, of a complicated time-space circulating around each other of the 'I' and the 'Me' unknown to the depthless (largely timeless) Cartesian cogito. It is unsurprising, therefore, that such an approach should attract criticism from those influenced by Wittgenstein, ethnomethodology and social constructionism. Mills, following this line, sees different vocabularies of motive corresponding to very different institutional situations. Douglas indicates that certain strands identified in phenomenology and ethnomethology (i.e., by the late sixties) seem tempted to think that by making everything externally observable 'one would never have to ask whether or not what is spoken and done is in some way the result of some unseen phenomena "inside" the actors' (Douglas, in Douglas, 1971, p. 33). In drawing attention to the prioritisation of indexicality and contextualisation in ethnomethodology, Douglas contends that the greatest problem facing us lies in analysing the interdependencies and complex relations existing between situational aspects of social meanings and those aspects largely independent of such situations. Understanding these interrelations is the means to deal effectively with Members' ordering of their social lives trans-situationally. Although it is couched, here, in terms of man the symbol maker and user bringing to bear on the immediate situation a wealth of experience from which to construct meanings and action, Douglas is drawing attention to man's 'awesome' capacity to transcend that immediate situation and 'himself' in the process, to coordinate the immediate situation with those beyond his momentary grasp and to project himself into an anticipated future. Such capacity does not depend on language alone but the means to use meaning transcendentally through consciousness, including memory, imagination and projections of the self and identity. In addition, as Mills's later work confirms, it is the means whereby man makes those crucial connections between himself, beset in his immediacy, and a larger world of uncertain constituency and presence pressing for attention.

6

THE SUPERSESSION OF CONSCIOUSNESS IN SOCIAL THOUGHT

'The word is available as the sign for, so to speak, inner employment: it can function as a sign in a state short of outward expression. For this reason, the problem of individual consciousness as the *inner word* (as an *inner sign* in general) becomes one of the most vital problems in the philosophy of language'.

(Volosinov, 1973, p. 14)

The attempt to transcend the subject–object dichotomy as the legacy of western philosophy has resulted in an emphasis on language and discourse, on being and on the body. Each has been seen to effectively supersede the problematic of consciousness. In fact, post-metaphysical thought has inherited a legacy of a philosophy or sociology of 'consciousness' *in action* (from Hegel on down) and there is continuity even between Hegel and Nietzsche in emphasising the self being *in* the deed. It would now seem to be conventional wisdom in this area of social thought to aver that the individual does not enjoy a privileged access to the meaning of their own mind or privileged access to the meaning of their own behaviour. The following discussion explores some of the main reference points in the 'post' consciousness debate by considering the emphasis that has been placed on language, on being, on the body and on discourse. Though from a variety of perspectives, theorists who prioritise these concerns share one thing in common: a total rejection of consciousness and all its works.

RYLE AND WITTGENSTEIN

The legacy of Cartesian body and soul dualism, with the soul (consciousness) preaching to the body, has met with a response from
anti-Cartesians, such as Ryle, who have sought to ground consciousness as that which is exhibited in behaviour. Ryle rejected the idea of
a person preaching to themself before they practice and the idea that
learning skills needs to be preceded by learning rules. According to
him overt performances are not clues to the workings of mind; they
are the workings. There is no double operation of understanding and
execution and 'knowing how' is not the stepchild of theory. Ryle says
that when people are described as exhibiting qualities of mind this
does not refer to an 'occult' and covert cause of which the behaviour
is an effect, but to the quality of the overt act itself. Mind really is *in*
action. In addition, will and emotions, moods and motive, are ultimately modes of communication and symbolic gestures. He remarks
that the term 'experiences' is spoken of, however glibly, as 'a plural
noun commonly used to denote the postulated non-physical episodes
which constitute the shadow-drama on the ghostly boards of the
mental stage' (Ryle, 1963, p. 63). He says: 'Motives and moods are
not the sorts of things which could be among the direct intimations of
consciousness, or among the objects of introspection, as these facti-
tious forms of Privileged Access are ordinarily described. They are
not "experiences", any more than habits or maladies are "experiences"' (p. 111). Though 'experiences', for Ryle, tend to designate a
special kind of mental operation, there is no means of acquainting
ourselves with such a world; the self is *systematically* elusive. Ryle's
view is that it is not only theorists who are mistaken, for the lay
person, too, works with a mind–body dualism. They are thus left
with the problematic task of making inferences, by analogy with their
own conduct, from observed behaviour to impute states of mind, i.e.,
something is signalised by the behaviour. Ryle indicates that people
are strongly drawn to believe, in the face of their own daily experience, that there are two separate processes of theorising and doing.
They too, he concludes, are implicitly wedded to the 'ghost in the
machine' dogma inherited from Descartes. This is extremely paradoxical because Ryle himself, like the other ordinary language philosophers and like G. E. Moore before them, had ultimate recourse to
common sense as 'proof'. Although Ryle chooses not to confront the
problem head on, the inherent paradox is that if ordinary language is

stacked full of phrases that refer to an inner life of the psyche how could Ryle, or others, gainsay that without jeopardising the security of the linguistic beachhead in the assault on cartesian 'ghost in the machine' dualism. How could the authority of ordinary language users in their reference to interiority, itself come to be questioned without undermining the hallowed ground of ordinary language? This objection, however, has not proved decisive. Ryle once referred to the legacy of cartesianism as the 'official doctrine' (p. 13) but in the last half century the tables have turned. It is testimony to its pre-eminent position that this new orthodoxy has been neither shaken nor, particularly, stirred by several frontal assaults which would have seen off less self-assured opponents (most notably perhaps by Gellner in Giddens, 1974, for example and Nagel, 1986). The reasons for this will not be explored in this discussion, nor will there be a further attempt at a foundational attack. What will be considered, rather, will be the marginalisation of the constituency for consciousness as seen from this particular corner.

It may well be appropriate to discuss Austin (1962) and Strawson (1959) at this juncture but attention really needs to turn to the most influential contribution to this kind of approach – that of Wittgenstein. Without engaging in the ultimately fruitless task of tracing the philosophical influences on Wittgenstein's thought, two undoubted points of reference are worth pinning down in that they also bear on this discussion of consciousness. Kant says in his 'Transcendental Logic' that ' [t]houghts without content are empty' and that 'intuitions without concepts are blind' (Kant, cited in Lukács, 1971, p. 133). 'Thoughts die' opines Schopenhauer 'the moment they are embodied by words' (Schopenhauer, cited in Sacks, 1991, p. 41). The relevance to Wittgenstein's thought of each maxim will become clear but in the case of both Kant and Schopenhauer there is also the notion of a metaphysical self, the transcendental ego, as the limit – not a part – of the world, which also becomes Wittgenstein's legacy; he says that there is no such thing as the subject or the soul that thinks or entertains ideas – rather the metaphysical subject is not a part of the world but the limit of it. Ultimately, this becomes for Wittgenstein a staged disappearance of the independent subject which thinks or entertains ideas. In addition, Hacker confirms that 'Wittgenstein was willing to adopt a neo-Humean analysis of the empirical self. There is no empirical soul-substance thinking thoughts, there are only thoughts' (Hacker, 1997, p. 86). When taken together the above two considerations form the mutually related axes of his position for the purpose of this discussion: what can or cannot be said in language and the superfluousness of the subject. In the *Tractatus* Wittgenstein (1961) arrived at his concern with the world as a totality of facts rather than things by a sequence of steps: the substance of all possible worlds is comprised of relations, unanalysable properties and spatio-temporal points – what Hacker refers to as 'the totality of sempiternal simple objects' (Hacker, in Honderich, 1999, p. 226). The combinatorial possibilities with other objects characterises the form of simple objects with any possible arrangement constituting a state of affairs. Such a state of affairs, when obtaining, comprises a fact. Wittgenstein then moves on to his critical statement on propositional forms via an assertion of the pertinence of isomorphic and logical representations of 'reality' and by increments he moves away from a spatial-relational, *real* world. By realising that one cannot step outside logic to describe it, he had arrived at the conclusion that there are no higher or lower or more foundational levels (or no meta language). Yet, at the same time he wanted to identify the unsayable with what is most important in life. In his early work he had in effect placed aesthetic, moral and religious questions beyond the limits of language though in his later work the language game, ironically enough, lies on the surface open to view and, more importantly, use. The only meaningful move or take up in use is within the accepted parameters and practices of the rules of the game.

Wittgenstein is concerned with a world of meaning simply because it is the only world available to us. He admits, and was acutely aware, of a world confronting us of sheer immediate existence; the silent face being a particularly potent and, for this discussion, relevant symbol (see also Schopenhauer, 1969, pp. 56–57). The world of the unsayable countermines the world of language. We cannot name any aspect of this meaningless world beyond language; it is too near, too suffused, far too naturally lucid. Existence, *per se*, apart from a world of meaning does not exist, does not exist for us and is ultimately inaccessible. What language cannot distil in the realm of meaning cannot be anything at all. The 'faced-world' cannot be entered into without being turned into the 'said-world'. As Wittgenstein, wrestling with his own paradox, stated the case classically and epigrammatically: '*The limits of my language* mean the limits of my world' (Wittgenstein, 1961,

5.6); 'What we cannot speak about we must pass over in silence' (7); 'the inexpressible is – inexpressibly – *contained* in what is expressed!' (Letter quoted in Schulte, 1992, p. 75); and 'Since everything is plainly there, there is nothing to explain. For what is concealed does not interest us' (Wittgenstein, 1958, p. 126). Indeed, Wittgenstein appears to go to extraordinary lengths to demonstrate that neither the world nor human beings have hidden depths – there is nothing, as it were, on the inside. He contended that language does not describe an inner state of the subject but constitutes public expressions of judgement, feeling or opinion, i.e., not descriptions, then, but avowals. His later works devoted attention to examining how our 'public' language operates when talking about our 'mental' states, i.e., thoughts and feelings. Whilst introspection appears to provide privileged access to the immediacy of inner mental states, this experience of a 'private' hinterland is, itself, misleading according to Wittgenstein. It is, in fact, composed throughout by the significances of social context and our thoughts can only have meaning in terms of public language shared with others. Winch says in setting the tone for much of what was to come to galvanise social thought: 'The concepts we have settle for us the form of the experience we have of the world' (Winch, 1958, p. 15). For him, following Wittgenstein, there is no way of stepping outside of the concepts in terms of which we think about the world and when our concepts change our concept of the world is also thereby transformed.

Gellner indicates that the 'forms of life' Wittgenstein and Winch have in mind – unspecified, without exemplar, abstract and unchanging – constitute in this approach a special variant of solipsism in which cultural collectivities of some sort replace individual islands of consciousness. In consequence, in Gellner's view, Winch 'in accordance with the principles and customs of his movement, does not operate with notions such as "consciousness", "inside", etc.' (Gellner, in Giddens, 1974, p. 135). The substitution of 'forms of life' for the Cartesian cogito is, however, ultimately illusory, forming only an allusion to real, social and historical conditions. Gellner asserts that with Wittgenstein 'a vision of society is smuggled in on the coat-tails of a theory of language' (Gellner, 1992, p. 122), though it is not the purpose here to uncover precisely how Wittgenstein channelled himself in this direction (see Gellner, 1992; Sass, 1994). This approach sets a scene that is simultaneously *too* socially determined and not socially determined enough. Ordinary language is mired in mystification and it is the forms of life it reflects that systematically resource it. Likewise, if a social, historical and overtly political world is a problem for the approach inspired by Wittgenstein, so, too, is a world at all. As Nagel says: 'The idea of objectivity always points beyond mere intersubjective agreement, even though such agreement, criticism, and justification are essential methods of reaching an objective view. The language that we can have because of our agreement in responses enables us to reach beyond the responses to talk about the world itself. . . . That world is not dependent on our view of it or any other view: the direction of dependence is the reverse. Even though we must use language to talk about the world and our relation to it, and even though certain conditions of agreement enable us to have this language, the areas of such possible agreement are a limited part of the world' (Nagel, 1986, pp. 108–109). If it cannot be assumed that there is a deeper, hidden, more authentic and more coherent mental realm lying behind what people actually end up saying, so, too, by the same token, it cannot be assumed that what people say – language or discourse – is equivalent to, or *is*, the world itself. If, following Wittgenstein, language is the limit of a person's world, then can it be the case, in turn, that the world is the limit of a person's language? In some quarters this may be conceded only reluctantly with 'the world' being reconstructed into language, discourse or semiotics with the resulting tautology of 'language is the limit of a person's language'! But there are, in any case, other strongholds of the position so averse to consciousness.

HEIDEGGER

It has been said that 'Heidegger does not ground his thinking in average, everyday *concepts,* but in average everyday *practice;* in what people do, not in what they say they do. This leads him to abandon our pervasive Cartesian way of thinking of human beings as subjects who represent objects to themselves . . . Thus, like Ludwig Wittgenstein, Heidegger finds that the only ground for the intelligibility of thought and action that we have or need is in the everyday practices themselves, not in some hidden process of thinking or of history' (Dreyfus and Hall, 1992, p. 2). Thus, as with Marx, the practical takes ontological priority over the theoretical. Neither theoretical activity nor the theoretical object is primary and theoretical seeing and knowing is displaced. The self and the world are jointly actively determining and not two separate entities like subject and object. Instead, Heidegger sought to frame human existence – *Dasein* – as a window through which Being could be beheld. If there is no *Dasein* there can be no understanding of Being. Whereas the subject was formerly viewed as essentially outside and distinct from the world, in Heidegger it becomes being-in-the-world. There is no soul or self that underlies and endures in Heidegger's view and identity means to take an authentic stance as we choose our own way of existing. This is the removal of everything potentially 'inside' to the 'outside' of *Dasein*. We are inescapably social beings bound to our culture and community in their entirety and 'the *world* is structured as a field of *reference*-relations' (Polt, 1999, p. 90). Unlike Kant, for Heidegger there is no world known to us (or appearing to us) as distinct from the one in which we act. The Cartesian legacy of the world as somehow apart from us where we remain for ever subject as over and against object is rejected with equal conviction. And from that same tradition he is critical of all dualisms and dichotomies: subject/object; self/other; mind/body; and ourselves as consciousness in opposition to the physicality of the world (the myth of presence). Whilst for Husserl the mind might be seen to move out to become one with the object, in Heidegger the direction of influence is reversed: essents – things that 'are' – 'jut' in and dawn in us. Indeed, the early Heidegger seems to turn Husserl's *intentionality* into the problem rather than the solution.

Dasein, for Heidegger, would appear not to be the 'go-between' twixt subject and object but their very fusion; for him the self and the world together in practice *are Dasein*. In effect there is a unity of purpose in being-in-the-world, which in turn, imports the sociality of 'being-with'. *Dasein* is the nature of ongoing human existence whereby human beings interact intentionally with the world in which they exist; *Dasein* always finds itself amidst an already existing world of *equipment* with each thing in that world being experienced as a significant something. The emphasis is then placed upon the world disclosing function of practices in the everyday world, revealing the concealed order of intelligibility known to Heidegger as *Being*. *Dasein* – being there – is the brute fact of active engagement with the world and is, as such, prior to all else. Our Being in the world is a seamless totality for Heidegger and in that is reminiscent of Hegel. Although in some of his writing it appears to be identified with the human subject *Dasein*, for Heidegger, is more primordial than humanity. Indeed, it is not clear that Heidegger differentiates sufficiently between Being and beings as Rorty has indicated (see Rorty, in Dreyfus and Hall, 1992). Heidegger's point is that *Dasein* is only ontically distinguished when in its very Being, that Being becomes an issue for it, but nowhere in this does consciousness have a role. In Heidegger's radically anti-subjectivist philosophy there is no place, no space left, for consciousness to *be*. Yet in Being I cannot escape my mood as, by the same token, I cannot escape my past. When my past and my future become at issue for me in the present in the mood of anxiety, the interconnectedness of the world and its fragility weighs in on me intensely. Anxiety makes Being aware of itself; *Dasein* is, thus, for the first time, brought before beings as such. In a situation of breakdown, Being remains, but stripped of its ordinary familiarity. In anxiety, this withdrawal from speech, we lose our foothold in the epochal world. In effect, anxiety sits between inauthenticity and authenticity and Heidegger's inauthenticity connotes the custom and practice prescribed by the condition of the world – an incessant average everydayness. Authenticity, conversely equates with choice – *Dasein*, leading a life of its own.

In a definition that he stuck to over time, which departs from Hegel but invokes Nietzsche's 'Superman', Heidegger states: 'Spirit is neither empty cleverness nor the irresponsible play of the wit, nor the boundless work of dismemberment carried on by the practical intelligence; much less is it world-reason; no, spirit is a fundamental, knowing resolve toward the essence of being' (Heidegger, 1959, p. 49). The self, of which we become aware primarily, is defined by others and framed in their expectations so that in this state (*das Man*) we do not have selves or our own self. As *das Man* is forged by community and history, which is the only possible crucible for Heidegger, the equation then becomes drift or choice. But with Being having become hidden from us the question seems to be how do we get (back) from *Dasein* to Being after our fallenness from Being? On the ground, Heidegger's paradox appears to be how can we be caught up in the moment and not caught up in it at one and the same time with the forgetfulness of engagement with the world of *equipment* holding recollection in abeyance? Ironically enough Heidegger's before/after transference problem, notwithstanding its status as a dichotomy, seems to be as pressing as it is in classical marxism: to be over-determined by the social world *and* be destined to overcome it! So how is it conceivable that human beings can live both inside and outside of history like Being? He says: 'Only as a questioning, historical being does man come to himself; only as such is he a self. Man's selfhood means this: he must transform the being that discloses itself to him into history and bring himself to stand in it. Selfhood does not mean that he is primarily an 'ego' and an individual. This he is no more than he is a we, a community' (pp. 143–144). He says that his usage of 'transcendental horizon' in *Being and Time* is not that of subjective consciousness but 'rather, it defines itself in terms of the existential-ecstatic temporality of human being-there' (p. 18). This amounts to an awareness of Being when the essential historical relation of Being in general and of human being are bonded.

Heidegger does not want to dispense with thinking altogether but to realise a stricter more radical thinking as part and parcel of Being that overcomes the dualistic legacy of subject and object realising a reciprocal bonding for the unfolding of Being. Habermas asserts that '[t]he path-breaking achievement of *Being and Time* consists in Heidegger's decisive argumentative step towards overcoming the philosophy of consciousness' (Habermas, in Dreyfus and Hall, 1992, p. 190). Yet, elsewhere, Habermas considers that Heidegger never really broke free from the philosophy of consciousness (Habermas, 1990, p. 138); nor despite apparent evidence to the contrary, did he study language systematically. Heidegger's philosophy of emancipation is not realised through rational communication as Habermas would like but nor, for that matter, *is* it a philosophy of emancipation.[1] Although Herder (see Taylor, 1992b) claims that language makes possible 'reflective' consciousness, Heidegger, conversely, who has is own very original position within this tradition, comes to see language as opening up access to meaning. Language is not merely an instrument of thought and communication, it is the 'house of Being' and the crucial condition of *Being*. Language is seen as the condition of the disclosure of the human world, a disclosure which is not 'intra-psychic, but occurs in the space between humans; indeed, it helps to define the space that humans share' (Taylor, 1992b, p. 256). However, Heidegger's later work appears to despair of language ever accessing Being and, ultimately, there is finally an ambivalence in his attitude to language not unlike that of Nietzsche.

POINT, COUNTERPOINT - SARTRE AND MERLEAU-PONTY

Whilst being within the ambit of Heidegger, both Sartre and Merleau-Ponty develop their own angle on consciousness. In the work of Sartre, the 'I', self and personal identity are not of the same order as consciousness. In contradistinction to Husserl, self and consciousness have quite different properties for Sartre. Consciousness exists confrontationally with the world whilst the self, in Sartre's view, is to be found in the world just like the self of another. In search of the self, consciousness reaches ahead of itself in the lived world of actions and relations with others discerning meaning in a world against which it is interminably set. The fact that the subject–object legacy is of immediate relevance to Sartre becomes apparent in his version of Hegel's master–slave, self–Other dialectic which unfolds with tenacious ingenuity. When confronted with the Other, the objective world I thought exclusively mine has to be acknowledged as also existing from their point of view – they become the object which perceives what I perceive. The uncomfortable prospect is that I find myself amongst the objects they perceive. This stage facilitates a crucial turning point. I, that cannot be an object to myself, am rendered an object for the Other who, in that possibility, then reveals themself as a subject. I, in turn, become self-conscious by being looked at and aware of the de-limitation of my freedom whilst held in the Other's gaze. Consciousness of my feelings at this state begins to induce myself as a subject which facilitates the re-objectification of the Other – thus regaining my subjectivity. In effect, in such a play, the meeting of minds in an I-subject in liaison with an Other-subject remains perpetually in abeyance.[2] But Craib describes the inherent contradiction highlighted in Sartre's dialectic of the self and Other in the following way as 'the more I try to establish myself as an object in the eyes of the other, the more I am thrown back on my own subjectivity; the more I try to transform the other into an object, the more he reveals his subjectivity' (Craib, 1976, p. 26).

In the analysis of Sartre's early work when we recall a memory we do not call it forth but betake ourselves to where it is awaiting us and this is what distinguishes memory from imagination. To imagine, in contrast, consciousness must be able to form and posit objects as unreal – the hypothesis of nothingness in relation to reality or the whole. Consciousness must be able to deny the reality but only by retreating from reality grasped as a whole. For consciousness to imagine 'it must be able to posit the world in its synthetic totality, and it must be able to posit the imagined object as being out of reach of this synthetic totality, that is, posit the world as a nothingness in relation to the image'(Sartre, 1972, p. 213). From being 'in-the-midst-of-the-world', as Sartre terms it, where it is 'engulfed' in the real and 'enmired' in the world, consciousness, by its very nature, must be able to escape or withdraw from the world in order to imagine. But in order to embark on this sequence the imagining consciousness has to be 'situated in the world' or 'be in-the-world' which forms the motivation for the creation of any unreal object and though 'consciousness can appear momentarily delivered from "being-in-the-world", it is just this "being in the world" which is the necessary condition for the imagination' (p. 215). Imagination must be free from all specific reality and we have here freedom defined by a 'being-in-the-world' at one constituting and negating the world which is surpassed in a concretely motivated movement towards the imaginary. Sartre concludes that 'imagination is not a contingent and super-added power of consciousness, it is the whole of consciousness as it realises its freedom; every concrete and real situation of consciousness in the world is pregnant with imagination in as much as it always presents itself as a withdrawing from the real. . . . The unreal is produced outside the world by a consciousness which *stays in the world* and it is because he is transcendentally free that man can imagine' (p. 216). Imagination is a form of intentional consciousness whose contents are not to be considered as if they were inner objects.

In Sartre's account consciousness is emptied of a shadowy inside of inner 'content'. There is no *centre* to consciousness as it is totally in the world in being relational to an object. There is no underlying self as he removes the substance from subjectivity and leaves immanence of the self to itself. We have not a self but a presence to self as definitive of human reality. This underscores the impossibility of someone being an object for themselves and suggests a limit to the possibility of reflective withdrawal (though Sartre does hold that we can detach ourselves from the roles we occupy). Consciousness is fundamentally impersonal and makes itself personal by the pure nihilating movement of reflection. Consciousness opens up the world to us and it is our means to access an independent reality, otherwise this would be nothingness. If this *is* the case, having consciousness entails being a subject and possessing a point of view. Yet, this point of view can never be of itself. Sartre's idea is that reflection forever turns the subject into an object, leaving consciousness unable to ever grasp itself. (Ground already covered by Hume, James, Mead *et al.* as we have seen.) It is not an object of any kind and is totally empty, i.e., consciousness cannot be an object for itself, though it can negate the present world by envisioning the future and by imagining other worlds. Consciousness's ambiguous status as nothing in itself and yet anything and everything imaginable, leads consciousness to aspire to be something that it is not: god, king or a better person. Yet, consciousness is faced by an obdurate world and our 'facticity' (a term taken by Sartre from Heidegger) – the immediate determinacy of who and what we are garnered through our past – tilts a human being's face to the facts. Whilst 'facticity' is the limit of possibility, 'transcendence', an idiosyncratic term in Sartre's hands, is the opening up of possibilities through linking imagination to action in the formation of intentions. *Bad faith*, for Sartre, is when one has recourse to one's 'facticity' to excuse not actively courting the future. As consciousness has no content whatsoever, motives, emotions, will and desire are objects *for* consciousness not *in* consciousness and we are able to take a position on them as we would on any external force. Though consciousness is the very motivating power of motives as it brings about that motives motivate (see Flynn, 1984, p. 5) it is our choice whether we are overwhelmed or overcome them. To follow Sartre's train of thought is to recognise that what we are (the self) is a function of what we do (i.e., action). This, in turn, is girded by our working out the extent of our freedom. Sartre's position prohibits him from envisioning the emergence of man's true essence out of their existence as a before–after projection. He stops short, then, of charting a shortfall between one's essential nature and one's actual condition in the fashion of Marx. There is no disparity to be overcome in Sartre. In an existential sense he might only sanction the realisation of one possible course of action rather than any other.

Contra Marx, Sartre rejects the dualism of appearance and essence, i.e., the 'thing-in-itself'; appearance reveals essence for Sartre rather than acting to conceal it. Human existence has no essence other than individuals being essentially free to choose what human being will be: we are always what we make of ourselves. In Sartre, the 'for itself' of consciousness amounts to freedom plus awareness of all else independent of consciousness (the 'in itself'); consciousness is nothing but an opening on to things. Freedom, thus conceived, is voluntaristic and self-deterministic, whereas in Heidegger by comparison, we have no such unfettered control over our own destinies. Sartre's self is free and undetermined whilst consciousness *is* freedom to choose and not a great deal else. Consciousness is the freedom of *nothingness* in the midst of *Being*; it is undetermined and projects range before it as choice. Consciousness, being empty, amounts to an awareness of a relationship to *Being*; the connection itself being open to variation. In this view, consciousness 'is capable of imagining a situation which *is not yet* the case and which, because a question is asked about it, might not become the case' (Craib, 1976, p. 17). For Sartre, it is *nothingness* that divides consciousness from the world; it is a hole in *Being* that is no more than a relation to *Being*. Consciousness is a flight into the future. For Sartre 'pre–reflective' consciousness is a simple consciousness of something whereas 'reflective' consciousness is consciousness of being conscious of something. The 'choices' in question are set out for consciousness by the world around it and at a 'pre–reflective' rather than a 'reflective' (i.e., rational, self–aware) stage. Craib says that what he has been describing in Sartre's thought is a 'progressive–regressive movement: from situation to project and from project to situation – a *movement* as opposed to the *state* of shared rationality, shared meanings implied in Weber and Schütz. The movement of understanding is grounded in the structure of consciousness itself as a project from a specific point of view on the world, and this basic structure of project–situation is common to each consciousness. This is what Sartre calls 'human reality', the nearest we can come to a 'human nature', and it means that all human action is, in principle, understandable' (p. 36).

An appeal to empathy was regarded suspiciously by Sartre who viewed the essence of the relation between consciousnesses as conflict. In Hobbesian fashion there is opposition among individuals and conflict involved in Sartre's being-for-others. From the early work onwards, Sartre suggested that collective consciousness is an impossibility. The common transcendence of the community and individuality in its plurality are mutually exclusive and collective action remains a futile ideal. Class consciousness appears to be a particularly strong version of the 'Us' relation in response to a plainly structured collective situation with the contingent possibility of 'Us' turning into 'We' (which remains, however, a purely subjective experience (*Erlebnis*)). Certainly in Sartre of this period there is a stress on a public realm of inter-subjectivity and the inter-personal and a claim that the choice of self (i.e., subjectivity) implies inter-subjectivity. As Sartre moves towards Marx (Sartre, 1976) he introduces facticity and the given in accounting for the existential situation against which freedom must define itself. The utilisation at this point of the 'practico-inert', which subvert the purposes for which they were intended as institutional and cultural forms, connects Sartre immediately with alienation and reification. He contemplates the brute giveness of the 'in itself' as countervalent or indifferent to our projects. It is at this point that Sartre introduces a range of concepts to recognise the power of directly encountered circumstance, i.e., the practico-theoretical legacy of Marx. Inner and outer life come to be determined by *objective possibility* (an expression to be found in Weber) and the objective social situation features in high profile in Sartre's later work. Material conditions of existence circumscribe a highly structured field of possibilities, depending, in turn, on social and historical reality. Such fields of possibilities are systematically limited as objective contradictions of material conditions are interiorised. *Disalienation*, as a heightened sense of collective identity, is faced by this prospect as it is by exploitation and mystification and against this backdrop synthetic situational thinking must emerge as characteristic of revolutionary thought. Yet, only individual praxis is seen to be constitutive of social reality and collective consciousness is not a hyperorganism (in the fashion of Durkheim). It is Sartre's 'dialectical nominalism' which saves him from the 'organicism' of Hegelianism, though sympathetic commentators such as Schütz (1982) and Flynn (1984) remark on a flawed attempt to galvanise a dialectical union of subjectivity and collectivity.

The undoubted counterpoint to this kind of legacy from Sartre is the work of Merleau-Ponty, who as well as drawing on obvious points of reference – Descartes, Husserl, Sartre and Heidegger – also draws most noticeably upon Hegel and Marx. From the former he takes the idea of Being instantiated in the act itself and from the latter the implication of man's objective nature lying sensuously outside himself. Merleau-Ponty (1962) remained critical of Sartre's emphasis on consciousness. He points out that whilst idealist reflection reduces the proletarian condition to an awareness at which the proletarian arrives, *objective thought*, as he describes it, derives class consciousness from the objective condition of the proletariat – both of which remain in the realm of abstraction and leave us torn between the *in itself* and *for itself*. For him, evaluation of the present operates through one's free projects for the future – the free act but lived through in ambiguity. This is the pursuit of a goal both determinate and indeterminate accompanied by the exchange of individual and generalised existence. Choice is based on a certain givenness of the extant projects into which we are thrown. We are our acts – chosen and willed – and in them our significance streams effulgent. My identity thus comes to me on the day I take my stand and my decision lends the motive its force; if I elect to view history in terms of the class struggle it is the decision to will revolution that makes a proletarian of me. According to Merleau-Ponty collective consciousness is characterised first by experience then by long periods of gestation and latency with emergent properties that burst into explosive activity in reactive social and historical circumstance. Merleau-Ponty, unlike Sartre who he accuses of remaining wedded to the dualism of subject and object, sees consciousness as fully embodied with its originative feature being 'I am able to' rather than the Cartesian 'I think'. He seems to grasp, in a way that eludes Sartre, Heidegger's drift: an active, emotional, embodied being in the world with tasks to be done with their attendant means. The opposition of subject and object, self and the world, cannot be overcome by consciousness and (self) knowledge because it is not ordered in that way: life's 'problems' are proximate and pass away with no possible removed participation.

Merleau-Ponty recognises that the opportunity presents itself to leave behind the traditional subject–object dichotomy once and for all by embarking on the attempt to describe the phenomenon of speech and the specific act of meaning. He says: 'We must recognise first of all that thought, in the speaking subject, is not a representation, that is, that it does not expressly posit objects or relations. The orator does not think before speaking, nor even while speaking; his speech is his thought' (Merleau-Ponty, 1962, p. 180). In this view, speech *accomplishes* rather than translates ready–made thought. The one is not a sign of the other as the two, rather, are what he calls 'intervolved'. Speech is the presence of thought in the phenomenal world: 'Thought is no "internal" thing, and does not exist independently of the world and of words. What misleads us in this connection, and causes us to believe in a thought which exists for itself prior to expression, is thought already constituted and expressed, which we can silently recall to ourselves, and through which we acquire the illusion of an inner life. But in reality this supposed silence is alive with words, this inner life is an inner language' (p. 183). Language's content is not self-subsistent and self-conscious thought but *is*, actually, the subject's taking up of a position in the world of their meanings. The linguistic, inter-subjective world is, thus, indistinguishable from the world itself. Merleau-Ponty affirms that language is a worldly institution. He says 'as, in a foreign country, I begin to understand the meanings of words through their place in the context of action, and by taking part in a communal life' (p. 179). Indistinguishable in many respects from Wittgenstein, Merleau-Ponty's account of language stresses that speech is no mere clothing or would-be fashion for ready-made thought, but, in fact, makes thought its own. The self is an outcome of expression. Ideas are necessarily linked to acts of expression to which they owe their appearance of autonomy. He says that '[i]n fact analysis demonstrates, not that there is behind language a transcendent thought, but that language transcends itself in speech, that speech itself *brings about* that concordance between me and myself, and between myself and others, on which an attempt is being made to base that thought' (p. 392). Although it is not the purpose of this discussion to connect up direct points of influence and cross-fertilisation, ideas such as these from Merleau-Ponty dating from the early 1940s are contemporaneous with the similar sounding theses of C. Wright Mills, of Wittgenstein just a few years before and of Ryle a few years later.

Whilst in the process of doubting Descartes, Merleau-Ponty distinguishes his own position from other more recent contributions: ' "My life", my "total being" are not dubious constructs, like the "deep-seated self" of Bergson, but phenomena which are indubitably revealed to reflection. It is simply a question of what we *are doing*'

(p. 380). This embodies a consummate rejection of the subject–object legacy of western philosophy and he goes on to state that: 'Inside and outside are inseparable. The world is wholly inside and I am wholly outside myself' (p. 407). I belong to myself only whilst belonging to the world. Self consciousness is an *act* – the very being of mind in action. In this regard he talks about the *acts* of the *I* outstripping themselves and leaving no interiority of consciousness. He ultimately directs our gaze away from private states of consciousness – from inner perception – as we make our reality and find ourselves only in the *act*. We know ourselves through our doing, through our relation to things; inner perceptions come afterwards. We are a project directed at the world with objectivity conceived as inherence in that world. Significantly, Merleau-Ponty refers to us having no option but to 'have it out' with the world. We live in an *interworld* along with others of concrete human inter-subjectivity. The embodied subject is engaged with the world and in incessant dialogue with it: 'What remains, on the hither side of my particular thoughts, to constitute the tacit *cogito* and the original project towards the world, and what, ultimately, am I in so far as I can catch a glimpse of myself independently of any particular act? I am a field, an experience' (p. 406). His version of Husserl is one that holds on to the idea of returning to all the living relationships of experience in a world that precedes knowledge, i.e., the practical before reflection upon it with emphasis on perception preceding knowledge as an *intentional* way of being in the world. He says that truth does not just 'inhabit' the 'inner man' as, there 'is no inner man, man is in the world, and only in the world does he know himself. When I return to myself from an excursion into the realm of dogmatic common sense or of science, I find not a source of intrinsic truth, but a subject destined to the world' (p. xi).

Merleau-Ponty concludes that man amounts to a network of relationships which, alone, matter to him. For him man *is* but a network of relationships – to be lived not thought. Man's abode is the act itself and that act is what man is and his significance. Around his absolute individuality, Merleau-Ponty concludes he must apprehend a kind of halo of generality or atmosphere of sociability: 'I must apprehend myself from the onset as centred in a way outside myself, and my individual existence must diffuse round itself, so to speak, an existence in quality . . . [m]y life must have a significance which I do not constitute; there must strictly speaking be an intersubjectivity; each one of us must be both anonymous in the sense of absolutely individual, and anonymous in the sense of absolutely general. Our being in the world, is the concrete bearer of this double anonymity' (p. 448). Yet, he still refers to a 'subject' destined to that world and the point he makes to great effect against Heidegger, is that once the Genie of subjectivity is out of the bottle – to mix metaphors with Wittgenstein – no amount of coaxing, cajolery or wishful thinking can reconfine it. Nor can we return to a pristine time, somehow, before our encounter with subjectivity. Perhaps we no longer wish to believe in such an apparition but that does not alter the fact that we are in denial. Nevertheless we are not just left with a dry husk stripped of all but the idea of subjectivity, as the body itself holds a germ of truth.

THE POLITIC BODY

The phenomenological reduction of Husserl is predicated on the method of Cartesian doubt and, again like Descartes, there is no 'body' to be found. Ironically it is Husserl's disciple Merleau-Ponty who has been taken as being the tincture of the 'body' position despite his excellent summative definitions of consciousness. Crossley, for example, makes the point that the corollary of Merleau-Ponty's thought, as it is of Wittgenstein's for that matter, is to challenge the notion of a substantial difference between body and mind: 'In opposition to such separation Merleau-Ponty focuses upon *behaviour* which is simultaneously meaningful, embodied and intelligent. In behaviour, Merleau-Ponty argues, the mindedness and embodiment of human life are inseparable. The implication, moreover, is that the subjective or mental states of others are available to us, directly, and that ours are available to them, directly, in the form of our behaviours; subjectivity is not private and inaccessible, it is worldly and publicly available. Further to this, the suggestion is that, in focusing upon behaviour, we arrive at an understanding of ourselves and of others by the same route; we do not enjoy a privileged access to our own minds' (Crossley, 1995, p. 143). Crossley maintains that mental predicates for Merleau-Ponty (like Ryle and Wittgenstein) are to be understood not as standing for (incorporeal) inner mental states but, instead, as referring to embodied behaviour or conduct that is publicly verifiable. The division between subject and object is thus unsustainable at the level of ontology.

Crossley allies Merleau-Ponty with Goffman who came to argue that the very orderliness of the interaction order 'is dependent upon the mutual, public availability of participants' subjective "states"' (p. 142). What they share additionally, for Crossley, is an emphasis on a shared 'intermundane space' in which we all participate though which belongs – unlike the penchant of subject–object – to none of us. Thus perception is not the realm of the inner and private but is shared visual space whilst the social world is shared practical–perceptual space centered on the ongoing relations of sentient–sensible bodies. Goffman begins by questioning the utility of the 'self-as-character' housed in the body to which a self is imputed in recognition of a performance. In fact, such an imputed self is a *product* of a successful staging not a *cause* of it where the self as a performed character 'is not an organic thing that has a specific location, whose fundamental fate is to be born, to mature, and to die; it is a dramatic effect arising diffusely from a scene that is presented, and the characteristic issue, the crucial concern, is whether it will be credited or discredited. In analysing the self, then, we are drawn from its possessor, from the person who will profit or lose most by it, for he and his body merely provide the peg on which something of collaborative manufacture will be hung for a time. And the means for producing and maintaining selves do not reside inside the peg; in fact these means are often bolted down in social establishments' (Goffman, 1971, pp. 244–245). Goffman's view would be that there can be no sacred space for the real, authentic self, no 'alone zone' where we can truly be ourselves. Even here, such that it is a 'here', Goffman identifies a variable formula for stage-managing oneself in such situations not a substantive entity in the process of 'unconcealing' itself. The idea of 'role-distance', too, dismissed the prospect of knowing, self-conscious, often ironic, declarations of something more behind the role. The 'person' *in* the performance – albeit only glimpsed – is party to the way the role is brought off and, as such, part of the role itself. 'Role-distance' is a means of commenting on the role whilst playing it, not an extra-social, deeper dimension.

As has been seen at various points in this discussion a concern with the 'body' goes back further and ranges wider than theorists working on this issue sometimes care to acknowledge. In the irrationalist tradition, Schopenhauer, for example, saw the body as the will's phenomenon; the will being objectified in the body. Affirmation of the will is affirmation of the body in Schopenhauer's view. Nietzsche saw that the body harbours much of the wisdom exploited by us in the decision making of everyday life: 'Behind your thoughts and feelings, my brother, stands a mighty commander, an unknown sage – he is called Self. He lives in your body, he is your body. There is more reason in your body than in your best wisdom' (Nietzsche, 1969, p. 62). Bourdieu, influenced by Nietzsche remarks that the centrality of the intellect for intellectuals in combination with the 'prejudice inherent in the science which takes as its object the psyche, the soul, the mind, consciousness, representations, not to mention the petit-bourgeois pretension to the status of "person", have prevented us from seeing that, as Leibniz put it, "we are automatons in three-quarters of what we do", and that the ultimate values, as they are called, are never anything other than the primary, primitive disposi-tions of the body, "visceral" tastes and distastes, in which the group's most vital interests are embedded, the things on which one is pre-pared to stake one's own and other people's bodies' (Bourdieu, 1986, p. 474). A position adopted, to a large extent, by Foucault for whom human subjects are more suggestive of body than of consciousness: 'It is the element in which are articulated the effects of a certain type of power and the reference of a certain type of knowledge, the machinery by which the power relations give rise to a possible corpus of knowledge, and knowledge extends and reinforces the effects of this power. On this reality-reference, various concepts have been con-structed and domains of analysis carved out: psyche, subjectivity, personality and consciousness; on it have been built scientific tech-niques and discourses, and the moral claims of humanism . . . The soul is the effect and instrument of a political anatomy; the soul is the prison of the body' (Foucault, 1987, p. 30). Rather than conscious-ness the human subject is 'body' whose existence is limited by discourse.

FOUCAULT AND POST-STRUCTURALISM

With the emergence of the human sciences from the nineteenth cen-tury an abstract, idealised concept of Man is centred as subject as concrete individuals increasingly come to be decentred. The will to knowledge (or truth) which accompanied this, already tried and tested in the natural sciences, prescribed what would count as truth and verifiable and useful knowledge, the vantage point from which the world could be seen and ultimately what was 'thinkable'. Aware of the positivistic pursuit of truth pertaining to objects lying beyond discursive accounts of them and a transcendental teleological system like that of Marx and Comte, Foucault suspends the recentring of the knowing, human subject and confronts, instead, discursive structures. From Foucault we have inherited the idea that, such as it exists, the subject is the focus of multiple, decentred discourses and in his analysis there is no constant human subject throughout the life-course or history for that matter. Foucault has been associated with debunking the project of self-revelation and self discovery of an internal entity – a deeper and truer self (quite rightly he associates such a construct with Christianity). There is no inner self, then; the self is constantly invented and reinvented: 'Where the soul pretends unification or the self fabricates a coherent identity, the genealogist sets out to study the beginning. . . . The analysis of descent permits the dissociation of self, its recognition and displacement as an empty synthesis, in liberating a profusion of lost events' (Foucault, quoted in Habermas, 1990, p. 250). It is not a question of uncovering underlying truths or logic in his view, but, rather, one of a recognition of the emergence of historically contingent competing interpretations – each and every one of which will be attempting to seize the right to dominate. Foucault's is not the historiography of a linear, evolutionist unfolding of inevitable or necessary causes but a hunt back along the genealogy of difference until we finally lose our hold on our cherished point of view. In addition, he avoids globalising, totalising and systemic analysis, preferring, instead, the singular rather than the spectacular with shadow replacing highlights and distant detail overtaking foreground. Here, will surface the intimate, the fragile and the forsaken. The emphasis is 'localised' in every sense of the word, alongside contingency and complexity, mischance and misrule. With this type of analysis any concern with consciousness very quickly, too, decomposes.

In his earlier work the individual subject was created at the intersection of discourses and was otherwise empty; later, his view shifts to one where individual subjects are constituted by relations of power in every fibre of their being. Thus, the 'transcendental subject' from Kant to Sartre invested with the authority of knowing, reflecting and willing, is decentred or disappears altogether. If we are talking about the psychic formation of the individual at all here, discourse and/or power are omnipotent and omnipresent with Foucault providing for us the point of entry to this peculiarly modern subjectivity. Internalisation has replaced external forms of violence. Foucault's concern with the prison and the asylum symbolises the constitution of consciousness in the modern world; the chains are mental as much as material. Each person becomes their own warder with the interiorisation of a system of surveillance; bars and keys are transposed into recognisable melodies of manipulation. Both Nietzsche and Foucault embrace the idea of the internalisation of morality, where control of behaviour becomes restraint from within, stemming initially from overt coercion or the threat of it. Self-policing, isolated subjects become responsible for their own subjection which is a far cry from the autonomously responsible human subject of the rationalist philosophical tradition. In the famous debate on Dutch television between Foucault and Chomsky, Foucault expressed his suspicion of universalism both as a claim to universal truth and as represented in universal conceptions of justice or human nature. He did not believe, it became obvious, that there was any universal understanding to be had beyond the social and historical and he refused to use universal notions advocating, instead, giving up first principles for the focus on the operation of power and knowledge in society. Chomsky, in contrast, wanted to hold on to universals like justice and human nature arguing that scientific understanding would be impossible without a fairly fixed human nature. Foucault suggests there is nothing sufficiently stable in man (sic) – including the body – to serve as the basis of either self-recognition or understanding of others. However, does Foucault's critique of the philosophy of consciousness and the attack on the 'great myth' of interiority mean there is to be no identity carried over from one subject position to another and no transcendental continuity as the subject is produced through, within and as the effect of discourse and set discursive formations?

Both Merquior and, more recently, Hall detect that Foucault's later work accommodates subjectivity and seeks to account for the practices of self-constitution of the subject. This amounts to the recognition that although the subject has been 'decentred' it has not been, thereby, altogether destroyed particularly when, as Hall says, the 'centring' of discursive practice is unable to work without a constituted subject. Though not the adoption of 'agency' the practices of self-constitution in this view include recognition and reflection in the production of self as an object in the world. Hall recognises this as a significant advance 'since it addresses for the first time in Foucault's major work the existence of some interior landscape of the subject, some interior mechanisms of assent to the rule, as well as its object-ively disciplining force' (Hall, in Hall and du Gay, 1996, p. 13) which saves the account from a 'behaviourism' and objectivism which threatens certain parts of Foucault's earlier work. Whilst stopping short of deploying the term 'identity' the later work does allow for the apparatuses and capacities of subjectivity and does account for individuals' recognition of their self-constitution as a 'performative' subject. It has been contended that the self in Foucault's early work was seen as a tool of, or a prey to, power and his preoccupation is with the replacement of group identity typical of traditional society with identity as a private 'property'. But the story of the Self's pro-duction by power comes to be 'told from the inside' with ' "technolo-gies of the self" envisaged in their own inner space' (Merquior, 1985, p. 119). Foucault's long-standing subject-phobia through which he encouraged us to despise subjectivity as a metaphysical mirage, is, according to Merquior, replaced by a view of subjectivity not as a dependent variable (formed as an historical product of power) but as an independent variable of a genuine force that, itself, shapes con-duct. In fact 'could it be that, in Foucault's work in the 1980s, the subject – and, together with it, plain human agency – was eventually, if tacitly, vindicated, or re-entered the scene by stealth?' (p. 138).

Foucault's supersession of the problematic of consciousness has been linked with the project of post-structuralism more generally. Lacan's contention in his early work is that the ego is a product of a series of imaginary identifications with the Other (initially a mirror image of itself with which the young child identifies). The subject, constructed in childhood, proceeds as discourse and comes to life in ongoing social interaction and the forms of the person we would recognise as self are called forth in social situations. The ego, then, is not a unity by its very nature. Persistent attempts to encourage the subject to render the self a coherent whole is seen by Lacan as inher-ently elusive and self-defeating. The conscious speaking subject is ensnared in untruth, unable to piece together the accumulated frag-ments of biography. The paradox is that language does not act neu-trally, helping us back to ourselves, but, is, instead, the impersonal medium of the very constitution of our subjectivity. Language is the limit of our world not a transparent medium for accessing deeper 'truth' about ourselves. Nor is there a world there to be retrieved that is somehow of a quite different order (of reason). But whilst Lacan is intent on decentring the rational, conscious subject (the ego), tending to produce a universal subject not situated historically, the real, anyway, for him, lies beyond language and beyond our ken. What we assume to be 'the real', or perceive as such, ultimately defies the reach of the symbol. Nor can it be experienced directly but is mediated by the imaginary and symbolic orders. In such a situation the subject is engaged in an ongoing quest for a 'lost' object, that it has never actually possessed and which the Other is at a loss to provide. Such is the impetus of unfulfilled desire (see Sarup, 1993).

For Husserl, for example, the datum of *self-presence* was the inner voice of the conversation we have with ourselves in consciousness – the soliloquy of an interior mental life. The self, for poststructuralists ranging from Lacan to Deleuze and Guattari (1977) is not its own 'centre' being rather a decentred subject lacking coherence, autonomy or normalcy though positively fragmented and in a state of perpetual flux. There is no such entity, then, as a *whole* person who can reach out to others in human relationships. Deleuze and Guattari provide a variant of post-structuralism which draws on Lacan's concept of the 'imaginary' stage prior to the acquisition of language with the subsequent transition into the symbolic world of language, structure and society registering as an ineluctable and tragic loss. What is envisaged is a return to the 'imaginary' in retreat from the symbolic; to recapture freedom from repression in direct, unmediated and spontaneous desire. They posit two poles of *delire*: that based on the authoritarian structure of the hierarchical state which they associate with reaction and paranoia and centered on flight, the real *delire* of schizophrenia. For them it is the mad who remain in touch with the power of presymbolic desire. Desire in the passionate 'animal' emerges as a productive force of libido – all pervasive, mysterious and unsettling. Its possibilities and potentialities are lauded by Deleuze and Guattari. According to them human beings are 'desiring machines' with *delire* being the outward, linguistic manifestation and effectual product of the machinery of desire. In their terms there are just sparking connections made between 'desiring machines' out of which reality flows molten. There is no true dichotomy between the collective and the individual or the social and the personal as the same form of energy, libido, permeates the psychological and political fields which interpenetrate producing both individual (*delire*) and political (class struggle) effects. They aver that collective action is produced out of the revolutionary desire flowing through individuals and small groups. Its genesis is within individuals and outside of them and in that sense it is wrong to conceive of collective action as an abstraction elevated above individual members. Even should it appear to be produced by an individual they emphasise the social and collective nature of *delire* – though the trend in recent times has been for it to be privatised. In the belief that we somehow construct our own versions of reality – largely through the medium of language – anti-realist approaches deny knowledge as a direct precipitate of reality. There is a rejection of the complexity of both external and internal reality to be replaced by a world *sans* things but replete with words. In variants of post-structuralism the deconstruction of the world flows from the deconstruction of text.

POST-MARXISM

The Frankfurt School – reification and rationality

It is difficult to pin down the origins of post-marxism with any degree of accuracy but perhaps it begins with the Frankfurt School who somewhat anticipated the substantive priorities and systemising reticence of poststructuralism (see Craib, 1992, pp. 208–227). There is certainly a similarity of style and, in part, of substance. The Frankfurt School emphasised the domination of various overarching forces which take over – and analytically takes over from – the individual. They refused to 'connect up' the 'big' picture and engage with class and the mode of production with a critique of its cultural forms sufficing. To engage in structural analysis seems to be seen as giving in to instrumental reason and there is limited development of a theory of action in their work. This, itself, is characteristic of their critique of Enlightenment thought and method which led them latterly to be critical of Marx's emphasis on science and his own use of instrumental reasoning in his critique of capitalism. For the Frankfurt School – in the Hegelian tradition – consciousness is constitutive of the world and they were particularly drawn to the distinction embodied in the idealistic division of *Verstand* (understanding) and *Vernunft* (reason). By the former, Kant and Hegel had meant a lower faculty of mind which structured the phenomenal world according to common sense. It thus failed to penetrate immediacy to grasp the dialectical relation beneath the surface. *Vernunft* on the other hand, signified a faculty which went beyond mere appearances, to the deeper reality. Hence, there was a rejection by the Frankfurt School of the identification of reason and logic with the limited power of *Verstand*. In science and technology, positivism, not surprisingly, had always denied the validity of the traditional idea of reason as *Vernunft*, which it dismissed as empty metaphysics. Adorno and Horkheimer (1972) distinguished between 'subjective' and 'objective' rationality where the former is the instrumental means–ends reason increasingly characteristic of western culture, whilst the latter is concerned with ends and, as an outlook, has become increasingly eclipsed. Whilst subjective reason concentrates upon faculties of mind in the selecting of appropriate means to ends, objective rationality seeks to discover the irrationality of these ends and what constitutes reason itself. Indeed, the fundamental assumption of the Frankfurt School was that irrationality had corrupted rationality. Adorno emphasised immediate authentic, contextual experience (*Erfahrung*) over the fragmentation of 'imagined' experience in late capitalism (*Erlebnis*). This dichotomy is to be found in the thought of Walter Benjamin (1973) who adduced a division of the integration of events into the memory of collective and personal traditions in a meaningful communal or individual context (*Erfahrung*) as opposed to that which has increasingly come to supplant it – isolated, disconnected, incoherent, meaningless, impoverished narratives that typify everyday discourse and representation of events in late capitalism (*Erlebnis*).[3]

The Frankfurt School argued that contained implicitly in the Cartesian legacy was the reduction of reason to its subjective dimension – the first step in driving rationality away from the world into contemplative inwardness. It led to an eternal separation of essence and appearance, which fostered the non-critical acceptance of the status quo. In the tradition of Lukács and the Frankfurt School there is the theory, criticism and practice of rationality as opposed to illusion, manipulation and passivity of irrationality. From this perspective it is not so much a before/after, or coexistence, model of consciousness, as irrationality having swallowed rationality whole in late western capitalism.[4] The Frankfurt School adopted the emphasis of a dominant culture engendering false consciousness, with dominant culture being linked to commodity fetishism as the means by which the subordination of the working class is enacted, with Marcuse (1964) identifying false consciousness as abounding in a situation where reified relationships permeated through to all levels. He stressed the effect of language on consciousness, and the manipulative role of the mass media, believing that, words such as 'freedom' and 'fulfilment' had become meaningless through debasement in propaganda. Marcuse seemed to be saying that if supplied with the right tools to interpret reality (i.e., concepts), there would be a need expressed for de-alienation. In consequence, although this analysis begins with monolithic reification in society, it ends by stressing the role of language and mind. From this perspective a precondition of overcoming reification is to fully *understand* that it is in evidence. Adorno (in Arato and Gebhard, 1978), too, emphasised the importance of subjectivity, both individual and collective, stressing collective subjectivity's role in potential emancipation and the transcending of the status quo, but for him cognition was dependent upon the collective – ultimately to be superseded by truly transcendent subjectivity. Adorno was as wary of social nominalism as he was of the social realism which gainsaid a role for individuals and he was not impressed by the empathic understanding of *Verstehen* as a method or by pursuing the subjective meaning of the actor. For him social practices were not to be grasped from within as a product of deliberate intentionality. He saw the subject as the object's agent rather than its constituent and recognised the fallacy of 'constitutive subjectivity' which had to be broken through by the strength of the subject. Unlike Benjamin, who had always appeared hostile to individual subjectivity, Adorno clung on to a concept of subjectivity as both individual *and* collective, being, as such, the precondition for overcoming extant relations. Experience, in its reciprocal relationship with knowledge, is a dynamic force and Adorno's retention of the Hegelian concept of Totality holds on to the prospect of an all embracing grasp of the nature of society and social structure, whilst the space for our standing back from our predicament is created in his positing of thought in constant oscillation between the concept (language) and (objective) experience. Nevertheless, structure and language remain largely unresolved in Adorno's artful interpretation; not so, it was to become obvious, as post-marxism proper emerged.

The legacy of structural Marxism – the undoing of subjectivity

The nadir of a Hegelian or humanist Marxism and the critique of consciousness is associated with the name of the French philosopher Althusser (1969, 1971) who sought to rank ideology along with the economic and political as of equal theoretical importance, as well as a condition of their existence. In this view, ideology is the variable through which individuals are related to their world which, in turn, has to be set in the context of the reproduction processes of capitalism including the legitimation of capitalism and the reproduction of agents, where existing social relations are reproduced as consciousness is shaped. From Althusser's viewpoint, ideology is not simply imposed from above, but is the medium through which everyone experiences the world. It is a framework of understanding through which men interpret and make sense of experience and live the material conditions in which they find themselves (including misrecognition). Although his analysis is internally inconsistent, ideology for Althusser equals practices rather than systems of ideas that act to reproduce the relations of capitalism. He indicates that ideology is a system of representations that has nothing to do with 'consciousness' and it is as images and concepts but above all structures that they impose on human beings, i.e., not via their consciousness. Hence, this is ideology producing the subject rather than the subject producing ideas through consciousness, i.e., ideology as the practice of creating subjects. Therefore, ideology comprises the images, representations and categories through which men 'live', in an imaginary way, their real relation to their condition of existence, and it forms the constitution or interpellation (the hailing) of subjects in all given society.

Ideology performs the function of concealing real contradictions whilst reconstituting on an imaginary level a coherent discourse serving as the horizon of individual experience. Solved in consciousness rather than practice, contradictions of consciousness are thus concealed and negated. Individuals are born into an ideological situation just as they are born into economic and political relations, i.e., they inherit given representations of the world and relations between men who are themselves constituted as subjects ideologically, which gives them and their reality an appearance of coherence. Individuals are constructed ideologically out of contradiction. They form the commodities of capitalism, yet, are, necessarily, beings with choice who appear to themselves as wholes. Ideology tends towards structural closure, defining the limits and fixing the individual within a certain mental horizon. This closure by casting the relationship by which individuals represent themselves in the world of objects, provides positions from which they act and represent themselves and others. Ideology equals common sense and the natural, hence, it is not perceived as a 'closure'; it fixes the individual as the subject of meaning and provides individuals with a consistent subjectivity, subject to social structure with its contradictory relations and powers. Ideology, then, leads to the homogeneous, non-contradictory, coherent, consistent, 'free' subjects in the face of the contradictions of capitalism who appear in control of their own destiny. Ultimately Althusser rejects the class–subject conception of ideology and instead substitutes the structure of society as subject with an all-pervasive and enduring ideology which acts to reproduce the relations of production and the class structure.

Developing the tradition of structural marxism, Balibar has contended more recently that human beings cannot maintain an invariant 'essence' whilst engaged in changing their conditions of existence. Therefore what should replace the question of human essence is 'to think humanity as a *transindividual* reality and, ultimately, to think transindividuality as such. Not what is ideally "in" each individual (as a form or a substance), or what would serve from outside, to classify that individual, but what exists *between individuals* by dint of their multiple interactions' (Balibar, 1995, pp. 30–32). In this view, then, the self is nothing if not in transformation and humanity is necessarily *transindividual*. Balibar sounds remarkably close to Wittgenstein when he asserts that *'the limits of communication between individuals* (what might be called their practical universe) *are also the limits of their intellectual universe'* (pp. 47–48). This, for him, is a question of situation or existential horizon before being a question of interests. Marx in Balibar's view produced a theory of the class character of consciousness with the division of society into classes reflecting and reproducing the limits of communication and intellectual horizons, rather than a theory of a system of ideas – consciously held or not – expressing the 'aims' of a particular 'class consciousness'. He makes the point that Marx never invoked the notion of 'false consciousness' or spoke of 'class consciousness' or, for that matter, 'proletarian ideology' and claims it is the division of labour in Marx's view which accounts for the 'gap' between consciousness and life and the 'contradiction' between general and particular interests with the division of society into classes becoming the structure or condition of thought itself. For Marx, according to Balibar, the world is constituted not by the work of a subject but subjectivity is itself generated as a part and counterpart of the social world of objectivity. Subjects are constituted rather than being constituent: they are, in Balibar's interpretation of Marx, 'economic subjects'. The constitution of the world does not arise out of the activity of any subject which could be conceived of in terms of consciousness. Such sentience is given only as part of objectivity alongside and in relation to the world of commodities. In fact, subjects, forms of subjectivity and consciousness are constituted in the very field of objectivity.

Marxism and the philosophism of language

The subsuming of consciousness to language has featured consistently in the development of Marxist thought. Volosinov, as long ago as the 1920s, had stated unequivocally that '[t]he only possible objective definition of consciousness is a sociological one' (Volosinov, 1973, p. 13) and that '[c]onsciousness becomes consciousness only once it has been filled with ideological (semiotic) content, consequently, only in the process of social interaction' (p. 11). What 'sociological' is taken to mean here is, undoubtedly, an organised group in the process of its social intercourse as the social, ideological medium that constitutes the vantage point for explanation of individual consciousness. Volosinov's main criticism of idealism and psychological positivism is their lack of concern with inter-individual territory organised *socially*. Significantly, he saw consciousness as having meaning given to it only in terms of the medium of ideological signs, i.e., semiotic communication. Drawing on the work of Saussure and the American Pragmatists (in particular C. S. Peirce) he equates ideology with signs but he is in no doubt that both exist as part of reality. He says '[a] sign does not simply exist as a part of

reality – it reflects and refracts another reality' and '[e]very ideological sign is not only a reflection, a shadow, of reality, but is also
itself a material segment of that very reality'(pp. 10–11). There can be
no understanding without semiotic material as we move from one
link to the next and 'nowhere is there a break in the chain, nowhere
does the chain plunge into inner being, nonmaterial in nature and
unembodied in signs. This ideological chain stretches from individual
consciousness to individual consciousness, connecting them together.
Signs emerge, after all, only in the process of interaction between one
individual consciousness and another' (p. 11). Ideology is not local-
ized *in* consciousness construed in conformity with laws of individual
consciousness; individual consciousness itself is a social – ideological
fact. Consciousness, then, is to be explained from the vantage point
of the social–ideological medium of communication, whence the
word remains the primary medium of individual consciousness.

More recently, and following Marcuse in the tradition of the
Frankfurt School, Habermas (1978) has drawn on Freud's interpretation of institutions as a power having replaced acute external force
with a fixed internal compulsion of self-limiting, distorted communication. The institutional framework of the established society
appears to the individual as an immovable horizon and any wishes
incompatible with the prevailing outlook are located beyond the
bounds of possibility. Yet, such impulsion, retaining the dimension
of fantasy, are transposed into substitute-gratifications. In fact,
Habermas draws a distinction in some detail between discourse and
communicative action. Discourses are practices that systematically
reproduce the objects to which they refer and the means by which the
subject is reproduced in the process of the sustaining of the social
order. Discourses, in his view, are purged of experience and action
and produce nothing but arguments, the force of which is a definitive
attribute. In contrast, communicative action belongs to experience
and action and the practice of life. In Habermas's view the objectivity
of experience consists in it being shared inter-subjectively and if
experience is to be deemed such it has to claim objectivity for itself.
He stresses the significance of the interpenetration of linguistic inter-
subjectivity and cognitive abilities and action motives where psychic
processes are transformed from inner states into intentional contents when they enter the structures of linguistic inter-subjectivity.
Inasmuch he wants to retain a reflexive foundation lost in the long

haul from Comte to Mach to the Vienna Circle and Wittgenstein. But this is not a reflexive foundation based on a transcendental subject and a transcendental consciousness, as the 'paradigm of language has led to a reframing of the transcendental model in a way which makes it unnecessary to add a transcendental subject to the system of conditions, categories or rules established by linguistic theory' (p. 377).

The nature of social reality is misread, according to Habermas, if there is an attempt to isolate the analysis of social action from linguistic meaning. In effect, for him the boundaries of action are inevitably drawn by the boundaries of language which, of itself, makes action possible. The understanding of social action is thus assimilated to the interpretation of linguistic meaning. The 're-enactment' model of phenomenology – and for that matter, Weber's *Verstehen* – is deemed surplus to requirements. The 'problem' of consciousness has been reinterpreted by Habermas as the capacity to engage in symbolic thought, to create meaning, to communicate, i.e., the use of language. Instead of a theory which 'represents the relation of ego to inner nature in terms of a philosophy of consciousness – on the model of relations between subject and object – we have a theory of socialization that connects Freud with Mead, gives structures of intersubjectivity their due, and replaces hypotheses about instinctual vicissitudes with assumptions about identity formation' (Habermas, 1987, p. 389). He states conclusively that the theory of consciousness and the subject–object metaphysical legacy of western philosophy has been discredited and superseded: 'There is no pure reason that might don linguistic clothing only in the second place. Reason is by its very nature incarnated in contexts of communicative action and in structures of the life world' (Habermas, 1990, p. 322). The mediating role that Marx and western Marxism had reserved for social practice is overridden by an interwoven life world and everyday communicative practice: 'The communicative practice of everyday life is, as it were, reflected in itself. This "reflection" is no longer a matter of the cognitive subject relating to itself in an objectivating manner. The stratification of discourse and action built into communicative action takes the place of this prelinguistic and isolated reflection' (p. 323).[5] The part of the self which is cut off from the growth of conscious agency becomes a 'delinguistified steering media', in Habermas's terms, remaining unconscious and unarticulated, whilst directing the actions of the personality.

Here, then, we have the legacy: language and transindividuality.[6] In fact, the transformation of the Marxist project was presaged by the Frankfurt School's attack on the legacy of the Enlightenment definition of reason and given enormous impetus by the disappearance of the individual in Althusserian structuralism – all that was required to complete the revisionist transformation was the substitution of discourse for dialectics. Eagleton is particularly critical of the post-structuralism and post-Marxism of Hindess and Hirst (1975; 1977) wherein all 'necessary' links between social conditions and political interests are severed and reality, before it is constituted in discourse, is that ineffable something *à la* Wittgenstein. In Laclau and Mouffe (1985) the distinction between non-discursive and discursive practices is collapsed with the former being subsumed to the latter and whilst not denying the existence of a 'real' world this, itself, it is confirmed, is constituted as a symbolic order. What human beings are, their needs and interest, flows not from biology or the relations of production but from the discursive practices which produce them and issue solely as struggles over meaning. Eagleton remarks that with the 'Humean' Laclau and Mouffe 'what Perry Anderson has called the "inflation of discourse" in poststructuralist thought reaches its apogee. Heretically deviating from their mentor Michel Foucault, Laclau and Mouffe deny all validity to the distinction between "discursive" and "non-discursive" practices, on the grounds that a practice is structured along the lines of discourse. The short reply to this is that a practice may well be organised like a discourse, but as a matter of fact it is a practice rather than a discourse' (Eagleton, 1991, p. 219). He remarks that in the neo-Neitschean language of post-Marxism little or nothing is "given" in reality: 'The category of discourse is inflated to the point where it imperialises the whole world, eliding the distinction between thought and material reality. The effect of this is to undercut the critique of ideology – for if ideas and material reality are given indissolubly together, there can be no question of asking where social ideas actually hail from. The new "transcendental" hero is discourse itself, which is apparently prior to everything else' (p. 219). Nevertheless, Eagleton attests: 'Talk of signs and discourses is inherently social and practical, whereas terms like 'consciousness' are residues of an idealist tradition of thought' (p. 194). Quoting Volosinov (1973), Eagleton states that the 'logic of consciousness' ' "is the logic of ideological communication, of the semiotic interaction of a social group. If we deprive consciousness of its semiotic, ideological content, it would have absolutely nothing left". The word is the "ideological phenomenon *par excellence*" and consciousness itself is just the internalisation of words, a kind of "inner speech". To put the point differently, consciousness is less something "within" us than something around and between us, a network of signifiers which constitute us through and through' (p. 194). Here, he himself renders consciousness as just the 'internalisation of words' and the external network of signifiers which constitute human beings. The spatial metaphor of thought somehow lying behind the utterance, has, for Eagleton, been perpetually obfuscatory, it being totally unhelpful to think of words concealing thought.

Though critical of consciousness other Marxists of the last generation have not been so persuaded by 'language'. Sève, for example, refers to 'a condemned philosophy of "freedom", "subjectivity" and "consciousness"' (Sève, 1978, p. 404) and rejects a central role for consciousness seeing, rather, *personality* and *biography* being of pivotal significance for a Marxist theory of man. Yet, language cannot be sustained as a singular solution – the essence of everything human – for it is not self-evident that language by itself, separate from labour as well as from the relations of production, can account for social life. Lefebvre, too, holds that neither consciousness nor language can stand alone in an attempt to overcome the subject–object legacy of western metaphysics. In fact, 'the unification of subject and object in such notions as "man" or "consciousness" succeeded only in adding another philosophical fiction to an already long list of such entities' (Lefebvre, 1991, p. 406). Nevertheless, language alone is no substitute, for whilst the world of images and signs exercises a fascination, it diverts attention from the 'real' (i.e., from the possible) with linguistics establishing 'a void, a dogmatically posited vacuum which, when not surrounded by silence, is buried in a mass of metalanguage, empty words and chit-chat about discourse . . . it is impossible to put such a high value upon language, on speech, on words. The Word has never saved the world and it never will' (p. 134). Words about words are actually consumed as metalanguage – itself a grand substitute for historical missions left undone. Likewise Bourdieu (1986) introduces the idea of the creation of a 'market' of discourses generated by the owners of the means of production of legitimate problems and opinions where power to produce a *judgement* is, in fact, production by proxy. There is, thus, a delimitation of the universe of the (politically) thinkable. Bourdieu sees an essential indeterminacy in the relationship between experience and expression with the prospect that language may not engage with reality – in fact, things named may be 'de-realized' or transmuted. Though the social order is inscripted in people's minds he refers mainly to this functioning below the level of discourse with the sense of social structure removed from any act of cognition. Such practice does not engage consciousness; this is the unconscious and unreflective rather than goal-directed, person-centred level of analysis.

Ironically, it may be back to Volosinov for the most heroic attempt to give language *and* consciousness their due. Consciousness, in Volosinov's estimation, is on the borderline, the cutting edge, between social reality and the individual subject, yet the problem of subjective consciousness does not disappear. It is not, then, a question of the non-existence of consciousness but one of its location and its latitude. He *is* concerned with the role of the semiotic material of inner life – of consciousness (inner speech). The word becomes an inner word and is an accompanying phenomenon, an obligatory presence, in each conscious act; the word is the primary medium of individual consciousness in this view comprising the semiotic material of inner life, i.e., consciousness is inner speech. He seeks to break down the dichotomy of the psyche as individual and ideology as social. They are, in fact, interpenetrative in a dialectical interplay of inner and outer signs. The direction is from the outside inward though involving participation of the individual psyche. He transforms dialectically a uni-directional subjective–objective relation by returning the ideological word to the psyche. In fact, Volosinov's definition of 'inner experience' includes it within the unity of objective, outer experience. 'Inner experience' is defined by the word and experience *per se* exists only in the material of signs. Despite the governance of the ideological informing spirit and the framing of the word, he sees the psyche as a special, systemic unity in possession of its own set of laws and in his view the ancients were not too wide of the mark in referring to inner speech as an *inner dialogue*. He leaves space for introspection which for him is aimed at elucidating the inner sign, but orientation in 'one's own soul' cannot be parted from the specific social situation of that experience. He writes 'any

deepening of introspection can come about only in unremitting conjunction with a deepened understanding of the social orientation'
(Volosinov, 1973, p. 37). The sign and the social situation are
inextricably fused, to the extent that in each speech act 'subjective
experience perishes in the objective fact of the enunciated word-
utterance, and the enunciated word is subjectified in the act of
responsive understanding' (pp. 40–41).

CONCLUSION

The unsubstantive self was not a discovery of poststructuralism,
deconstructionism or postmodernism but was partially unearthed by
the under-labouring spade work of Locke and ultimately recovered
and classified by Hume as we have seen. The unsubstantive self has
been 'known' to social thought for over two hundred and fifty years,
at very least notwithstanding Buddha, though this has largely gone
unacknowledged in recent work in this area. This 'fact', itself, has
made even less impression over that same period on people in everyday life who view themselves as singular, coherent and enduring –
unto death and beyond. The 'unsubstantive' self, is considered
incontrovertible in certain quarters yet that would appear not widely
known abroad. If references to interiority of various kinds accompany ordinary language and discourse, then advocates of the
exclusivity of this medium cannot gainsay such turns of phrase without undermining their own case. Not only is this a question of terms
of reference used in forms of life, but, in addition actual instances of
people evincing their belief in the existence of an enduring substantial
and substantive self. The second-guessing of the existence of selves or
souls (immortal or no), seems to be an accomplished aspect of human
being in the world. Ryle admits the ordinary person works with a
mind–body dualism, perceiving two separate processes of theorising
and doing, i.e., people believe there really is a 'ghost in the machine'.
As has been seen, this is not actually the case but it is fortunate for us
in Hume's view that we believe it to be. Both Wittgenstein and
Heidegger, in their different ways, dispense with a need for an enduring, underlying self. In as much for both of them, too, our *acting* in
the world is everything – there is no detached standing back.
Thoughts, images and memories, in the tradition of Wittgenstein, are
not to be considered as being seen or observed in some private

'screening' in an inner cinema or theatre but are being *constructed*, as it were, on the hoof. They are not being *re*-viewed but are being made. As Louch (1966, p. 156) remarks, an image is something *done not* watched. Yet, a sociological perspective was anathema to Heidegger who was anxious to distance his philosophy from any similar sounding projects elsewhere. Perhaps that is just as well because the social world conjured up by Heidegger is bogus and empty – redolent of, in that absence of anything genuinely social and historical, Wittgenstein's 'forms of life'. The illusion of social and historical specificity in Heidegger, despite its invocation of 'historical man', is pure legerdemain and it is not the purpose, here, to engage hermeneutically with the Heideggerian text which he would bequeath us as an alternative.

Wittgenstein and Heidegger have influenced inordinately the priorities of the last generation of theorists and a wide range of contributions can be brought together as exemplifying a view that the concern should not be with inner (incorporeal) mental states to which mental predicates appear to refer but, rather, with their real point of reference – embodied behaviour and its publicly verifiable aspects. Included here along with Wittgenstein would be Ryle, Goffman, Merleau-Ponty and Coulter according to Crossley. The least likely name to be included in this company is Sartre and there is perhaps no other philosopher whose stock has been at such a low ebb in the last generation. Guilty by association with consciousness, Sartre's view is, in fact, a minimalist interpretation with consciousness an opening onto the world framed by the reach of freedom; a world where appearances are revelatory of the reality. Perhaps some of the disrepute is because Sartre baulks at the prospect of a world of shared meanings. It is of course the case that social reality is concept and people dependent, but it is not exhausted by them. The question is whether structures, conscious or social, are real? Wittgenstein accommodates a relational real world and Heidegger's account reveals a complex mutually revelatory relation between appearance and reality. Foucault, too, appears to refer to an external world replete with power and conflict but what brings post-structuralist thought together with the position of Wittgenstein and Heidegger is that they recognise no independent arbiter – no master game that evaluates all other games.

Phenomenology was criticised by early Frankfurt School critical theory because of its idealism and its preoccupation with 'essences' and later because the phenomenological perspective was still seen to stand within the ambit of the problematic of conciousness – a limitation only to be transcended by the linguistic approach originating with Wittgenstein according to Habermas. Ironically, the Frankfurt school still plies the subject–object dichotomy and itself remains bound by the problematic of consciousness. In contrast, what disappears from structural Marxism is any concern with the emergence of self-consciousness, the nature of human subjects and the projected relation of individual subjects to inter-subjective contexts. It is now clear that in varieties of post-Marxism, transindividuality serves further to keep at bay such issues. Post-Marxist musings about the constitution of the subject in capitalism in and through ideology and language are overlaid upon the already difficult legacy of voluntarism versus determinism in Marxism. The problem is compounded because there is no 'real', corporeal human being that might pass for a subject in this view. Just as Schiller considered that the idealist thought so highly of mankind that they ran the risk of despising 'single men' (quoted by Simmel, 1964, p. 70), post-Marxism and post-structuralism are in danger of doing something similar. What appears to be the case is there has been a recognition of the myth of the substantive self: 'The continuity of the ego is a myth. A man is an atom that perpetually breaks up and forms anew' (Brecht, quoted in Coward and Ellis, 1977, p. 75). Yet, along side this, a 'continuity of the ego' has been identified as a product of the work of ideology at the individual level where the individual subject appears the origin of their own activity and responsible for its consequences. But, ironically, ideology presupposes a consistent subject and capitalist social relations are only possible with this notion of the subject as consistent and 'free'. It is ideology that fixes the subject in the fast dye of discourse; though consistent subject-ivity is an imaginary wholeness.

But this subject, such as it is, has survived only, it would seem, *en passant*. Ryle, Wittgenstein, Heidegger and Merleau-Ponty all reject the subject–object legacy and substitute a network of relations of a field of experience. Here we have language, relationality and intersubjectivity. Recent Marxist thought concurs. From its 'transcendent' or 'transcendental' position, subjectivity has shifted into a position of effect or result of the social process: 'The only "subject" Marx speaks of is one that is practical, multiple, anonymous and by definition not conscious of itself. A *non-subject* in fact, namely "society" . . . . And it is this non-subject or complex of activities which produces social *representations* of objects at the same time as it produces representable *objects*' (Balibar, 1995, p. 67). In Balibar's view Marx is not concerned with representation and the life of the mind, i.e., not with consciousness but with production and praxis. Habermas's departure from Marx's view of the self-creativity of labour and the substitution of his own concern with communication is so radical that it reformulates the original problem whilst not being able to serve as a solution in its own right. Critics such as Theunissen (writing in 1969, see Habermas, 1978, postscript) had already remarked on the tendency evident in the work of Habermas to subordinate a 'spurious' subjectivity of the individual to the inter-subjectivity of the human species, ignoring how the grounds of a subject *per se* might be established. True, Volosinov has warned us that outside of objectification and embodiment in the inner word, consciousness is a fiction. But, he says consciousness as organised, material expression 'is an objective fact and a tremendous social force. To be sure, this kind of consciousness is not a supraexistential phenomenon and cannot determine the constitution of existence. It itself is part of existence and one of its forces, and for that reason it possesses efficacy and plays a role in the arena of existence. Consciousness, while still inside a conscious person's head as inner-word embryo of expression, is as yet too tiny a piece of existence, and the scope of its activity is also as yet too small. But once it passes through all the stages of social objectification . . . it becomes a real force, capable even of exerting in turn an influence on the economic bases of social life' (Volosinov, 1973, p. 90). In fact, he stresses how in an 'unremitting conjunction' introspection is deepened through a deepened understanding of the social orientation. Although there is no exegesis of the classical Marxist texts in Volosinov, the underlying sentiment, here, is faithful.

7

THE 'NEW' CRITIQUE OF CONSCIOUSNESS

Our tales are spun, but for the most part we don't spin them; they spin us.
Our human consciousness, and our narrative selfhood, is their product, not
their source.

(Dennett, 1991, p. 418)

THE RANGE OF OPINION

The following discussion considers the state of the debate on consciousness via reference to recent contributions from sociology, anthropology, philosophy, psychology and social psychology. In each case a particular polemic or exchange of ideas will be reviewed as typical of the range of views or perspectives, whilst stock will be taken of ancillary contributions. The cases considered in this chapter feature not because the combatants have locked horns in itself but because they invariably champion and defend territory laid out and covered throughout this discussion: Locke, Hume, Kant, Hegel, Marx, phenomenology, symbolic interactionism, Wittgenstein/ Winch and Heidegger, amongst others, all become antagonists by proxy. The scene will be set for each intervention in the debate to make the connection with what has been ascertained of consciousness in this discussion thus far. The restatement and reassertion of ideas that are, by this time, already familiar to us will be the first and perhaps most obvious manifestation of this exercise.

SOCIOLOGY - SOMEONE ELSE IN MIND

Not only has the problematic of consciousness been superceded according to the lights of certain perspectives but so, too, has the penchant in social thought of playing off subject and object as ego against alter. At its most complex this entails not first person second-guessing, as with Weber's employment of *Verstehen*, but, rather, 'third-person'-guessing: me monitoring you monitoring me monitoring you. Models of this kind of dialectional exchange can be found in Hegel, C. S. Peirce, Husserl, Mead, Heidegger, Sartre and recently Dennett (1996b, p. 121). Schütz (1982) spends a great deal of time discussing the various attempts to cover this issue in European social thought, including detailed discussion of Scheler and Sartre – the latter ultimately failing to provide a model of future-bound inter-subjectivity in Schütz's view. It is Mead who is widely credited with the resolution of this question, not least by Habermas (1995) who appears to suggest that anything approximating *Verstehen* – present even in the work of C. S. Peirce – is a problem in that it dissolves the language-created individuation on which communicative action depends. What is required is not a metaphysical 'oneness' with others but, rather, an inter-subjective orientation to others – each with a 'mind' of their own. The trick of 'living' in someone else's brain as well as your own, as described by Peirce, is more trouble to Habermas than it is worth; this, despite the fact that Mead tended to see being able to adopt the Other's point of view as the basis of morality. Giddens, for his part, is persuaded that the social world 'should not be understood as a multiplicity of situations in which 'ego' faces 'alter' , but one in which each person is equally implicated in the active process of organising predictable social interaction' (Giddens, 1991, p. 52).

Giddens confirms how the question of other persons has endured in social thought with no issue being more thoroughly explored in early phenomenology where Husserl drew on Cartesian rationalism for his formulation of interpersonal knowledge, a position where '[a]ccording to Husserl, we are aware of another person's feelings and experiences only on the basis of empathic inferences from our own. As is well known, the inadequacy of this view proved to be one of the intractable difficulties of his philosophy. A transcendental philosophy of the ego terminates in an irremediable solipsism' (pp.

50–51). This difficulty was avoided, according to Giddens, from the perspectives of the later Wittgenstein and more sophistical versions of existentialist phenomenology, where '[s]elf-consciousness has no primacy over the awareness of others, since language – which is intrinsically public – is the means of access to both. Intersubjectivity does not derive from subjectivity, but the other way around . . . . Learning the qualities of others is connected in an immediate way with the earliest explorations of the object-world and with the first stirrings of what later become established feelings of self-identity' (p. 51). More recent contributions from hermeneutic phenomenology 'have reworked the notion of *Verstehen* in such a way as to detach it from its dependence upon the idea of the "reenactment" or "reliving" of the experiences of others. Thus, for Gadamer, *Verstehen* is to be treated not as a special procedure of investigation appropriate to the study of social conduct, but as the ontological condition of inter-subjectivity as such; and not as founded upon an empathic grasp of the experiences of others, but upon the mastery of language as the medium of the meaningful organization of human social life' (Giddens, in Bottomore and Nisbet, 1979, p. 279).

For the later Heidegger, language itself speaks not the individual subject. This becomes Gadamer's legacy to which he introduces in addition the idea of dialogue through which truth is disclosed. Without this dialogical process, where the stock of opinion, persuasion and prejudice is high, the self-reflection of the subject is a mere 'flickering' in historical life. Understanding is less a subjective act than a 'conscription' into effective history and its contexts of tradition (i.e, it is an event). Truth, rationality and justification have the same function in all linguistic communities despite specific nuance. The merging of 'interpretive horizons' for Gadamer is a convergence; a learning process in which learning itself belongs to neither party and in which both sides are caught up equally. Thereby, an appeal to common reference points for any possible consensus is mounted. In drawing upon Heidegger's model of understanding and in its application to hermeneutics there is obvious continuity here between Gadamer and thinkers such as Habermas, Apel and Rorty (see Giddens, in Bottomore and Nisbet, 1979). As Habermas says what needs to be examined is whether those who hold to this position 'do not have good reasons for according philosophical status to "third" categories, such as "language", "action," or the "body". Attempts to think of transcendental consciousness as "embodied" in language, action, or the body, and to "situate" reason in society and history, are supported by a set of arguments that is not entirely insignificant. These arguments have been developed, from Humboldt through Frege to Wittgenstein and through Dilthey to Gadamer, from Peirce through Mead to Gehlen, and finally, from Feuerbach through Plessner to Merleau-Ponty' (Habermas, 1995, p. 19). What has accompanied this preoccupation with language at the expense of the subject–object opposition has been the cultivation of a biographical self strung together by self narration rather than being itself the object of consciousness.

THE IDENTITY OF THE NARRATIVE BIOGRAPHICAL SELF

What is astonishing is the sheer range of opinion taken with the idea of the 'biographical self' of which only a few examples, here, will have to suffice ranging through symbolic interactionism, hermeneutics, marxism, phenomenology and perhaps most strident in promoting this view, the work of Giddens.[1] For him 'identity' does not refer to the persistence of the self over time but, in fact, presumes reflexive awareness; identity is not a possession but is the self understood reflexively by the person in terms of their biography. It is that of which the individual is conscious in terms of 'self-consciousness' and as such has to be routinely manufactured and monitored through the reflexivity of the individual. There is continuity over time in terms of identity but as interpreted reflexively by the person themselves. Giddens contends that to be a 'person' is to have a concept of person applied to self and others in addition to being a reflexive agent. He describes this as a 'cognitive component of personhood' which is not only created and sustained in a routine way by reflexive individuals but suggests inheritance of a biographical past, maintenance in the present and projection into the future – all conceived as a worthwhile project across time and space and checked dialectically with the external world. Feelings of self-identity, in Giddens's view, are both fragile and robust. Fragile because the 'story' reflexively held in mind as the biography of the individual is only one of potentially many other story-lines and, simultaneously, robust enough to weather changes in the individual and in the social life through which they move. It is the self-identity and emotional commitments emerging out of early trust relationships with carers which develops a sense of security that helps individuals withstand, throughout the life-course, the dangers which threaten the self's integrity in the encounters of everyday life. Hence, resistence is fashioned to being overwhelmed by anxiety and dread – rising levels of which threaten awareness of self-identity. States such as trust, belief and conscience, whatever their distinctive features, have in common a projection into the future that banks on an eventual outcome. Knowledge and sense of power vis-à-vis the external world depending upon early trust relationships determine whether the world has a shadowy existence or is something that is taken as a given. That is, basic trust relations and routinised activities sustain ontological security.

Giddens's discussion of motives, the self and identity is, thus, predicated upon factors pertaining to child development and language acquisition. He proposes that the production of interaction as 'meaningful' can be usefully analysed as depending upon 'mutual knowledge' drawn upon by participants as an interpretative scheme. Yet he considers actors' conduct may be opaque to themselves at the level of motivation. For him motivation refers to the wants which prompt action which, in turn, are connected to the affective elements of personality inaccessible to consciousness – the 'well-spring' of action. Nevertheless, he states that '[n]eeds are not motives, however, because they do not imply a cognitive anticipation of a state of affairs to be realized – a defining characteristic of motivation' (Giddens, 1991, p. 64). Giddens has consistently drawn a distinction between motives and reason giving, but whether he is discussing motives or reasons or intentions or purposes each is subsumed to the continuing successful monitoring by the actor of their own activity. However, it is not always clear whether this is an 'inward' or 'outward' process. Do the 'grounds' with which agents 'keep in touch' (i.e., 'monitor') amount to awareness and reflexivity or to that which is variously referred to as 'conduct', 'behaviour', 'doings', 'agency' and 'activity'? Is it apperception, perception or both, or really always a question of discourse? Whilst Giddens does emphasise how individuals forge their self-identities and how this is defined by reflexivity, self-narration and self-monitoring, he also sees this as involving individuals in knowing, virtually all of the time, what they are doing and why they are doing it and with good discursive reason.

Elsewhere, theorists such as Ricoeur (1991; 1992) and Taylor (1985; 1992b) have sought to interpret the self as a structured unity maintained by an ongoing narrative project through which identity is constructed. Ricoeur adduces that human social action should not be approached by way of the psychology of the actor as the generated meanings and effects always outrun the intentions of their author. Like a text, human social action leads a life of its own independently of what was scripted. Life stories are formulated which, through the mediation of the narrative, lend themselves to interpretation by ourselves and others. Actual life stories, then, inform our sense of identity. The idea of a core self asking the question 'Who am I?' is retained in Ricoeur and in Taylor who says that we are selves in that certain issues matter for us. Things matter and have significance for the self which exists within, and only within, a web of interlocution. Identity, here, refers not to a uniquely individuating collection of physical or mental properties, nor to 'character' as behavioural traits formed by habit, but to the background distinctions of worth which enable people to react to certain kinds of questions of a fundamental nature: how is right to be told from wrong; is life worth living and so on. Taylor's version of identity emphasises what might be missing for the person unable to orient themselves to such questions. In such an 'identity crisis' there is no identity shaped by an ideal and no moral evaluation on which to draw. The social world for Taylor is constituted inter-subjectively through language but in addition it is a shared acceptance of some ultimate good that makes human agency, knowledge and identity thinkable at all. Relationships with our fellows over the highest good are constitutive of our identity. Personal identity and social reality are just that by dint of self-interpretation which is, itself, constitutive of society and identity. Language encodes a shared world of inter-subjective experience, i.e., a common world. It is in this context that strong *evaluation* occurs where things of greater worth or higher standing are picked out and, in turn, pick us out, i.e., we define ourselves against them. Just as individuals orient themselves in physical space they have, of necessity, to orient themselves in this moral space in which they define themselves and others in relation to their conception of the *good*.

An interesting point of comparison with this kind of approach is Melucci, for whom identity is permanence of a subject over time comprising the unity which establishes the limit of a subject distinguishing it from all others facilitating recognition as identical. So we have here continuity of the subject over time, their delimitation with respect to others together with the ability to recognise and be recognised. This is how we actively continue to be the same person, an achievement itself dependent upon the recognition and affirmation of others. In adults new identities can be produced by an integration of the past with choices available in the present into the unity and continuity of a person's history. It is above all, Melucci holds, in situations of crisis that the question of identity is intensified. He says identity is the product of our conscious action and an outcome of self reflection and it is we ourselves who construct our coherence in which we recognise ourselves (within biological and environmental constraints). Thus, identity is in the process of being redefined in terms of self-awareness or a pure reflective capacity. But who or what is it in us that recognises ourselves as the authors of our action? The problem for Melucci seems to be who, or what, asks the question 'who am I?'. He refers to a capacity to shift our point of view and adopt a perspective. The continuity of identity relies not on specific contents but on 'a formal and processual capacity which enables the individual to assume a situational identity without a loss of a deeper sense of continuity of her/his personal existence' (Melucci, 1996, p. 52). Yet, quite remarkably, he suggests that '[o]pening and closing become necessary capabilities if we are to preserve our unity in the flux of messages and in the interminable sequence of changes. In the alternation between noise and silence, we can create an inner space which persists even if languages and interlocutors change, and even when communication itself breaks down' (p. 53). Something, then, is to resist becoming submerged by the flood of messages; closure, withdrawal, cessation of communication fail to annul our presence to ourselves.

Melucci is undoubtedly envisioning an outer and inner reality whose boundaries are at issue, where the self-reflective orientation is directed towards our personal quest of closer contact with inner experience. The 'inner world' is described in terms of a 'container' of different and contradictory elements of personal experience to which it lends unity: 'The capacity of being present to oneself as a body, mind and soul is the thread that stitches together the fragments of the individual life' (p. 54). He is convinced that 'we know that the point-like moment of the present condenses the fullness of our

experience . . . [but] the flux will be interrupted if we prove unable to
tie the threads of the past and the future in the "now-time" in which
we are immersed' (p. 12). It is interesting to consider how far this
'stitch in time' metaphor is removed from the figures of speech of
Locke, Hume and James. In relation to Wittgenstein, by the same
token, Melucci feels confident in referring to both an 'incommunic-
able circle of inner experiences' and to 'our inner life that speaks our
own secret language' (p. 55). We posses our own discourse on the
'inner planet' in Melucci's view. The 'inner planet' is not an essence or
a Cartesian 'I' in the dualistic premises of philosophical debate, as the
mind–body relation has come to be framed from entirely new perspectives with alternative conceptions of the relationship between
biological life, mental experience and social reality coming into
prominence. He says: 'The experience of each one of us, our conscious scrutiny of our own selves, are precious and inexhaustible
sources of knowledge' (p. 68). His position at first blush so similar in
its particulars to Giddens's train of thought, ultimately develops
away from it at a sharp tangent to leave space finally for a private self
and a role for consciousness.

CONSCIOUSNESS - POINTS OF THE SOCIOLOGICAL COMPASS (ELIAS, GIDDENS, ARCHER AND CAMPBELL)

Echoing a kind of interactionism and constructionism Elias and
Giddens differ markedly from Melucci in articulating a critique of
consciousness. Elias's term *figuration* suggests networks and interdependence and the intermeshing and interweaving of process. Here,
agency and structure, individual and society are collapsed into the
(often unintended) moment and in that there are echoes of Simmel's
formal sociology and an anticipation of Giddens's theory of *structuration* – discussed below. In Elias's view the individuals are not
somehow separate from the *figuration* of social relations they
form. He describes *figuration* as a ' flexible lattice work of tensions'
(Elias, 1978a, p. 130), though the pattern may be shifting , in which
people are engaged in terms of their whole selves in the totality of
their dealings with each other. This social *relationality* is both suffused and structured by a fluctuating and uncertain balance of power.
The mind constitutes a function in the orientation of social action,
acting as a means in orienting the self and the dialogical structure of

the inner conversation (identified variously by Mead and Vygotsky) constitutes the activity of 'thinking'. The inner dialogue held with ourselves in a soundless rehearsal of symbols is the activity to which the concept 'mind' refers, which as human psychology and personality, can be explained not by metaphysics but in terms of social action within *figurations*. Elias points to how inappropriate to the human situation are our habits of thought which portray the 'I' or self as secluded from other people and as resident within the individual person. He is against the 'me as closed box' view of the self and advocates a degree of detachment from the feeling that all other people exist outside whilst we ourselves exist as a person within. In the work of Elias, individuals are not so much decentred as dissolved into social process. He rejects the idea of a dividing line between an inner self and an outside world. By drawing on the idea of *figuration* – social networks or interdependent chains of acting human beings – false dichotomies between subject and object and inner and outer are, it is claimed, finally overcome. In Elias's view the emergence of the idea of the enclosed ego shut off from the rest of the world was extremely historically specific. Coming from the period of the Renaissance the idea of the primary reality of the individual ego came to be embodied in the philosophy of Descartes, Leibniz and Kant. Yet, Layder says in criticism of Elias that '[s]ome account is needed of the contribution of the unique psychobiographies of the real and describable human actors involved as they criss-cross and intertwine with the emergent and unfolding elements of the situation' (Layder, 1994, pp. 119–120). In fact, in this radical view, biography is as much in danger of subsumption under relationality as is consciousness.

In contrast, Giddens has drawn a distinction between *practical* and *discursive* consciousness; the former designating that of which we may be unaware as we are focussed on the task in hand whilst the latter is framed – and only framed – in language and discourse. He describes *practical* and *discursive* consciousness as coexisting, come alternative, modes of awareness. The former is what actors know about the situation as they routinely monitor events in a business as usual kind of way, though such a stock of working knowledge cannot be articulated or expressed discursively. Conversely, the latter is the verbal communication of the individual and social conditions of ongoing action. *Practical* consciousness cannot be 'held in mind' as its tacit, taken-for-granted dimension underpins all ongoing activity.

Being able to 'go on' is carried on at the level of practical conscious-ness which demands the bracketing-off of a whole range of possi-bilities to make headway and where there is a tacit acceptance of the self. He infers that the knowledgeability of agents is not, however, limited to a discursive consciousness of the conditions of their action, as: 'Practical consciousness is integral to the reflexive monitoring of action, but it is "non-conscious", rather than unconscious. Most forms of practical consciousness could not be "held in mind" during the course of social activities, since their tacit or taken-for-granted qualities form the essential condition which allows actors to concen-trate on tasks at hand. Yet there are no cognitive barriers separating discursive and practical consciousness, as there are divisions between the unconscious and consciousness taken generically' (Giddens, 1991, p. 36). Either we are present with the world and practically preoccupied or we are parts of speech; there is no room, in this view, for a disengaged standing back and taking stock. He is certainly against any vestige of a 'transcendental subject' and for 'knowledge-able subjects' – though he is not persuaded by ethnomethodology (nor by postmodernism or poststructuralism). In articulating his view of consciousness Giddens contrives equidistance from both struc-turalism and symbolic interactionism. In rejecting a conscious/ unconscious divide his usage of *practical* consciousness is not con-sciousness as commonly understood in structuralism, whilst the adoption of reflexivity (or 'reflexive monitoring') is against the back-drop of the discarding of the reflexive relation of the 'I' and the 'me' in post-Meadian symbolic interactionism in favour of a *social self*. Giddens is also equally anxious to distinguish his position from the legacy of Cartesianism by stressing that 'it is essential to grasp the importance of the thesis that we have to reject any conception of a subject that is "transparent to itself"' (Giddens, 1979, p. 255).

The idea of a practical consciousness unaccompanied by awareness can also be located in Mead and has the same problem and criticism has been levelled at Giddens to the effect that 'the person' in his early work lacks any psychological depths which could hold in abeyance the normative nature of social life and respond emotionally (Craib, 1992). Layder, in response, suggests that this has been put right in Giddens's later work on 'self-identity' which becomes, in the light of circumstances, a reflexively revisable project creating further strands in the narrative of the individual's biography and their sense of self. In Giddens's view the person is totally socially located and only locateable as such. Though there is no room for disengaged consciousness in his analysis he remarks in his substantive discussion of anxiety that this 'derives from the capacity – and, indeed, necessity – for the individual to think ahead, to anticipate future possibilities counterfactually in relation to present action' (Giddens, 1991, p. 47) and elsewhere considers what it is that the individual holds in mind reflexively. Though 'fateful moments' can often be dealt with within the bounds of such systems in Giddens's view, at such times 'individuals may be forced to confront concerns which the smooth working of reflexively ordered abstract systems normally keep well away from consciousness. Fateful moments necessarily disturb routines, often in a radical way. An individual is thereby forced to rethink fundamental aspects of her existence and future projects' (pp. 202–203). Nevertheless, despite this tacit acknowledgement of the capacity to 'rethink', the view exemplified by Giddens has begun to attract further sustained criticism reflecting, if implicitly, an alternative approach to consciousness.

THE ALTER-EGO – CONSCIOUSNESS AND THE NON-SOCIAL WORLD

In recent British sociology there has been a reaction against the over-social view of the person in social theory and its penchant for dismissing 'consciousness' out of hand. Layder considers it a mistake to rule out the prospect of early experiences imprinting themselves on the psyche of the individual feeding then into behaviour, and he observes that 'any fieldwork that purports to give a balanced view of the form and direction of social behaviour must at least acknowledge the possibility of the subtle interplay of psychological interior and social environment on an individual's behaviour' (Layder, 1993, pp. 77–78). In a more radical statement than Layder, Archer makes reference to selfhood in terms of individual psychology as well as social influences and states that 'personal and social identities are not synonymous' and that 'our humanity is prior to and primitive to our sociality and that social identity is emergent from personal identity' (Archer, 1995, p. 284). In Archer's view the capacities of consciousness, in Kantian fashion, discriminate in the objective world and reflect on the properties thus ordered, including ultimately social roles and collective life about which creative judgements can thus be made. Consciousness, too, here, seems to be able to realise both an anthropologically universal, constant sense of self – the *moi*, of which Mauss (in Carrithers *et al.*, 1985) remarks, with all human beings, wheresoever, having been aware of being physical and spiritual individuals – *and* a supremely social and historical process of individuation of personhood. Archer's emphasis on the direction of influence is outward from a primal, pre-social human being which is first outside of, in order to be at all *in*, the social world. Personhood is a body-plus-consciousness which brings with it non-social parameters of possibility. Not only is this sequence of events a challenge to social constructionist and Foucauldian accounts but, also, to Giddens too.

Archer rejects the usage of the terms 'agents', 'actor' and 'person' as somehow interchangeable. For her, each of these stratified levels has emergent properties and is, as such, not reducible one to another. The sequence is human being – agent – actor without personal identity being subsumed to social identity. In addition, 'social agent' in the plural is not synonymous with 'social actor' in the singular – we become agents before we become actors in Archer's view. But the transition from agent to actor does not exhaust our humanity as it is always human beings who do the *becoming*. It is essential then when considering that it is actually 'someone' who does the *becoming* not to collapse the capacities of human beings into a social being *per se*. Positing a gap between personal and social identity implies that private consciousness and public character are not one and the same, thus opening up the prospect of a space in which the former can usefully reflect on the latter. This is allowance for the inwardness and privacy of a self capable of resisting collapsing into the 'social' whilst actively working out a social identity. It is, therefore, inappropriate to consider a homogeneous, unified power interminably and unremittingly engaged in society. What she is sceptical of is the emphasis on an unstratified social self which denies personal psychology by insisting on the ubiquity of the social mediation of reality, i.e., we are denied unmediated relations with the objective world. In summary, her case is that there has to be something, relatively enduring, which recognises itself in relation to security and insecurity, trust and anxiety and so on. The approach she is challenging rejects the possibility of treating inner projects and outer expression as separate entities.

Archer quotes Shotter (1993) – though we would recognise it from C. Wright Mills and elsewhere – to the effect that such things as motives are not 'in' human beings but exist 'between' them as mediatory activity and, although not referred to at this juncture by Archer, only instantiated in discourse. She says in criticism: 'If inner visions cannot be conceived within our private lives, then how can those human intentions which repulse their social context be construed as being 'specified' within it?' (Archer, 1995, p. 129). How else could subjects set their face against the unacceptable? She is referring, here, to the possibility of authentic inner experience. In addition, we need to have and refer to a continuous personal identity in order for there to be someone – a knowing subject – who is aware of the frustration of failure: 'After all, talk of "dehumanization" only makes sense if it does mean something to be human, and to experience it only makes for grief if there is a self who can sense its loss' (p. 257). For Archer, processes such as self and social monitoring or strategic reflection on means–ends relations are contingent upon more primitive properties of persons. The approach Archer is criticising prioritises history at the expense of its makers and decentres subjects by truncating their own biographies. Instead, she seeks to hold on to evaluation by reflective subjects who weigh up their own experience of emergent structural influences through their own emergent properties of self-monitoring and self-consciousness. This self-modificatory process is an emergent human capacity of transformation and what she sees as needed is the logging of prior structural conditioning against individual differences between persons.

Referring to the theories of both Locke and Kant, Archer remarks on the significance of a continuous *sense* of self for the existence and persistence of individual and social life but it is the continuity of consciousness which secures personal identity and defines the person. The *sense* of self which is universal – and she quotes Mauss in support of this – cannot be subsumed to socially and historically specific constructions of the person which vary over time. The latter is seen by Archer as dependent on the former and she is making a clear distinction, here, between our personal and social identity. A sense of self is *a priori* to recognisably social action an Archer's view. Quite crucially, she also distinguishes between the capacities of the human mind and its social contents. We are embodied as a species being but human beings have imagination which over-reaches this animal status. She argues that things the self senses and that constitute personal identity are not exclusively social nor mediated through society. Rather, she is intent on considering non-social relations with non-social reality as part of our consciousness and what we are as persons. The supremacy of the idea of society as the 'gate keeper' of the whole world, usually in the guise of social relations and language, is challenged in Archer's analysis which she connects firmly to Marx's 'insight that we are committed to *continuous practical activity in a material world*, where subsistence is dependent upon the working relationship between us and things, which cannot be reduced to the relations "between the ideas of man". In this case, cumulative experiences of our environment will foster propensities, capacities and aversions which sift the social practices we later seek or shun, and thus the social identity which we then assume because of something that we already are as persons' (p. 291). She sees Marx as positing a direct connection between reality and (embodied) consciousness in the production of the means of subsistence.

Whilst Archer's work as we have seen invokes Marx, a not too dissimilar critique has been plied from a Weberian perspective. Drawing directly on the work of Weber, Campbell has identified the emergence of a new orthodoxy in social thought which he describes as *social situationalism*, resulting from the confluence of apparently diverse academic trends and traditions of the kind discussed in earlier chapters of this account. The concord between certain positions – as that between Mills and ordinary language philosophy – seems almost uncanny. What is most characteristic of this position overall, Campbell remarks, is the overt denial of consciousness and its subjective location. Whilst interpersonal processes are embraced, intra-personal considerations are designated off-limits by *social situationalism*. Weber's emphasis on motivational understanding is rejected as for *situationalism* motives are plainly mislocated in an 'internal state'. In effect, actions are deemed to be without subjective import because action itself has largely been adopted in a way that cannot be made to 'square' with the existence of an actor's subjective world. *Situationalism* exhibits anti-mentalist assumptions and neglects the role of causality and Campbell regards it as an approach inherently unable to account for the aetiology of actions. The emphasis on the inter-subjective denies individual human beings the capacity to engage in voluntary and purposive action – willed and responsible behaviours – involving the prospect of human beings, unlike animals, having the choice to act differently and, moreover, *knowing* they have the choice, i.e., the ability to stand back and take stock. He explains that, in his view, the concern with inter-subjectivity accounts for the lack of a theory of action in contemporary sociology and a lack of concern with consciousness. Instead, the preoccupation is with language and communication *as* action: 'Social situationalism is a perspective which, although overwhelmingly concerned with cognition, actually eschews the study of mind. It is ostensibly concerned with meaning yet eschews the study of consciousness; it disparages the 'scientific' causal-style form of analysis and yet has clear behaviouristic and deterministic overtones. It also involves privileging the public over the private, the overt over the covert, the inter-subjective over all other forms of meaning' (Campbell, 1996, p. 154).

He claims that communicative acts constitute a small proportion of all human action and that *socially* constituted communicative acts comprise an even smaller part and declares that to assume an 'extensive parallelism' between action (events) and language (symbols) is deeply misleading. A consequence of the rise of *situationalism* is that non-social action has been defined out of existence and action and social action have been confounded. In addition, all action performed in a social situation is seen to have social meaning which in turn invokes inter-subjectivity and the most socially situated of phenomena – language. His point, then, is that the distinction between *action* and *social action* in the work of Weber has been elided in subsequent interpretation, and C. Wright Mills and Schütz, in particular, are castigated in this regard. He argues that 'the original Weberian emphasis on "subjective meaning" has been displaced by one on "inter-subjective" and "communal" meaning, thus breaking the intimate connection between action and the actor's viewpoint' (p. 30). He says Weber's concept of motive was formulated to accommodate a non-interactional purely private or personal dimension which, as we have seen, Mills conveniently ignores. Schütz, in contrast, renders social action necessarily the interpretation of another's subjective meaning not Weber's 'taking others into account'. Campbell, in fact, points out at one juncture that Schütz's work has been used by others to the end of 'desubjectivizing' the actor and he refers to John Searle (see this chapter below) in support of his contention that every action is identified by reference to an actor's subjective state – though this constitutes a mindless prospect according to *situationalism.*

Campbell infers that because we possess the capacity to view ourselves as objects it does not follow that we see ourselves as the same object that others see. Adult selves are not framed entirely by the way they are seen by others but are conducted independently. He views Mead as being quite explicit on this point and quotes him as saying: 'After a self has arisen, it in a certain sense provides for itself its social experiences, and so we can conceive of an absolutely solitary self' (Mead, quoted in Campbell, 1996, p. 109). Campbell indicates that authors such as Goffman and Mills, for example, stress inordinately the import of *situations*, the *situated* and the *situational* where people are in visual and aural range of each other. But even so, a whole range of human actions can be performed at such proximity without being oriented to others – communicatively or otherwise. Men may live in immediate acts of experience as Mills suggests but these do not have to be *socially* informed. In both Giddens and Habermas, in Campbell's view, a theory of action is eclipsed by emphasis on inter-action and communication – though Giddens may hold on to the idea of reflexive monitoring. Habermas's abandonment of a paradigm incorporating individual, subjective consciousness – Weber's original brief Campbell would argue – is unequivocal.[2] He says: 'The error has been in studying action as if it were language and, in particular, treating its quality of "meaningfulness" as if it resembled that which is embodied in language, whilst also taking communicative actions to be paradigmatic of actions as a whole . . . It is not the study of language as action which is needed; it is the study of the role which self-directed language plays in enabling individuals to accomplish their actions which should be the focus of study' (Campbell, 1996, p. 139). This kind of re-introduction of consciousness onto the agenda of modern sociology has proved telling and as a trend has been reflected elsewhere in social thought.[3]

ANTHROPOLOGY – PROLOGUE

Not only were Durkheim and Mauss influential in setting the agenda of early anthropology but the *Geisteswissenschaften* approach, in the guise of Dilthey, indicated to early anthropologists such as Boas that the study of human society was a predominantly cultural affair. Boas

interpreted the evolution of mind and society in terms that were specifically cultural and historical and raised questions that were inherently psychological in cast. For him, the same mental processes were
shared by people the world over, but the 'emotional associations' of
pre-literate peoples failed to differentiate between aspects of their
cultural life thereby merging the disconnected and unrelated. He
differed from Lévy-Bruhl, who was in turn much criticised by
Durkheim and Mauss, on the issue of primitive mentality. Lévy-
Bruhl initially saw a transition from a 'pre-logical' to a logical form
characteristic of modern society but later saw the two types as coexisting side by side. In relation to the idea of a moral community he
saw virtue in variability and the importance of local social circumstances. For Boas, culture was essentially a mental construct and in
that respect he anticipates Lévi-Strauss (1963), who was influenced
by Durkheim and, in particular, Mauss, whose work *The Gift* (1970)
treats gift-giving as a total social fact whose functionality is to be
interpreted within the totality of the institutional relations of society.
More to the point for our purpose, Mauss related the facts of individual consciousness to collective representations hazarding that one
may pass from one to the other through a continuous series of inter-
mediaries. What Lévi-Strauss recognised here was that Mauss was
acknowledging the existence of inner, hidden, deep structures of
the human mind causally antecedent to collective representations
of objective social facts. Mauss, in Lévi-Strauss' estimation, was
responsible for setting in sharp relief the unconscious teleology of
the human mind and, as it turned out, setting in motion the general
direction of French 'structural' anthropology.

In the work of Lévi-Strauss, language – wheresoever – structures
thought and all human minds think alike, creating an iron-clad law of
restricted reciprocation. He advocates analysis of unconscious infrastructure rather than conscious phenomena and variables, for him,
have a positional meaning in a system. Collective modes of thought
and systems of representations, though invoking Kant, are detached
from a Kantian 'transcendental subject'. Lévi-Strauss would contend
that what has replaced the subject, *per se*, is the relations of communication between subjects. Though anthropology is fundamentally the study of 'thought' for Lévi-Strauss, his withering criticism of
Sartre's emphasis on subjectivity and consciousness led to the eclipse
of those priorities for over a generation. Sartrean phenomenology

(and existentialism) and its supersession by structuralism (Lévi-Strauss) and post-structuralism (implicitly in Foucault) are, in turn, concerned with abstract freedom, the isolated individual and consciousness, and objective, impersonal and unconscious structures. Here we have 'on the one hand the effort to account for man in his concrete reality, an effort which gets lost in arbitrary philosophical abstractions without managing to discover the real basis of social and personal life beyond the illusions of subjectivity; on the other hand the rigorous approach to scientific analysis, but acquired at the expense of its object, man, who is dissolved in structures, reduced to nature and denied the meaning of history and his own biography' (Sève, 1978, p. 406). Sève proclaims how it is 'possible to think the relations between biography and individual consciousness without consequently reducing the latter to the former and also without losing the infrastructural role of biography. But the difficulty which usually appears insoluble arises from the fact that mental activity and the movement of consciousness are in a relation of functional determination with *two* orders of infrastructures: the infrastructure of society and those of the personality' (p. 412). This is resolved by an approach to the individual founded on the social relations within which it is formed and transformed and the social relations which functionally determine individual consciousness initially through biography but without diminishing their social objectivity. But the tensions between structure and subject, culture and agency as modes of explanation have continued to engage anthropology.

THE REHEARSAL OF THE DEBATE

It is uncanny how the attack on essentialism and interiority and the acclamation of a linguistic, public world has been rehearsed, with slight variations in theme, in each of the social sciences. A classic instance in anthropology is Geertz (1975), who, playing on examples such as a Beethoven quartet, demonstrates, at least to his own satisfaction, that such a sample of culture has to be seen to be out-in-the-open, shared and public. Culture, then, is not instantiated in thought and action in this view; culture, instead, consists in socially established structures of publicly sanctified meaning. Nothing cultural is hidden and private as might be posited by essentialist claims to a mentalistic world, but is evident in knowing how to perform and construe in a public world. In contrast, others have sought to forge an interactive connection between the phenomenal social world and interpretive individual psyches and to move away from the stress on either universal needs and drives as the source of motivation or human action as a direct precipitate of cultural constructs. When 'cognitive' anthropologists refer to 'cognitive representations' or 'mind' they are indicating the linking up of thought and feeling in psychic states and processes. Whilst, in some instances, retaining a place for universal drives and needs (and unconscious desires) in their theoretical armory, such approaches stress that 'social action is the result of a process by which public events are turned into private representations and acted on, thereby creating new public events' (Strauss, in D'Andrade and Strauss, 1992, p. 16). This theory of motivation, as such, builds in space for an essential world of mentality. Cohen and Rapport (1995) have indicated that consciousness has not traditionally been a problem for anthropology – despite the legacy indicated above – and has been explained away in other terms usually of a socially deterministic nature. Cohen says that '[w]hat consciousness of the self and of the philosophical problems of personhood *should* have taught us is that, by failing to extend to the "others" we study a recognition of the personal complexity which we perceive in ourselves, we are generalizing them into a synthetic fiction which is both discredited and discreditable. We fall back too easily on the assumption that in important matters the members of collectivities think alike' (Cohen, in Ingold, 1996, p. 29). Cohen (1994) promotes a position that argues for both selfhood resting on the essential privacy of meaning and for the ultimate primacy of the self whether construed as mind, spirit or soul. In this view there is something on the inside of individuals. Jenkins (1996) has pointed out that the emphasis in Cohen is not only on private thoughts but on thinking rather than doing. In contrast, Jenkins emphasises a narrative self taken alongside the social construction of identity. He is persuaded, on balance, by the social constructionist tenet that the division between society and the individual is a nonsense (see this chapter below). Unsurprisingly, Giddens is also a consistent point of reference for Jenkins for whom the self is not a 'thing' but a process best captured by the term *selfhood*. Craib (1998), whilst agreeing with Jenkins that identity is a process rather than a thing, criticises him for eliding identity and social identity thereby ignoring half the picture and rendering everything social. What is missed is any idea of what goes on on the 'inside' for the bearer of the identity.

At this point it is worth considering two quite radical contributions to the anthropological theorisation of self and identity to further illustrate the opposition of a public world of social relationality and interiority. In his discussion of consumption, self and identity, Munro reviews the anthropological contributions of Douglas and Strathern. He says that the former analysis prioritises identity but stops short of an analysis of the self whilst the latter position, though not setting out to theorise the self *per se*, rejects the idea of a core self to which we retreat – in fact, the only thing we are ever 'in' is *extension*. What he means by this is that there is no prospect of repairing from extension to a core self but rather there is exchange to another configuration. This is not the taking on of roles then returning to a pristine self but circulation around and around from figure to figure. Though perhaps we imagine the connection with Elias, Munro's objective is to articulate a novel theory of the self drawing on the work of Strathern: 'Movement among figures, for Strathern, is not, as Plato had it, a will to recover the magnificence of a prototype from its diminishment as a shadow on the wall. An endless process of "repair" between an ideal and practice. Between the core self and its diminishment in a "role"; a vain process of "recovery", where the appearance is created of particulars that travel (badly) and a universal that always remains "in place" as the same' (Munro, in Edgell *et al.*, 1996, pp. 266–267). This is what Munro refers to as an age-old myth of 'reversability' – a movement of going out from the self to the social, before an inevitable return as the self recovers itself *as* self. It is from this position that he is seeking to move on. Though Munro does secure a place for the sedimentation of 'selfhood' through experience, the metaphor is that of the river—we may never step into the same self twice (though this is not news, as we have seen, to Hume and James). Munro reflects on whether evacuating social thought of the 'logic of presence' need necessitate being sold on the 'roller coaster' of identity. He muses further on the merits of the stark choice of either centring or decentring the subject and reflects that 'we seem to be too quickly caught here into taking sides. On the one side, the end of culture, bringing in an "anything goes" notion of identity that would so disperse self, as if to delete it altogether ... And on the other side, essentialist versions of the human, notions of a core that continue to delete materiality from agency?' (p. 270).

In Munro's eyes, Strathern offers a more 'potent' version of what might be meant by the decentered self than other types of analysis available. In this view, even in moments of despair suffering a 'loss of self' is still to remain in extension; but there is still a self as an 'amalgam' varying from moment to moment and place to place. The question is, has the thesis of the continuous transmography of the self out of the consumption of goods obviated the need for a person? Munro contends that by rejecting out of hand notions of a centred self, and by choosing to ignore issues raised by Cohen on self-consciousness for example, postmodernism has deleted debate about the self. Cohen's concern is perhaps too much with a core self for Munro's taste as his own emphasis is on movement that is 'never a travelling to and from a core self, but always movements *around* the "surplus" of a rim : we move endlessly from "figure" to "figure", not so much inchoate as undecided and undecidable' (p. 271). Strathern, indeed, has an antipathy to the rigid dichotomy of the individual in contradistinction or opposition to society, yet, though being wary of landing in the morass of social constructionism as she puts it, she stresses that social relations are intrinsic, not extrinsic, to human existence and that they are a primary not secondary phenomenon. She says that persons conceived as individual entities are not the proper object of anthropological study; instead, the significance of relationships to human life and thought has to be conveyed: 'We have now reached the point of having to tell ourselves over again that if we are to produce adequate theories of social reality, then the first step is to apprehend persons as simultaneously containing the potential for relationships and always embedded in a matrix of relations with others' (Strathern, in Ingold, 1996, p. 66).

Further to this, Hastrup has sought to combine ethnography with a view of collective consciousness whilst exploring the relationship of human agency and articulation to be found in the work of Taylor discussed above. The anthropological preoccupation with agency is thus transferred on to the ground of distinctions of worth where definitions of a competent human agent are to be located, i.e., they are socially and historically constructed. Following Taylor, Hastrup argues that with St Augustine's 'radical reflexivity', knowledge and awareness became a property of the agent. Not only does one's own experience become a matter of reflection but what is brought to the fore is a presence to oneself, as Taylor puts it, in interfusion with one's being the agent of such experience. With this came an irresistible language of inwardness in Taylor's view, with a being speaking of itself in the first person. 'I think', came to flourish as an act outside of the world and inside the self. After Descartes, 'control' of ourselves – firmness of will – as a moral resource became located on the inside. The intra-psychic world of the person replaced the cosmos as the loci for the very notion of "idea", in order for it to become a thing one had 'in mind'. Inspired by the work of Taylor, Hastrup makes the case that motivation is not to be located in the disengaged mind, that there are no selves beyond any particular social context and that identity is wedded to orientation in moral space. In practical life cognition and knowledge cannot be isolated from evaluation and emotion and the opposition of body and mind, still evident she remarks in received wisdom on the 'self' and all pervasive in medical language, is firmly rejected. In making an operative distinction between awareness (an explicit understanding) and consciousness (an implicit vector of knowing), Hastrup draws attention to their relative explicitness. Awareness is 'social, rather than individual, since explicating something, if only to oneself, of necessity involves particular cultural schemes and values. There is no "explication" outside a conversational community, whether this is actually addressed or not in the particular instance. While meaning is certainly always emergent rather than prior to events or phenomena, it must still in some sense be shared' (Hastrup, in Cohen and Rapport, 1995, p. 183). Awareness, for Hastrup, like meaning, is collectively premised and emergent; it becomes entangled in other projections as it projects itself forward. She refers to unknowable processes of understanding taking place within the self and remarks that consciousness belongs to a timeless dimension of knowing the world and the self whilst awareness is in time, relating to the historically specific moment. Though such consciousness is to be regarded as 'indistinguishable from our continuous being in between time past and time future. Awareness cuts us loose from this; just like narrative punctuates experience, awareness constantly arrests the flow of consciousness – to make room for action , as it were. Relating the question of consciousness and awareness to agency is to seek a theoretical understanding of motivation, constituting the link between culture and action' (p. 184).

In Hastrup the link is through Taylor to Wittgenstein and to the modelling of social reality as *language-in-action* – an agenda she shares with Giddens and, and as we shall see, Dennett.

THE 'NEW' PSYCHOLOGY AND PHILOSOPHY OF CONSCIOUSNESS – PROLOGUE

Often, the first name associated with the analysis of consciousness in early psychology is not that of William James (see Chapter Four) but that of Wilhelm Wundt. For Wundt, the ego is the lasting substratum of our self-consciousness; always there but always subject to change. This is not, however, a substance self but nor is it the 'sense-perception series' of Hume. Rather, the ego or self is neither a specific feeling nor an idea but is part of the process of consciousness identified with elementary volitional processes of apperception. Wundt saw no validity in a distinction between inner and outer experience and he did not view psychology as being concerned with inner conscious experience which is, itself, for him, not at all separate from our entire mental and physical being. Nevertheless, apperception, as used by Wundt, refers to an active structuring and selecting out of internal experience concerned, particularly, with focussing attention in the field of conscious experience. If apprehension is coming within the range of consciousness, then apperception is attention actively grasping that content. This is a highly focalised property of consciousness different in kind from the periphery of consciousness which is perceived. Apperception, then, is in 'active mode' which for Wundt gives direction and structure to experience and movement and, as such, approximates a manifestation of the feelings emotions and affectivity of volition or will. Whilst Wundt's reputation tends to be impugned by his constant attempts in the laboratory to break down experience into elements of sensation, William James, who despaired of ever gaining any critical purchase on Wundt's voluminous work, likened consciousness to a bird perching on an object then swooping in motion, i.e., as both selective and continuous. After James – the philosopher–psychologist – the way was left open for psychology to enter upon its endeavours as a hard, experimental science.

The confirmation of the status of consciousness as a 'nonentity' came with the work of John B. Watson and his followers who had no place for consciousness when systematising responses to external stimuli. Subsequently, in this tradition, B. F. Skinner believed the 'inner-man' was a mythical being and a convenient, yet self-deluding, creation to keep us away from the realisation that we are much less the masters of our individual destinies or captains of our own souls than we dare recognise or care to admit to ourselves. After this discarding of consciousness the dominant paradigm in twentieth-century psychology became behaviourism with its preoccupation with stimulus and response, and latterly stimulus–organism–response, and its penchant for applying models derived from animal behaviour to human beings. As a consequence, with the subsequent development of behaviourist orthodoxy in psychology, few psychology text books for over half a century referred to conscious-ness – forever associated with introspection. In Europe, roughly contemporaneously, Gestalt psychology argued that we perceive the shape or the form of the whole configuration initially and then its separate elements – including tasks and courses of action – with meaningful, immediate perceptions being arrived at through our mental ability to create and decipher relationships. Implicitly in the tradition of Kant rather than Locke, the emphasis, here, is on the fact that immediate perceptions become meaningful because of a mental ability to posit relationships. In their pure forms, neither of these approaches now finds general acceptance. A further point of juxta-position with the present discussion is humanistic psychology exemplified by the work of Carl Rogers (1961) who, though at first reluctant, came to take seriously the concept of Self because of his clients' recurrent reference to being, or not being, in touch with their 'real' selves. Rogers came to conclude that we live essentially in our own personal and subjective worlds where the perceived self is a phenomenological event – our perception of reality – which acts as a selective barrier to unacceptable perceptions; a barrier that is only dropped to let in *all* experiences under conditions of extreme onto-logical security. It should be recalled that R. D. Laing (1965) draws a distinction between a 'false' self governed by social relations with others and a 'true' (inner) self, though for him the self is only 'real' in relation to people and things.

In the last thirty years the issue of consciousness in psychology has been re-examined as part of the so called 'cognitive revolution' which once again, if indirectly, raised the question of consciousness. The foundations had been laid half a century earlier with the work of the 'cultural–historical' school in the Soviet Union. With the psychology of Vygotsky (1962) the classical opposition of subject and object (in this case often the child opposed to their world) is broken down and human beings are embedded and embodied beings *in* the social world. There is no transcendental distance to be accounted for in this view. In addition, consciousness and self are a product of practical and symbolic skills acquired in interaction with other social beings. Practical development thus comes before psychological or intellectual functions are differentiated. The classic illustration of this is in Vygotsky's stages of speech development in children which range, in sequence, from 'social speech' where the child is introduced to and taught words, to 'ego-centric speech' where the child talks themself through the situation, as it were, 'out loud', on to, finally, 'inner speech' which autonomously regulates and monitors behaviour. At this point speech is 'centred' in the personality as a self-conscious ego – the 'I'- and as the child becomes an object to itself it is able to carry on an inner conversation with that self. In Vygotsky's view, processes in the development of all higher mental functions appear first inter psychologically between people and then intra psychologically inside the child; they are, in fact, internalised social relationships. For Vygotsky desire and emotion are the well-springs of thought and language is the conduit they require, i.e., thought is restructured as it is transformed into speech. Vygotsky asks us to imagine, in a schematic way, thought and speech as two intersecting circles with verbal thought residing in the overlapping 'zone' where they coincide. However, inner speech for Vygotsky comes to be defined by 'word meaning' where the vocalisation of inner speech has died away leaving behind it a sense or image of a word rather than its full expression. Technically, it is contended, the syntax of inner speech, in a kind of mental shorthand, is different to its audible counterpart but it is also the medium in which we know the phrase we are after before we pronounce it. In a transformational process consciousness and the whole of the personality are focussed on word meaning. Emotions, memory, imagination and the will are all given form by it and with each stage of development the internal structure of consciousness is transformed.

In his own way Piaget, too, sought to overcome the subject–object and determined *or* determining legacy of western social thought, though Vygotsky and Piaget differed in their view of the stages of child development and on the direction of influence – particularly as regards language acquisition and speech. Piaget (1926), alongside the articulation of his developmental stages, argued that knowledge is acquired by attending to, moving about in and exploring the world and its significations. It is not a question of the acquisition of schemata for the construction of the world mentally but of plying the skills of direct perceptual engagement with the world and its social and non-social constituent parts. Certainly, Piaget's view accommodates an adult capable of both rational and intuitive thinking and combining or moving between the two. Human beings, then, are able to link different forms of understandings with different kinds of knowledge base, though intuitive thought – that which Hegel described as 'immediate thought' – has not received a good press and has been associated with credulity, superficiality and error. One crucial link with modern developments in this area is the work of Bruner who says of Vygotsky's work that: 'Consciousness plays an enormous role, consciousness armed with concepts and the language for forming and transforming them. About consciousness he says: "Consciousness and control appear only at a late stage in the development of a function, after it has been used and practised unconsciously and spontaneously. In order to subject a function to intellectual control, we must first possess it." This suggests that prior to the development of self-directed, conscious control, action is, so to speak, a more direct or less mediated response to the world. Consciousness or *reflection* is a way of keeping mind from ... shooting from the hip' (Bruner, 1986, p. 73). In Bruner's view the questions raised by Vygotsky cannot be divorced, it seems, from cultural and historical specificity as he says 'Vygotsky strived mightily (for he was devoted to Marxist theory) to provide a means of bridging the gap between historical determinism and the play of consciousness' (p. 78).

For his own part, Bruner seems to see consciousness as the lynchpin between reflection and action. But the relationship between these two aspects of consciousness is an exigent one. According to Bruner, perception is an instrument of the world as structured by expectations where human beings perceive feel and think all at once; whatever is perceived achieves its 'meaning' when it is placed within a class of percepts with which it is grouped. He questions the status of completely unique perceptual experience which if 'uncut' is doomed to remain gem-like encased in the silence of private experience. He contends that children are very quickly adept at following another's line of regard which requires a sophisticated conception of the other's mind to search for what is engaging their attention. The child is not as 'self-centered' as has been thought according to Bruner who sees the main issue as being rather what it might be that readies the child so early for transacting their lives with others based on workable intuitions about Other Minds in given social settings. It is only when the child fails to grasp the structure of events and context that they abandon taking another's perspective and have recourse to an egocentric framework. The pressing question then seems to be the extent to which this capacity is innate. Bruner says that 'human beings must come equipped with the means not only to calibrate the workings of their minds against one another, but to calibrate the worlds in which they live through the subtle means of reference. In effect, then, this is the means whereby we know Other Minds and their possible worlds' (p. 64). Nevertheless, he is not keen to have this capacity explained away in a singular manner by reference to 'empathy' and 'sympathy' and seeks to root it in the workings of language and the communication demands of a public world.

THE NARRATIVE, BIOGRAPHICAL SELF - REPRISE

Although uncomfortable with the idea of the self in his early work Bruner refers to the self in terms of 'text': 'I think of Self as a text about how one is situated with respect to others and toward the world – a canonical text about powers and skills and dispositions that change as one's situation changes from young to old, from one kind of setting to another. The interpretation of this text *in situ* by an individual *is* his sense of self in that situation. It is composed of expectation, feelings of esteem and power, and so on' (Bruner, 1986, pp. 129–130). In addition, he speculates on the actual, historical emergence of the self: 'It can never be the case that there is a "self" independent of one's cultural–historical existence. It is usually claimed, in classical philosophical texts at least, that Self rises out of our capacity to reflect upon our own acts, by the operation of "metacognition". But what is strikingly plain in the promising research on metacognition that has appeared in recent years . . . is that metacognitive activity (self-monitoring and self-correction) is very unevenly distributed, varies according to cultural background, and, perhaps most important, can be taught successfully as a skill' (p. 67). There is evidence that meta-cognition is present as early as eighteen months and its development depends upon, in Bruner's view, the processes mapped in symbolic interactionism. Providing further grist to the mill of the narrative self, Sacks, from a neuro-scientific background, has said: 'We have, each of us, a life-story, an inner narrative – whose continuity, whose sense, *is* our lives. It might be said that each of us constructs and lives, a 'narrative', and that this narrative *is* us, our identities . . . Each of us *is* a singular narrative, which *is* constructed, continually, unconsciously, by, through, and in us – through our perceptions, our feelings, our thoughts, our actions; and, not least, our discourse, our spoken narrations . . . historically, as narratives – we are each of us unique. To be ourselves we must *have* ourselves – possess, if need be repossess, our life-stories. We must "recollect" ourselves, recollect the inner drama, the narrative, of ourselves. A man *needs* such a narrative, a continuous inner narrative, to maintain his identity, his self' (Sacks, 1986, pp. 105–106). Yet Sacks does not appear to be in any doubt that there is an 'inside' to human beings which can be referred to in terms of consciousness.

For Dennett, too, the important thing is that we tell others – and ourselves – stories about who we are: 'These strings or streams of narrative issue forth as *if* from a single source . . . their effect on any audience is to encourage them to (try to) posit a unified agent whose words they are, about whom they are: in short, to posit a *center of narrative gravity*' (Dennett,1991, p. 418). In Dennett's view a self is 'an abstraction defined by the myriads of attributions and interpretations (including self-attributions and self-interpretations) that have composed the biography of the living body whose Center of Narrative Gravity it is. As such, it plays a singularly important role in the ongoing cognitive economy of that living body, because, of all the things in the environment an active body must make mental models of, none is more crucial than the model the agent has of itself' (pp. 426–427). In this view a defining story about ourselves is built up and organised around a basic blip of self-representation. Not a self then, but a *representation* of a self. Ironically Dennett refers to the self as a 'center of narrative gravity' and then concludes it a 'fiction'. He is not persuaded by the prospect of introspection wherein we can shift our attention 'inwardly' to become self conscious. As a marked departure from this, Searle defends the idea that self-consciousness is a correlate of consciousness and argues that there is no objection to introspection if this refers to thinking about our own mental states – this, he says, is decisive for any form of self-knowledge and is a regular occurrence. But he says it seems to him there could be no special capacity to *spect intro*: 'There could not be, because the model of specting intro requires a distinction between the object spected and the specting of it, and we cannot make this distinction for conscious states. We can direct one mental state at another; we can think about our thoughts and feelings; and we can have feelings about our thoughts and feelings; but none of these involves a special faculty of introspection' (Searle, 1994, p. 144). The two positions exemplified by Dennett and Searle, then, diverge in significant respects and as such typify recent debate in this area: the self in one case is viewed, primarily as narrative whilst the other sees the self as a product of consciousness which, itself, in turn, is seen in the one perspective as a multiplex phenonomenon and in the other as an incontrovertible 'unity'.

CONSCIOUSNESS – THE MIND SET OF THE 'NEW' PSYCHOLOGY AND PHILOSOPHY

It is worth turning at this point, after having set the scene, to review in rather more detail recent theories of self and consciousness on the cusp between psychology and philosophy. The themes themselves, as will be seen, are not noticeably new. In exploring the problem of mental causation which beset Descartes, Searle is convinced that brains cause minds; the way to dispose of the mind–body problem is to accept that minds are 'emergent properties' of brains, i.e., consciousness is one of the properties of minds produced by brains, it is just something that brains do. He seeks to explain a number of puzzles about mental experiences and views consciousness as central to being human because without it all of the other characteristic human aspects of our existence – including language – would be impossible. All consciousness 'of' is consciousness 'as' according to Searle. Not only does this imply language and concept acquisition (and, for that matter, memory), but also categories prior to perception. Dennett's view is that consciousness is not a single, autonomous entity but is, rather, a sum of many abilities or 'competencies' and intentionality is one crucial 'competence' in a multiplex of capacity. Of all the multiple drafts that are churned out, consciousness is the dominant mental state at any one point in time. Whether it be the processing of incoming information or recycling from memory, the point about his 'multiple drafts' model – of which consciousness is the most dominant or current version – is that such drafts are being prioritised, in as much worked up and worked over, on the basis of both factors integral to the organism and the appropriateness of the social setting and what is known of it. Through his embrace of Dawkins's idea of *memes*, Dennett's multi-drafts model of consciousness is matched in 'social and historical' space. Whatever the cultural trait it is passed on from one to another by imitation, each interpretation competing against the other for 'elbow room' until one – in true evolutionary style – inherits the future. Human consciousness is then itself rendered a massive complex of such memes. In a tradition that has been associated with Bergsonism (Watson, 1998), Dennett locates consciousness and its object 'out there', referring to things remaining out in the world where they can just 'be' – not entering our consciousness but simply being available. Things are not perceived, then, in ourselves but at the place where they are and qualities are in the world not representations in the mind. Yet, this radical anti-Cartesian position, which rejects the idea of sense data of the material world being seized upon by an occult mind in a representational form, sounds remarkably similar to terms of reference used by Cartesian phenomenologists like Husserl and Merleau-Ponty. Nevertheless, Dennett is critical of Descartes and phenomenology and philosophers influenced by it such as Nagel (1986) and Searle who are criticised for treating consciousness as 'foundational'.

Dennett has referred to Searle as being influenced by the Husserlian school of phenomenology leading him to suppose that consciousness is the source of 'intrinsic intentionality' of some special sort. Indeed, Searle does actually remark that 'the ontology of the mental is an irreducibly first-person ontology' (Searle, 1994, p. 95) with others having a subjectivity just like our own; a subjectivity where mood, though it is not itself intentional, colours consciousness and pervades all intentional states. He contends that intentional states do not function autonomously or independently as each intentional state requires a Network (a complex of beliefs and desires) of other intentional states which, in turn, only function in relation to a set of Background capacities as the condition of possibility of the flow of intentionality. Conversely, if intentionality is considered to be our intentions at any one point in time that orders our thought and directs it to the purposes in hand and where the relevance of the ideas and information of which we become aware is pragmatically related to the effects we intend, then the organic connection with Dennett's multi-drafts model of consciousness can be clearly detected. Both Searle and Dennett, then, consistently devote a great deal of space to intentionality, but with different emphases: Searle seeing it as an original mental property of mind ('intrinsic' definition) whilst Dennett views it as living our lives by the light shed by words and language – the 'understanding' of intentionality, thus, being a very social property ('derived' definition). Dennett, for his part and at his most influenced by Wittgenstein, Ryle and Winch, not only suggests that consciousness is a cultural construction but that we cannot have consciousness without a *concept* of consciousness.

Searle, in contrast to this, made a transition in his own academic career away from ordinary language philosophy to a position which acknowledged the importance of understanding both the fact of consciousness as a subjective biological phenomenon and that a real world exists independently of our own representations of it. Dennett, instead, emphasises how 'we persist in the habit of positing a separate process of observation (now of *inner* observation) intervening between the circumstances about which we can report and the report we issue – overlooking the fact that at some point the regress of interior observers must be stopped by a process that unites contents with their verbal expression without any intermediary content-appreciator' (Dennett, 1991, pp. 319–320). In this situation: 'Sometimes subjects are moved to revise or amend their assertions, and sometimes they aren't. Sometimes when they do make revisions, the edited narrative is no closer to "the truth" or to "what they *really* meant" than the superseded version . . . When we put a question to a subject about whether or not a particular public avowal adequately captures the ultimate inner truth about what he was just experiencing, the subject is in no better position to judge than we outsiders are' (p. 247). The message, here, is a familiar one from the work of Mills, Burke (1945) and Coulter and has now become an intrinsic part of the repertoire of debate in this more recent area of social thought. Ironically Dennett highlights the *stance* we utilise to make sense of and second guess Others's behaviour. This interpretative strategy is the perspective or attitude we adopt by which we regard Others as having a purposive mind acting in the light of beliefs and desires. They are treated by us *as if they were* a rational agent whose choice of action is governed by such considerations. This ascription is not a primitive form of *Verstehen*, however, as Dennett makes clear the *stance* he has in mind amounts to being prone to be described in terms of beliefs, etc. not a question of the Other really being *in* such a state. In this view a creature has a mind in that they are so regarded by us.

Locke's view of language has been superseded by that indelibly linked to the name of Wittgenstein. It is not, then, to be even a question of thinking aloud as Locke would have it – 'the *idea* in our minds of which the sound *man* in our mouths is the sign' (Locke, 1977, p. 160). Yet, it is quite astonishing just how much the name of Locke appears in recent social thought on the question of consciousness. As has been pointed out, there has been a 'strong intuition' dating back to the seventeenth century – with Locke's reaction to Descartes – that consciousness consists in a higher order *awareness* of ordinary mental states or processes of which it is not, in itself, actually a part. Consciousness, for Locke, is perception of that which passes in a man's own mind. Words that have come to be associated with this presupposition are apperception, introspection and, even, self-consciousness with consciousness coming to be portrayed figuratively as a scanner, a spotlight or a monitoring device (indeed, such metaphors and analogies abound because consciousness proves so consistently elusive to the grasp). Contributions to the new psychology and philosophy of consciousness seem to divide into those persuaded by the Lockean interpretation – thus creating a long tradition, in effect, back to ideas we have already considered in some detail – and those much more sceptical. For the motion are James (depending on where you look), Churchland, Lycan and, obliquely, Dennett. Other well known contributers to the literature in the area either give themselves a much more wide-ranging brief than the motion or work at a tangent to it: Dennett, in the main, Flanagan, Searle and Tye might be included here (all the above are referenced elsewhere in this text or are covered in Block *et al.*, 1997). Against the motion, at least in this particular form, would be Block, Guzeldere and Dretske, who argues that: 'Experiences and beliefs are conscious, not because you are conscious of them, but because, so to speak, you are conscious *with* them' (Dretske, in Block *et al.*, 1997 p. 785). Dretske is convinced that being aware of conscious experiences and beliefs is not what makes them conscious; they are conscious because they direct us to be conscious of something other – our bodies and the world we find ourselves in.[4]

THE SOCIAL PSYCHOLOGY OF SOCIAL CONSTRUCTIONISM AND DISCOURSE THEORY – KICKING OVER THE TRACES

In the last generation one of the most wide ranging challenges to the constituency of consciousness has come from *social constructionism*, which, wheresoever you turn, has certain characteristic features. All variants are: anti-essentialist, holding that there is nothing *inside* people that makes them what they are; anti-realist, assuming that there is no objective world or objective facts or truths (i.e. perspectivism), with the most extreme position construing reality as that which is constructed through language; and pro-language as a precondition of thought and an active, rather than passive, force to be reckoned with. There are wide ranging variants of this type of approach and the underlying influences are equally disparate: in some cases Marx, Mead, Berger and Luckmann, ethnomethodology, post-modernism and post-structuralism. It is from these latter, most recent, perspectives, that social constructionism acquires its disdain for hidden structures and meta-narratives (i.e., grand theories). What inevitably accompanies social construction is the problem of the nature of human agency once it has dispensed with – in anti-humanist fashion – a unified, coherent, rational person as its subjective point of reference. Despite what the person in the street might think about themselves, social construction is counter-intuitive and what we take for granted is rendered problematic. Notwithstanding the obvious clash with phenomenological sociology here, it is conceivable in social constructionism that objects of discourse (for example, 'ourselves'), whilst not actually internal and private, can be *held* in consciousness in a process ultimately dictated by the social realm. In the view of social constructionism we are a multiplex of selves in constant flux with any sense of continuity being illusory – itself a product of the artifice of memory or a product of language based social interaction. Thus mind is 'inter-subjectively constituted' in interaction with others and the 'self' boils down to publicly available context – bound discourses which should sound familiar from our discussion of Mills.

From a social constructionist point of view the 'I' is an indexical label attaching an utterance to a person and is not evidence of any inner property. Personality is a thing that exists *between* people if it has a place at all. Ideally, an essentialist tainted personality is replaced by a series of social identities in social constructionism. Our identities are made out of discourses grounded in power relations which discursive practices themselves uphold. The level of analysis is of competing discourses not attitudes and opinions which are essentialist concepts misconstrued as flagging a person's private world. What is said and done is a joint affair not a product of internal stuff. There are various examples in this tradition of how persons use and construe discourse. Gergen's (1989) idea of 'warranting voice' indicates how an individual or a party not only angle to have their say but also package their view as orthodox, authentic or legitimate when in competition with others. This suggests a movement away from single individuals to relational forms as the central unit of understanding. Despite what Derrida might conclude in rejecting binary oppositions, Billig *et al.* (1988) indicate that what we see as the two sides of an argument is shaped by our experience in society. Thinking itself is of a 'dilemmatic' kind as a two-sided equation and 'ideological dilemmas', at a social level, far from being a unified banner actually embody just such a mutually suggestive contradiction – selling the one thing automatically imports the contraband of the other. In Billig's view all properly social contexts are contexts of argumentation hanging on and locked into reason-giving, justification and criticism. Potter and Wetherell (1987) develop the idea of 'interpretative repertoires' to describe the linguistic devices that people use to get language to work for them and from their viewpoint the idea of an attitude as something enduring that lies within and which can be tapped into is totally misconceived.

Harré, perhaps our prime example here, influenced by Kant and Wittgenstein, sees the self as created through culturally specific language acquisition; talk of agency generates the sense of having agency in this view. A self, for Harré, is to be in possession of a certain kind of theory (one might almost say 'possessed by') rather than constituting a certain kind of being. Although his position has shifted over time Harré still gives house-room to the term consciousness. He says with Gillett that 'consciousness is best thought of as the capacity to focus cognitive abilities on a range of objects, events, and conditions around the subject . . . consciousness is discursive and loaded with conceptual content that may be well or ill defined but that expresses the discursive orientation of the subject. Thus the content of conscious experience is given not only by what it is one is conscious of but also by the discursive skills I bring to bear on it' (Harré and Gillett, 1994, p. 174). Of course, as was to be expected, language and discourse feature here, but so, too, does the idea of consciousness as 'capacity'. Consciousness, is seen in this view as 'the subjective springboard of agency' (p. 175) where conception of content relies on discourse-based skills. Additionally, consciousness is considered to possess intrinsically to it an evaluative structure and is, therefore, not just concerned with knowledge processing and representational activities. Interestingly, in this connection, when discussing self-consciousness Harré and Gillett draw attention to Sartre's model of self-awareness through recognition of becoming an object of which others are aware. This imports anticipation, reflection and evaluation as properties of consciousness of the 'knowing', socially engaged individual. Yet, it is thus far and no further, as they say that in their account they are focussing 'not so much on the entities lurking in the Cartesian interior of a human subject (because there are none) but on the significations that are available and permitted within a given moral reality. This moral reality is a discourse, elucidated so that its power relationships, positionings, and effects on human beings are exposed' (p. 179)

In this view everyone is in permanent dialogue with everyone else: thinking becomes argumentation, motives – never of anyone's making – become reason – giving and memory becomes socially constructed collective remembering. Nothing has depth or is hidden – neither psyche nor social relations – as there *is* no reality behind or beyond appearance and a public appearance at that. As Harré announces: 'Ryle and Wittgenstein both seem to me to offer convincing cases for treating some psychological activities as going on in public, with no private counterparts' (Harré, 1979, p. 423). Thus, mental activity is seen by Harré as available publicly in accountable activities in which people are involved together *not* a private state of mind. Thus 'the primary human reality is persons in conversation'

(Harré, 1983, p. 58) and in as much as individuals are complex 'mental' beings with unique 'inner worlds' it is because they have constructed a personal discourse modelled on public discourse. He is describing an intra-linguistic reality comprized spatially of locations or places; in effect a referential grid set out by moral and political considerations. Pronouns such as 'I' or 'me' do not refer to a subject but act to index temporal participation and location in such space. Harré *does* countenance unequal prospects of participation in conversational reality but not at the level of structural inequality actually reproduced in the very act of non-participation. For him, social actors and social worlds are a coproduction; social worlds are diachronic and have the form of a narrative with the persistence of practices reinforced by social skills. He points to Vygotsky as having the 'answer' on these issues. What is not the answer, Harré contends, is *structure* which cannot perform the work asked of it – the word itself referring to a cluster of practices not a unity of causal powers. Structure brings together under a superordinate category a whole lot of practices. In fact, structure has only a taxonomic role in his view. We are, in fact, reifying a taxonomic category. He contends we are trapped not in structure but in a complex pattern of narratives – the stories we have told ourselves since childhood.

Structure is rejected by Shotter (1993), too, because the property he is describing is always incomplete (the opposite of the state of affairs suggested by structure). Similarly relational fields are comprized of loci of activity not systematically ordered 'things'. He is talking, here, about the space for the novel, the original, the unforeseeable. He draws attention to Wittgenstein's contention that there is only an order of possibilities in language use; but so, too, though Shotter does not make the case, is it with reality. He quotes Volosinov sympathetically, that the *reality* of the subjective psyche is to be localised straddled on the borderline between the organism and the outside world – in more modern parlance it is in effect, the interface. Everything is located outside of the souls of the speaker. The idea of persons possessed of inner sovereignty, self-enclosed and essentially private is, from this viewpoint, totally illusory. It is an illusion, moreover, borne out of a misunderstanding of the nature of thought and language. Human beings are, in fact, an ongoing theoretical project on the boundary of themselves and others. Not at the centre, then, but on the periphery where the organism *becomes* through encounter with the other, with thought inevitably garbed in language. In Shotter's eyes Vygotsky, Volosinov and Bakhtin (the latter two, being one and the same author it is most often argued) are all passionate advocates of this case. To their concerns Shotter adds the preoccupation with context: the common-sense assumptions and accounting practices of given social settings which, ironically enough, can only be available from the *inside*. Also drawing on Volosinov, Burkitt indicates that conflicts in the psyche between different motives is an *inter*-psychological process rather than an *intra*-psychological one and, referring to Leontyev, he notes that: 'To understand motives clearly, one would have to undertake a study of a person's objective activity and not their inner feelings, needs and desires. These are only the psychological signals which direct actions and are themselves phenomena created in social activity' (Burkitt, 1991, p. 157). Nevertheless, individuals feel this impulsion as rising up internally from within their bodies and minds. The possibility that this feeling might, itself, be in need of explanation is not pursued by Burkitt. Although he says 'not only do people in the western world feel separated from the others with whom they live and who make up their society, they also feel divided within themselves, riven between the selves they present in relations with others and the individuals they feel themselves to be deep down inside' (p. 1) he moves quickly on to supersede this problem of the self-contained individual – the monad – to the question of the social construction of selves.

CONCLUSION

What has united a great deal of the social scientific literature reviewed in this chapter is an emphasis on the narrative, biographical self. Giddens has remarked on the self in modern society being seen from certain points of view as either delicately poised or hardly holding together at all. In the view of post-structuralism 'the only subject is a decentred subject, which finds its identity in the fragments of language or discourse' (Giddens, 1991, p. 170). It is against this backcloth that the narrative-biographical self makes its way in the world. But it is also both a post-Cartesian and post-Lockean self. In Taylor's philosophical anthropology, for example, there is no reality remaining aloof from self-interpretation, as reality exists as a result of the self-interpretations of human agents. Both reality and self-interpretations are constituted by language and are reshaped through our attempts at articulation of them in the germane discourse. This central insight of Taylor's ties him to the celebration of worlds from which it is impossible to be disengaged sufficiently to argue for better or different worlds or to judge one world against another. There is no mention of non-social dimensions of human existence, or of memory on which the self-narration must depend and no 'break-up' in linear projection. There is no disengaged standing back and no transparency to self. Consciousness if considered at all is a practical, discursive property of activity in the world; it is not generative of things from the inside as the direction of influence is from interaction to intra-responsiveness. The outer world is most often described in terms of relationality and relationships. Yet, as it takes shape the self can be thought of as the initial identity to which all subsequent identities will have to be accommodated; that first identity will remain the precondition of all that comes afterwards. This primary self offers a 'template' for later identities and a 'stem stock' on to which they will be grafted (Jenkins, 1996, p. 49). Identity would be thus a focus of consciousness like any other external object and not a composite part of the self; an adjunct, perhaps, but one that is a social acquisition: an identity can be let go but the self – albeit a changling – cannot. The lacunae between self and identity cannot be conflated by decree for: 'If some completion of identity is a necessary part of personhood, but no particular social identity is in itself necessary, then there will always be at least a potential gap between private consciousness and public character' (Collins, in Carrithers *et al.*, 1985, p. 74).

Consciousness in Giddens's view does not entail interiority and is instantiated in word and deed; consciousness, conversely, in Archer, involves distance to reflect in order to effect change. Unsurprisingly this very opposition is to be found replete in the corpus of marxism as has been seen. Archer claims that the success of the position held by Giddens depends on eliminating reference to a selfhood independent of social mediation which obviates the need for accounting for personal psychology in interplay with social factors and with non-social properties altogether. Her view is close to Campbell's at this point, but she tends to underestimate the demolition job done on the transcendental self by post-Wittgensteinian philosophy. The idea to be found in Archer that by nature people are reflective in thought and reflexive in action as inalienable emergent properties is in danger of providing a hostage to fortune. In fact, the difference between Giddens and Archer on the question of consciousness is profound and embodies a microcosm of the debate on consciousness right up to the last decade of the twentieth century. On one side, a range of heuristic distinctions have been worked tendentiously or conflated according to Campbell, including the social and non-social; the social and the human; the social and the cultural; the public and external world; and, perhaps most significant for our purposes, a public world as opposed to an internal, private 'world' and covert self. Despite mounting a telling clause by clause critique of *social situationalism*, Campbell does not really make play on the role of conflict in Weber yet the question of conflict in its own right is enough to undercut the constituency of *situationalism*. It is intriguing that Norbert Elias, the sociological doyen of the social constructionist fraternity, is not taken to task by Archer (or Campbell) for both his anti-essentialism and his inception of *figurational* sociology – in its basic principles a precursor to Giddens's theory of *structuration*. Taken from the work of Piaget (in the French), but influenced by Giddens's early work on Durkheim, *structuration* regards agency and structure as inseparable and mutually constitutive which appears to afford itself the luxury of structure only ever instantiated in social action, an all-pervasive social (real linguistic) world and purely practical, engaged consciousness. In a similar fashion, inner project and outer expression are also collapsed. In fact dispensing with structure whilst promoting language and discourse has been a consistent trait in this area of social thought.

We have observed in this chapter the keepers of the keys of some of the major intellectual traditions featured throughout this account. Though not exclusively, we see Locke in Archer, Armstrong and Cohen; phenomenology in Melucci and Searle; Wittgenstein and Winch in Elias, Giddens (alongside other influences), Dennett and Halstrup and the legacy of interactionism and constructionism at almost every turn. The new psychologists and philosophers of consciousness and recent sociologists are split between those harking back to past contributions and those forging resolutely ahead. Some, such as Armstrong and Archer, look back to Locke to inform their view of consciousness.[5] Others, ranging from Giddens to Dennett, see the discursive dimension as the prime mover. Here, the transcendental subject of metaphysics is as surplus to requirements as it was with Lévi-Strauss's prioritisation of structure. We have in both the new psychology and philosophy of consciousness and anthropology the rehearsal of the case for the supremacy of language and the counter-case which would seek to include consciousness as a prerequisite to being present with the world at all. Interestingly, and consistently, the former position cannot seem to confirm reality whilst for the later position reality is itself incontrovertible. Anthropology appears to have moved on from a concern with culture as a mental construct, or, for that matter, with culture itself as determinative. The awakening of awareness in *consciousness* in anthropology has been into quite alternative realities. The one stressing a private, essentially mentalistic landscape whilst the other recognises only a public world of social relationality and language, though the contributions themselves are diverse in their substantive concerns.

Searle has mustered for critical review the sheer range of contending paradigms in the new genre of psychology/philosophy of consciousness (see also Heil, 1998): views, as considered above, that say *either* that words that supposedly represent our inner states do not, in fact, do anything of the kind but just form a vocabulary – 'a manner of speaking' as Searle says – *or* that consciousness, as subjective, private and inner is not actually 'there', whereas the publicly, observable world 'is'; the 'eliminative materialists' who contend that mental states as such do not exist at all; 'functionalism' which holds that there is nothing specifically mental about so-called mental states; and 'computer functionalism', or what Searle dubbed the 'strong artificial intelligence' view, which equates properties of computers with the properties of consciousness. Searle has observed that few people nevertheless actually come straight out and say consciousness does not exist. What is admitted, he construes, is that Nagel (1986) and McGinn (1993) believe that the mind–body problem in terms of consciousness remains insoluble and that Dennett, despite all his apparent endeavours to the contrary, is not really persuaded by the idea of consciousness. McGinn, drawing on Kant, sees the mind as a noumenal realm with consciousness having a hidden structure not revealed to conscious beings themselves and suggests that Dennett is explaining away rather than explaining consciousness. (In recent times, it should be noted, Kantian Scholarship has entered into debate with the new theories of consciousness (see Ameriks (2000) on McGinn). By comparison Searle *is* convinced that we experience states of consciousness (subjective and qualitative) that are intrinsically mental and which cannot be reduced to other processes of objectively observable phenomena such as language. Jaynes, too, states that consciousness, although generated and accessed by language is not identical with it, though it is language that links into the characteristic spatial quality of consciousness in which introspection takes place – in turn, raising the question of exactly 'who' is doing the introspection: 'I', the self, an identity, for instance, in increasing levels of development. He says '[t]he basic connotative definition of consciousness is thus an analogue 'I' narratizing in a functional mindspace. The denotative definition is, as it was for Descartes, Locke and Hume, what is introspectable' (Jaynes, 1990, p. 450). With consciousness, in Jaynes's estimation, human beings can reflect on the past and 'look' into the future of imagination and have an apparent space to which they can return as they have a space in the physical world.

Social constructionism is characterised by both anti-essentialism and anti-realism; nothing goes on on the 'inside' of human beings and there is nothing on the outside in the material world of which we can be certain. In this view we exist at the linguistic interface of social relations (i.e., interaction) and we construct our own versions of reality. One dilemma, here, as Craib rightly points out, is how do we know we are constructing our own versions of reality if we have no direct sense of what that reality might be – or, it might be added, no 'sense' of *the* reality of which ours is a version? When everything is reduced to conversation or discourse the implication is that every morning we reinvent society. The fact that we are unable to do so suggests an implacable presence. Though Parker (1992) has attempted to arrest the apparent slide into relativism and has come up with a schema that he claims can account for reality existing outside of discourse, social constructionism sometimes appears to be intent on the reinvention of the wheel: rolling out the sociology of knowledge by another name, divested of Mannheim and Schütz; conveniently ignoring the 'essentialist' agenda of phenomenology; and reintroducing a disreputable *historicism* by the back door and so on. The idea that the external world exhibits *facticity* and the concepts of consciousness, reification and alienation rejected by social constructionism but used routinely by Berger *et al.*, suggests they, too, have been mistakenly co-opted as progenitors of modern social constructionism. Not only are philosophers and the work of theorists of language used selectively in this approach but the work of Mead is drawn upon in a tendentious fashion, largely ignoring the implication of the internal conversation in which the supra-personal 'I' is engaged. Craib points out that the capacity of subjective agency is denied by social constructionism leaving a similar conundrum to that bequeathed by Althusser and Lacan: for the subject to be 'hailed', 'interpellated' or recognise it is being called upon there must already be some properties of subjectivity in evidence. As Craib says, this dimension, the 'I' is 'that aspect of the psyche which might receive something from the outside and then make it its own, thus creating something different' (Craib, 1997, p. 5). The 'I', as the source of originality and creativity has been lost in social constructionism in Craib's view. With social constructionism perspicuity has replaced perspicacity and the opposition between social constructionism and realism is indeed 'sharp' (Shotter, 1993, p. 890). Though at some level language may be the technology of the self and we need language in full flow, it should not be a straight choice of *either* speaking 'out of' an inner plan of mental representation *or* 'into' an interpersonal, linguistic domain but *both*.

8

CONCLUSION

Whatever the subtle changes of meaning which have ultimately brought us, as a linguistic acquisition, the word and concept of consciousness, we enjoy direct access to what it designates. For we have the experience of ourselves, of that consciousness which we are, and it is on the basis of this experience that all linguistic connotations are assessed, and precisely through it that language comes to have any meaning at all for us.

(Merleau-Ponty, 1962, p. xv)

COMPONENTS OF CONSCIOUSNESS

This concluding chapter cannot hope to pull together all the threads woven throughout this discussion but a general pattern does begin to emerge with time. Consciousness cannot be dismissed out of hand because of its Cartesian 'infallible' past nor because it is seen to be just a rag-bag of properties (i.e., it can be nothing in its own right). We need to consider those properties anew including language which needs to be treated in a more measured way that may acknowledge flaws in its designs on the meaning of life. Its own variant on infallibilism cannot go unchallenged. This involves an attempt to 'conjugate' consciousness but in a quite different manner than has been the penchant of a great deal of recent social science which has looked askance at the prospect of thought reliant on memory and imagination and that a human being may be tired and emotional, deceitful and wilful and often lost for words. Hegel saw recollection, imagination and memory as steps on the road to thought, itself the last and main stage in the development of intelligence. The mind, by this token, cannot be grasped through compiling a catalogue of its capacities. These dimensions are present in the work of Hegel as part of the dynamic, dialectical unfolding of Reason and in Ryle in a much more static, though nonetheless heuristic, way. In contrast in this account they are referred to as co-present, component parts of consciousness not something to be transformed into something else by intellectual edict, i.e., less like the stations of the true cross history has to bear *or* self-sufficient, self-standing descriptions with no occult cause. Marxism, as a potential critical ally here, has tended to remain watchful but aloof: 'From the point of view of Marxism itself, nothing is more well-founded than Piaget's spirited comment in the name of the vast majority of psychologists, on how incongruous is the pretension of Bergsonism, existentialism or phenomenology, as philosophies, to construct a theory of memory, emotion or perception' (Sève, 1978, p. 391). But a materialist theory of these dimensions still requires articulation.

Self

If it is the case as James suggests – and Mead later concurs – that there are for a person as many different social selves as there are distinct groups about whose opinions he cares or individuals who recognise him and carry images of him in their minds, then the past 'self', too, when recalled to mind, informs the present self of its expectation. ('What would he think if he saw me now?') But can there be a self at 'rest' not caring for others' opinions, or would we be positing a void? Goffman's view is that to assume a self-conscious self behind a social self (or selves) would be to 'swallow' an empty PR operation when, in fact, there is no space for the deeper voice once language has been invoked. The alliance of self–identity–role, with the slippage from conscious self-narration to over-determined sociality, has not helped the analysis overall. But is the narrative self, as has been described in Chapter Six, the 'Non-substance self' of Hume? Indeed, Hume declared himself dissatisfied with the lack of internal consistency in his theory of personal identity. Is the stringing together of a 'silent' sentence of the same order as one thought inheriting the next ? The taking stock and the contrivance of distance between ourselves and any given *modus operandi* is not a deeper operator but one thought inheriting another thought – perhaps disconcerting and not germane to the performance – which, in turn, drags along other incongruous thoughts. The self is a pulse of recognition carried through memory. Parfit exclaims: 'The existence of a person, during any period, just consists in the existence of his brain and body, and the thinking of his thoughts, and the doing of his deeds, and the occurrence of many other physical and mental events' (Parfit, 1987, p. 275). He draws attentions to the Buddhist teaching that the individual is only a name of convention attributed to a set of elements and that actions and their consequences may exist but an acting person does not. The fire is not the same as it progresses, but overlooking such difference we indirectly call fire the continuity of its moments. In Parfit's view a person is that which has experiences, or is the subject of experiences, but not distinct from a brain and body and a series of mental and physical events. This reductionist view, however, is, according to Parfit, often hard to take in comparison with the non–reductionist view: most of us holding on to our continued existence as an all or nothing, deep further fact distinct from psychological and physical continuity. In contrast, Parfit declaims: 'I am not a series of thoughts, acts and experiences. I am the thinker of my thoughts, and the doer of my deeds. I am the subject of all my experiences, or the person who *has* these experiences' (p. 470). Parfit writes, movingly, that when he changed his view to accept the truth of himself in reductionist terms he found the realisation liberating and consoling, becoming more concerned about the lives of others and less so with the rest of his own life and his inevitable death.

Referring to the work of Parfit, who compares a person to a club that might go through different incarnations, lapses and reconstitutions, Dennett observes that this is the right kind of analogy, as 'selves are not independently existing soul-pearls, but artifacts of the social processes that create us, and, like other such artifacts, subject to sudden shifts in status. The only "momentum" that accrues to the trajectory of a self, or a club, is the stability imparted to it by the web of beliefs that constitute it, and when those beliefs lapse, it lapses, either permanently or temporarily' (Dennett, 1991, p. 423). Yet, Dennett remarks, if only in passing, that the belief in an enduring self where people are convinced that they are dealing with the same person come what may, could be well advised for its moral consequences. He says: 'There might even be good reasons – moral reasons – for trying to preserve the myth of selves as brain-pearls, particular concrete, countable things rather than abstractions, and for refusing to countenance the possibility of quasi-selves, semi-selves, transitional selves' (pp. 424–425). Notwithstanding the findings of philosophy and psychology, human beings work on the assumption that they have *a* self and that others are similarly so endowed. This is an assumed 'one to a customer' ration which stretches beyond quantity to quality in that the merchandise of the self or personality, however it is described, is thought to have the consistent brand of human nature. As has been seen, the substance self in this sense does not exist – even though it may be thought to. Should a reductionist view hold sway, the questions raised for consideration are, indeed, pressing: is a person sufficiently and enduringly the *same* to be accountable for their actions? does a person, on the reductionist account, have a sufficient interest and investment in their 'own' future? and how can sufficient space be conceived for the person to reflect on their actions or take disinterested stock?

In a recent account, Damasio (1999) tends to think of consciousness as the ability both to know of our existence and to know that the 'movie' being run in the brain actually belongs to us, i.e., a conception of the self. He suggests that we need a sense of our own self before we can know the Other, which tends to fly in the face of the findings of social thought, as we have seen, from Hegel to Mead which suggests that this process is, in fact, the other way around. Damasio is concerned to establish that not only do we have mental images, then, but that we know we are having them. He sees the self and the subjectivity it creates as the prerequisites of consciousness, with the self being constructed from the ground up – made up on the hoof and only problematised when things go wrong. Consciousness in this view is primarily creative, which enables the emergence of conscience (based on empathy). He contends a notion of identity can be reconstructed repeatedly on the basis of key events in an individual's autobiography, subjectivity depending, in great part, on the changes that take place in the body encompassing emotional states. This embodied self, thus aware, develops singularity out of the fact that we each have a body. Damasio (1996), admittedly, is close to Nietzsche, Merleau-Ponty and others here, though in contrast he divides consciousness into 'core consciousness' and 'extended consciousness', the former – not exclusively human – being concerned with the 'here and now' whilst the latter is individual identity which provides a sense of past and future.

Emotion

What we need to be clear about is that consciousness is a creature of mood and emotion. At one point Descartes remarks that 'the mind depends so much on the temperament and disposition of the bodily organs' (Descartes, 1997, p. 111) and the idea of 'will' in Schopen-hauer or 'life' in Simmel, forced kicking and screaming into the forms of concepts and culture, never forsakes an emotional, untrammelled dynamism. Emphasis on emotions as revelatory of our world is evident in Sartre, as it is for the existentialists more generally. Heidegger stressed mood, as does Searle, and emotion, in modern times, features strongly in a range of work stretching from Brentano to Damasio, most recently. Jaynes's view is that the self is forged as consciousness of who we are in relation to others but this occurrence is not cold and rational but essentially emotional, where images of an experience can be held in consciousness evoking a continuing response, though continuity in consciousness is illusory. Ornstein, too, stresses the role of emotions in consciousness, which operate on a different brain 'circuit' to the rational mind. He contends that emotions appeared first in human evolution and are at the front line experientially. They inform us as to what is important to remember and memory is ordered for recall by its initial emotional charge. Ornstein regards mental processes as being organised around emotional ideals rather than around thought or reason. Emotions are the chief organising system of the mind which they direct towards a particular outcome – short-circuiting deliberation. Bringing to mind Hume and Nietzsche, Ornstein remarks that emotions set our agenda without us being aware of them: 'Far from being disorganizing, they are the focal point of the mental system's activity: They govern our choices, they determine our goals, and they guide our lives. We are, for the most part, in most of life their servants and we are usually not conscious of them (Ornstein, 1992, p. 96). For many purposes, then, emotions *are* the mind.

Though he envisages a mismatch between the 'quicksilver' fast comprehension of images and emotions which are on the time scale of seconds and minutes, Damasio stresses the ability to feel emotions, with consciousness emerging from within based on emotions not resulting from a top-down process based on language. Consciousness is built on emotions and informs our reasoning capacity. Pinker, too, has contended that there has been an exaggeration of the influence of language on thought, which is all the more the case in relation to feeling. In Pinker's view emotions have been written-off prematurely as so much non-adaptive baggage. Yet, emotions work together with the intellect and are indispensable to the way the mind works as a whole: 'The emotions are mechanisms that set the brain's highest–level goals. Once triggered by a propitious moment, an emotion triggers the cascade of subgoals and sub-subgoals that we call thinking and acting' (Pinker, 1998, p. 373). Emotions mobilise the body and mind to meet the challenges of life, though this kind of sequence would no doubt be described by Ryle as a 'para-mechanical myth'.

Will

In their different ways, both Schopenhauer and Nietzsche, as we have seen, introduced *will* as the supersession of the problematic of consciousness. In fact, in Schopenhauer's voluntarism the *will* becomes reality. Nevertheless, the apparently radical legacy of irrationalism in cutting a swathe through consciousness was insufficiently swingeing for Ryle as it still considered volition an inveterate inner state (or, at least, a non-linguistic one). It would seem that even Spinoza's *conatus* would be rejected on the same grounds. Ryle makes clear that volition is *in* the mind as a species of conscious process and the output of internal forces. This is opposed to enactment and in Ryle's view the two have been linked in a mysterious connection. The mystery is soluble for Ryle if the first half of the nexus is dropped entirely; helped, no end, if we recite the mantra: no occult precursors to overt acts. He leaves us facing the prospect of only hazarded guesses that the action was ever willed and attests that the traditional tripartite split of mentality into Thought, Feeling and Will (or Cognitive, Emotional and Conative modes) is a curio of theory and a welter of confusions and false inferences. Departing from this model, the search for the final solution to the question of consciousness – resulting in *will* for Schopenhauer and Nietzsche, *Being* for Heidegger and *language* for Wittgenstein and Ryle – has led to a more exclusive essentialism. Alongside consciousness, the most obvious victims for redundancy have been memory and imagination with reason, too, not having any security of tenure. The worst of all possible worlds is where, within this sub-set, one power is seen to be in mutually exclusive partnership with another: rational knowledge and feeling in Schopenhauer, reason and the passions in Hume or imagination and reason in Vico, for example. Either one is seen as more primitive or powerful than the other or one an earlier stage of development to the other when, in fact, reason may temper passion and be fired by imagination at one and the same time.

Memory

In Locke and, particularly, in Hume, memory is definitive of self and identity and, therefore, consciousness – though it does appear to run counter to the discrete connectedness of the 'association of ideas' as presented by Hume and other British empiricists, where such ideas are represented as 'mental atoms which preserved their identity and integrity unmodified by their neighbours in the chain of association; they attract each other when charged by repeated and recurrent con-tinguities [sic], but they remain distinct like beads on a string. The opposing hypothesis . . . invokes Heraclitean and William Jamesian metaphors of rivers and streams, which represent our memories fusing with each other to form our consciousness of our own past experience – immediate, middle distant, and distant past: my continuous inner experience, the world as it presents itself to me but not to anyone else' (Hampshire, 1992, p. 121). Certainly there is a distinction to be drawn in the fashion of Kierkegaard, between recollection as an implicit, unmediated imprint of the past – a whole archive without index – and memory as an explicit, mediated worked-up remembering in narrative of experience which thus *becomes* memory. Memory is taken from history and is returned to it, whilst recollection remains outside of time; memory stands out noisily from a background of sitting, silent recollection. Yet, though memory may be mistaken or mislaid, recollection itself stubbornly remains. Hampshire's view is that although literal descriptions of memory can be utilised, this 'immense' and 'sprawling phenomenon', which comprises the largest part of our 'inner life', is captured best by use of metaphor. As Bergson found, the confused, emotionally charged, interpenetrating and unmechanical properties of memory and its constant accretions lend themselves, often, *only* to metaphor. Yet memory is so pervasive and predominant in connecting a large part of our mental lives that perhaps it is definitive: 'So dense and heavy are memories in the human mind, sustained by reflection and by description in a language, that some philosophers, conspicuous among them Bergson, have claimed that the memory-relationship constitutes the dividing-line between two categories of being, mental things and material things' (Hampshire, 1992, p. 120).

As described in the work of Bergson, Freud, Benjamin and others (Proust, for example, whose view was that memory was triggered involuntarily), consciousness can be seen as the capacity to prevent the world as perceived overloading memory and, in turn, to prevent memory pervading the living moment at will. A mechanism called *perceptual filtering* ensures that, of all the information arriving at one's eyes or ears at any given time, only a small proportion is actually registered and even briefly remembered. Memory can be divided into conscious memory and affective, emotional or unconscious memory, which unlike its conscious counterpart cannot be recalled to consciousness if not originally encoded in those terms. Psychology has identified eidetic (childhood) and linear (adulthood) memory; recognition and recall memory; working and reference memory; primary and secondary memory and, of course, most renowned, short- and long-term memory. In addition, the medium of memory has been seen to differ markedly: *verbal* as opposed to *visual* memory; *naming* in contrast to *doing* memory, and *declarative* as distinct from *procedural* memory. In addition, Tulving (see Rose, 1993, p. 120) subdivided such predominantly *declarative* memory into *episodic* (of one's own experience) and *semantic* (a wider historical context) memory. The very speed of language acquisition suggests that complex networking is set in train in the memory of a child, but the intensity, perhaps for survival purposes, does not last as we begin to select key features and prejudge the importance of in-puts – some things have to be forgotten in order to remember others. In adult life we selectively remember events to fit in with our self-perception and create and recreate ourselves through memory; in fact memory is selective, reconstructing history and biography in line with a project for the future. Memory is an active process and Rose says that 'one of the problems of studying memory is precisely that it is a dialectical phenomenon. Because each time we remember, we in some senses do work on and transform our memories; they are not simply being called up from store and, once consulted, replaced unmodified. Our memories are recreated each time we remember' (Rose, 1993, p. 91). Remembering, in Bartlett's view, does not involve retrieving a pristine memory trace from a memory store of one's past experience but is, in fact, constructed to order in the process of remembering itself. We fit our experiences into a mental template which Bartlett (see Rose, 1993) referred to as a *schema* wherein currently active information is what is available for recall and is often caught out by, for us, the non-sequitur emanating from someone else's current memory *schema*. Memory is responsive to our current predicament and priorities and is worked-up accordingly; it is not a store or a filing system or an archive in the basement of the brain. In fact classification is done differently on different days depending on circumstance, but most emphatically draws upon imagination.

Imagination

If one were to compare the approach of Sartre and Ryle to the question of imagination – writing in the same decade (1940s) – we would have a microcosm of the debate for and against consciousness right down to their respective styles of presentation. In fact, Schopenhauer's remark in chapter four on measuring the tower by its shadow comes to mind in Ryle's case. Drawing on symbolic interactionism, where all the acts of an individual in their public existence are set off against the gestures and intentions of their fellows, Robert E. Park suggested that individuals invade one another's lives and live in the minds of others. Echoing Cooley, he remarked: 'For man is a creature such that when he lives at all, he lives in his imagination, and, through his imagination, in the minds of other men, who share with him not merely their possessions, but their hopes and their dreams' (Park, 1927, p. 738). People *do* project outcomes in their imagination before execution *and* engage in occult operations. Though Marx may have been aligned latterly with the linguistic approach, he was, in fact, in no doubt whatsoever about the distinctive, mentalistic properties of imagination. Aristotle had considered that art consisted in conception of the intended outcome before its material realisation, and such insight influenced Marx. What distinguishes human creation from the instinctual forms generated by other creatures is the use of imagination. In Marx's example, before the architect erects the structure in reality, she has already raised it in her imagination. This is true, moreover, of every labour-process: conception in imagination before the task commences. With human beings work is both conscious and purposive, ordered by the power of conceptual thought. Human beings form in their minds the ends to which they labour and they are, at the same time, transformed by that labour: they are its special product. Labour, facilitated by imagination, is the force which created humankind. Moreover, with the separation of conception and execution, labour becomes a social phenomenon wherein the ideas of one may be realised by another. Symbolic representation and the use of language transform a rudimentary capacity into a world-transforming force. But imagination remains the power that transcends the instinctual and enables us to recognise Others as more than an instinctive force to be feared. Through imagination we have the means to enter into their lives, partake of their natures and cultivate fully social relations.

Language

In the last years of the twentieth century theorists of language – or of the body for that matter – have seen fit to rest their case without calling the unreliable witness of consciousness. In effect, the accounts of language and of consciousness are deemed mutually exclusive. It is intriguing to speculate whether post-Wittgensteinian philosophy of language can meet the disparate aspirations of the loose confederation and wide constituency who currently draw sustenance from it. It was, in fact, conceived less like manna and more like a crash diet. Though it is to be suspected that he associates post-Marxism with Lukács and the Frankfurt School rather than himself, the Marxist Balibar holds that there is no meta-linguistic level – an explicit insight he attributes to Wittgenstein. Similarly, Harré tends to imply that everything lies 'exposed', whilst Hastrup alludes to selves only solvent in social contexts and so on. Wittgenstein's point is that whilst there might be esoteric reaches of mental terms of reference, in general expressions allegedly alluding to *mind*, the place, are, in fact, really actions or descriptions of actions. The ability to say how things are is not to be confused with being able to 'perceive' or see that condition. We should not countenance a verbal 'description' of a private 'perception' to describe how things are with us (a privileged perception) amounting to descriptions of objects on a private stage; in fact we have 'manifestations' and 'expressions' as *criteria* of others having inner experiences. Wittgenstein is at pains to point up the misconception of the classical picture of the 'inner' as privileged access, as observations at a private peep-show, lying hidden behind the 'outer'. In fact, the 'inner' and 'outer' are not merely edged with metaphor but are made out of the whole cloth and as metaphor, as such, is unimaginable outside speech, so stands the décor of the mentalistic interior. Self-knowledge does not come out of a transparency of the mental and we mistakenly interpret a grammatical connection for a metaphysical one. By the same token the assumption that we can only *know* others indirectly, by analogy, is equally misconceived. It is permissible to speak of *knowing* what someone else is thinking if not what I'm thinking.

'Form of life' in this view amounts to the practices of a linguistic community with 'practice' and 'the practical' being stressed consistently along with the public criteria of its context. Goethe's ironic play that '[i]n the beginning was the deed' is embraced by Wittgenstein as company for his own maxim that people agree in language. But once the habitual 'form of life' has been invoked there is only description and acceptance. There is no transcendent impulse to overcome or even question, and any critique of custom in the modern world is, by implication, redundant. No sanction for reflexivity, then, but advocacy of self-justifying, uncritical, ordinary speech. We have here emphasis on the concrete practices of life as opposed to abstract thought, reason and a contested social order. It is no wonder that critics such as Gellner (1992) have levelled at Wittgenstein the charge of irrationalism and conservatism. The fact that utterances may be accountable at an interpersonal level does not logically gainsay this accusation. There may also be integrity in silence but the drift is toward uncritical acceptance, and not only in a political sense. Wittgenstein is concerned with what lies before us rather than with speculation on something mysterious. What is concealed does not interest us he says pointedly and it is the very fact of searching for the *essence* of a thing that has led us astray. In rectifying this perhaps Wittgenstein's concern was not to rule out of court that which cannot be said but to preserve and conserve it. It is to misunderstand him to assume he is fictionalising mental states of various kinds. Though behaviour might be seen as not distinct from the expression, minds or souls do not behave. The person is stressed by Wittgenstein *not* the brain and though it is not something necessarily inwardly critically resourceful or equipped for conflict in a contested social order we get a rounded view of the human being by these lights.

In Habermas's estimation, too, the transition from the exhausted paradigm of the philosophy of consciousness to the model of a communication community he proposes not only breaks out of the vacillation between metaphysical and anti-metaphysical thinking, between idealism and materialism, but makes possible an attack on a problem beyond the reach of the concepts of metaphysics: the problem of individuality. This appears superficially attractive, as it does with Wittgenstein, but Habermas's attack on consciousness is accompanied by an assault on a teleological, individualistic concept of action. In fact, the project of emancipation at a personal, psychological level seemed never Habermas's concern. We have, instead, the mutual understanding of inter-subjectivity as a replacement for the philosophy of the subject. Even in his early work we find the claim that autonomy and responsibility are posited for us in the structure of language with emphasis focused on understanding and coming to agreement. Variable contexts are transcended to leave room for the universal of the 'ideal speech situation' where the force of the better argument prevails. In the idealised world of Habermas's *Communicative Action* (c.a.) there is a presumption of a certain kind of *reason* which is not a function of the c.a. process itself for c.a. to work at all, i.e., certain mental attributes and capacities (for example the ability for judgement and juxtaposition) would have to be in evidence. At a further level this may encompass a predication on altruism or, at very least, require a rejection of out and out natural self-interest. Here, implicitly, might be the raw material for the emergence of the moral point of view c.a. seems to require. The catch-22 is that in his later work, Habermas (1995) sees c.a. actually creating this kind of post-conventional ego. There is no real conception of actors coming to that situation with their own unique 'back–pack' of experience, some aspects of which will have fallen short of the standards of c.a. Through the life-course this will range from exposure to inadequate child-rearing practice and socialisation (which will affect language acquisition) to lack of self-esteem and self-confidence. Limited material practice, insecurity and lack of trust – notwithstanding the effect of failure in education – will blight the prospects of c.a. for many. There is an assumption that c.a. forms a solution in its own right, applicable in

all times and places in the modern world but without any demonstration of any organic connection with real problems. In fact, c.a.
may form a distraction from real problems or act as a sop to
discontent.

It is almost as if there is a hypothetical, ideal state which is used as a
reference point or point of comparison against which the prevailing
situation can be judged. In this hypothetical state there is a rational
consensus against which all other claims to truth and knowledge can
be tested. Habermas, it seems, does tend to try to account for the kind
of social organisation that this would entail but rather than its scale
or context he is largely preoccupied with the 'ideal speech situation'
whereby truth and knowledge is connected with justice and freedom.
(In the way in which knowledge 'emerges' in this approach there are
marked similarities with Rousseau's idea of 'the general will'.) It
would appear undoubtedly problematic, however, to have the socialist project rest upon the construction of a hypothetical state of perfect
rationality totally disconnected from historical practice and for Habermas to flow from the very structure of language not just from the
'force of the better argument'. Unfortunately, for Habermas, and for
others who pin their hopes on the communicative act, the world is
not entirely tractable in that way. The utopian ideal of discourse
ethics envisages everyone's participation on equal terms but participation in the ideal speech situation is not a right, or a possibility, for
all. Theorists as divergent as Bernstein (1965) and Bourdieu (1977;
1986) have shown how language codes and cultural capital and competence get between those who need to talk and the conference table.
Gramsci and Bourdieu have both indicated that the working class are
deprived of a 'political tongue' and Marcuse saw ordinary people as
being deprived of language as a critical intellectual tool. Hegel,
Nietzsche and Heidegger each suspected that what language there
was available was in imminent danger of becoming a debased coinage
and Bataille informs us that '[l]anguage assembles the totality of what
has meaning for us, but fragments it at the same time . . . Our attention remains directed toward that whole which slips away from us in
a series of statements, but we cannot reach the point at which the
flashes of successive statements yield to the grand illumination'
(Bataille, quoted in Habermas, 1990, pp. 236–237). The echo of
Nietzsche here is insistent as it is in Foucault. There may be a
recognition in that quarter, too, that our political and moral world

is characterised more by a struggle unto death amongst moral opponents than it is by a conversation between them (see Benhabib, 1992, p. 33).

Sociology has traditionally been concerned with explaining the supervalence of the social order and, on occasion, most typically when inspired by Marx, has reflected on its supervention, and a sociological analysis of consciousness reflects this tension of being determined *and* determining. In fact, the question of order has been transformed from the Hobbesian conflictual idea of the war of all men against all men (with its attendant view of human nature), via functionalist emphasis on norms and values, to a state – with ethno-methodology for example – where order is an accomplishment of such accounting practices by which and through which it is articulated and justified. In addition, in the same period the emphasis has changed from the effect of the systemic level to that of the significance of rule – following as the real fabric of the truly social. In the post-Cartesian world the private, unspoken presence to ourselves is dis-interred into a public, linguistic behavioural world; the mutability and flux of thought (albeit thought being the thinker) is transfigured by the mutability and flux of discourse and identity, and the individual of choice and reason, even of *will*, is exchanged for the decentred party (line) to communicative action. It is forgotten that exploit (of word and deed) begets exploitation under precise social and historical conditions – largely without a 'by your leave'.

THE REACH OF REALITY

This discussion of consciousness has only indirectly constituted a platform for a realist social science but that is where its sympathies lie. However, what became clear from the review of a range of perspectives in chapter seven was that not only were mind and consciousness to be doubted but so, too, was reality. The magnitude of Berkeley's achievement in dispensing with reality is often remarked upon (Robinson (1995); Heil (1998)) as is how difficult it is, as a position, to refute. In effect, Berkeley closes off a real world to us as conclusively as Wittgenstein shuts off consciousness. Hume's rendering of external reality as a harmless illusion is equally hard to see off but fundamentally flawed as is his insistence on causation as a customary connection of a habit of mind. The idea of Hume's of the

Non-substance self can, though, be usefully retained. The means to
gainsay Berkeley and Hume is by rendering experience as a primarily
collective praxis in a social and historical world *not* an individualistic
and mentalistic phenomenon. The premise that things have no existence except in being perceived or conceptualised should now be in
jeopardy. So, too, should the insistent translation of questions about
being into statements about knowing (Bhasker's 'epistemic fallacy')
so that the problem of what there is is consistently subsumed to the
rather different problem of what we can know. Similarly, if we can
enter into relations only with meanings – as the Vienna Circle, for
example, contends – consciousness is not identifiable with what we
are. What needs to be contested is the presumption that language and
inter-subjectivity are the only levels of reality there are. Human
beings most certainly inhabit an inner-world and encounter an aso-
cial world surrounding them. The prospect is, then, human subjectivity and human life that is not entirely social. Additionally, the idea of
multiple realities in the work of James, Schütz and others can end up
as the social equivalent of living in our own removed, mentalistic
world. Though a useful idea, we should perhaps place the 'reality'
here in inverted commas. As it stands it is similar to the emphasis on a
range of social identities or of situated contexts where we are often
given the impression of transcendence and voluntary take-up in use.
Everyday life, as a supremely social phenomenon, is not *the* paramount reality, as that honour goes to reality itself which frames the
fortunes of social experience. Merleau-Ponty, in fact, says '[t]he real
is a closely woven fabric. It does not await our judgement before
incorporating the most surprising phenomena, or before rejecting the
most plausible figments of out imagination' (Merleau-Ponty, 1962,
p. x).
   Although Marxist realism introduces hidden structures, mechanisms and systems of relationships underlying and accounting for
observable consciousness and social relations, it is not clear that reality *is* always hidden. There are dissenters in the history of Marxism.
For Dietzgen, (see Pannekoek, 1975) phenomena appear or occur
and that is all there is to it. Whether in view by human perception or
no, there is only the totality of the world of appearances – a world in
a perpetual state of flux. Here meet in Dietzgen not only strands of
Marxism but those of Heraclitus in the distant past and Nietzsche of
the immediate future. Indeed, if it is assumed that the indubitable

reality is the experienced world of phenomena it is only a short step to conflate the opposition of appearance and reality. Heidegger and Wittgenstein may feature to some extent as realists. In fact, several of the theorists arraigned in this book for their anti-essentialism consider themselves, at least in part, realists. Taylor describes Heidegger as an 'uncompromising realist' (Taylor, 1992b, p. 163) and, indeed, the world exists and is what it is independently of people for Heidegger, but if there is no *Dasein*, no understanding of Being, there can be no conception of what it is independent things are. He is obviously plying a depth model with references to 'surface appearances' and 'moving on to a deeper plane' but he rejected the idea that appearance and reality are always in a contradictory, oppositional relation – appearance can be disclosive. Appearance is not merely imagined and subjective for Heidegger as it was for Kant. Sartre, too, believed that appearance revealed essence rather than concealing it. Real structures as existing independently of the patterns of events they generate and independently of our knowledge of them, as Bhasker (1989a,b) outlines, may not require hiddenness, however. The dammed realm of noumenal 'things-in themselves' is breached if things are seen to have manifestable latent and emergent properties including consciousness as emergent from the brain.

It would appear that one philosopher's hidden structure is another philosopher's noumenal realm. The fine line between these two has been redrawn in recent times in the new philosophy and psychology of consciousness. McGinn (1991) has traced back the divide to the work of Kant and Wittgenstein. He is of the opinion that whilst Kant's appeal is to a noumenal realm to span the gulf between consciousness and its physical embodiment (brain process), Wittgenstein's recommendation is not to let the gulf open up at all. In other words, avoid taking language on vacation to the resort of misplaced speculation and keep it employed in ordinary, everyday use. Though Wittgenstein, thus, turns away from the 'hidden' in the theory of mind, McGinn, concurring with Kant, is persuaded by the prospect of hidden dimensions of consciousness. In fact, theorists whose views diverge in their particulars have each described consciousness in broadly realist terms but their interpretation of what this might mean differs radically with one party despairing of an early solution, or a solution at all, to the problem of consciousness. Whilst Nagel (1986) advocates an integrated theory of reality to account for much of what

we do not know at present, McGinn holds that we can find intellectual significance in the existence of a reality we cannot know.
Nagel believes there will be some way forward that we now do not
yet understand, whilst McGinn is sceptical of even that level of progress. His belief in a mind-independent reality involves an acknowledgement that some reality will for ever remain beyond our ken – an
idea he traces back to Locke. In contrast, Flanagan (1992) and Searle
(1994), each in their different way, take both Nagel and McGinn to
task for mis-stating the nature of the mind–brain relation and, in the
process, confounding a realist approach to the problem, though they
themselves are far from being at one on the question of the 'hidden'
dimension of consciousness. Searle tends to talk in terms of higher
and lower levels of a system as a whole. Consciousness is a higher-
level feature of the brain and caused by its lower-level neuro-
biological processes just as the liquidity of water occurs at a "higher"
level than the microstructures (combustible gas molecules) that go to
make it up. There is nothing metaphysical about consciousness here,
then, for Searle; the appearance of consciousness *is* its reality. The
approach taken in this book broadly agrees with Flanagan and
Searle, though the mind–brain relation makes different kinds of
demands on realist method than when investigation is concerned
with the contents of consciousness.

What we cannot afford to do is to be content with the prospect of
distinct physical, mental (noumenal or ineffable) and social (multiple
real) worlds, with language and social interaction being the warp and
weft that weaves such reality together (see Hodgkiss in López and
Potter (ed.), 2001). We need to hold on to the physical, mental and
social worlds having peculiar emergent properties and potential
which may be unrealised in any of the other 'worlds' at given points
in time. Moreover, we should be concerned not with mere states of
affairs or existing practice but with how they come to pertain and,
thus, with the composition of their arrangement: poetically to look
into the seeds of time to say which grains will grow and which will
not. In depth realism the unfolding of multiple strata of ordered
layers is a far cry from models of multiple realities beginning with
James. In fact, reality *per se* does not lapse when our attention is
drawn elsewhere. However, within critical realism, the most recent
and most concerted assault on empiricism, idealism and social constructionism, opinion is divided on consciousness: Archer (1995) and

Bhasker seem to court a reflexive consciousness whilst others, such as Collier (1994), are less persuaded. This may well be symptomatic of critical realism's anxiety about consciousness *reflecting* the reality of which it is a part without the space for an inward reflexivity. The approach taken in this book has tended to look towards a successionist-emotional self were one thought is not only inherited by the next but is subject to its critical scrutiny. Nevertheless, the case for realism, which has to be pressed at every opportunity is helped by recognition of collective consciousness as a confirmation of the world beyond the individual and inter-subjective level.

THE INSIDE-OUT OF COLLECTIVE CONSCIOUSNESS

Nicholas Humphrey has charted the change of meaning of the word *conscious*. Deriving from the Latin, *conscious* suggests to know together with others, i.e., to share knowledge with people (Hobbes, as we have seen, was familiar with this sense). Humphrey suggests that the import of this changed over time from designating a potentially wide circle of persons to indicate, instead, a small circle of confidants. He says the circle came to be drawn tighter and tighter, narrower and narrower, until it encompassed just a single person, i.e., a subject who was conscious. The meaning of the word *conscious* underwent a further shift when it was introduced into English in the Middle Ages. Knowledge of one's own secret actions, *conscience*, came to be split off from being *conscious* of one's innermost private feelings and thoughts. The meaning of the word *conscious*, then, has undergone a volte-face from having shared knowledge to having only intimate and exclusive knowledge of oneself. Humphrey concludes that 'it is clear that by far and away the more common modern English meaning of "to be conscious" is to have knowledge of one's own private feelings and thoughts. Most of the earlier uses are not only no longer current, they are not allowable. Indeed today it would generally no longer be considered either natural or correct (although it might be understood) to say "I am conscious of" about anything other than a personal fact' (Humphrey, 1993, p. 101). It is not possible with consciousness, however, out of perversity or preference, to jettison essential dimensions of analysis on grounds of intellectual integrity or economy. After remarking, quite correctly, that consciousness, designating a shared social or communal knowledge was the earliest usage of the term, Guzeldere (in Block *et al.*, 1997) says he will put aside the *social* conception of consciousness – to concentrate on the more *psychological* conception – thereby approximately halving the size of the literature in need of examination. He is not untypical of his school in this, as has been seen, but it won't do. There are, however, precious few exceptions. As someone who is persuaded of the incontrovertibility of external reality, Searle (1999) allows himself the luxury of positing *collective intentionality*. The traditional choices seem to have led to becoming mired in either methodological individualism or, conversely, an ethereal, Hegelian Absolute Spirit in which we all, perforce, partake. Searle's view is that rather than beginning with a first-person-singular position, the idea of 'we-believe', 'we-intend' and so on is, in fact, primitive and a fundamental social building block. The *social* conception is essential to our understanding of what consciousness might be and he is convinced, quite rightly, that we need to rediscover the social character of the mind.

How to get from the singular to the plural is, however, perhaps *the* most difficult problem facing any analysis of consciousness. The recent history of social thought has witnessed, not the connexion of these two 'parts' of experience, but, instead, the abandonment of the *inner* realm to the constituency of the *outer* inter-subjective, linguistic domain. The problematic legacy of Cartesianism for the way in which inter-subjectivity is conceived is that mind and subjectivity are viewed as a private 'substance' directly accessible by means of introspection and that we know the existence of other minds by analogy with this process. Whilst our own minds can be known, others can be inferred. In consequence, those following Descartes have countenanced the connecting up of the subjectivity of one mind to another in seriality, whilst approaches critical of that assumption (culminating in Wittgenstein) have registered, instead, recognition of common appropriation from a public realm. If consciousness has been propelled on to the 'outside', as is clear from much of the debate reviewed above, we have to be pretty sophisticated about what we take the 'outside' to be. This is all the more imperative if the 'turning-out' of consciousness has been accompanied, as it so often has, by theories of the social construction of the self. Concepts such as the self at one level and motives at another have been relocated in social-linguistic space, yet the exorcising of consciousness from its lair has left the social objective world, ironically enough, as depthless and empty as its subjective alter ego. Though consciousness has been driven out into the open, the exact dimensions of that extension have remained largely closed to scrutiny. The models that reduce all to language not only deny depth to human beings but also deprive social reality of inherent quality. The social world does not, and cannot, exist independently of the striations of power, conflict and struggle – that is what it is.

In the history of sociology an imputed relation between the collectivity and consciousness has often featured in high profile. For Marx as for Durkheim, in their different ways, consciousness is the necessary product of the collective experience – whether it be the mode of production of material life or society. To entertain consciousness independently of the wider constituency does not, then, make a great deal of sense. Yet, as he has been seen, once that fact has been established there is scope for consideration of how the primary determination might be overcome or transcended. Marx's projection of a 'class for itself' emerging from a 'class in itself' is of this order, though how this emancipation actually comes about in practice is a highly contingent and historically specific affair. In contrast, not only is it an aggregate of individuals who come to constitute a class for Weber, but class cannot be construed as a class 'in itself' in the fashion of Marx and, by the same token, never amount to a class 'for itself'. Classes are not communities in Weber's estimation and consciousness of common life chances is, therefore, unthinkable. (For Weber's individual, too, consciousness of life chances is severely limited.) Reflecting this, in the phenomenological tradition, Schütz remarked that we should not forget that 'whereas the conscious experiences of typical individuals are quite conceivable, the conscious experiences of a collective are not' (Schütz, 1967, p. 199). In reading off the one from the other people have been led to take the imputed metaphor too literally, but what is missing in a concept of 'action' of a social collective is a subjective meaning-context that is at all conceivable. Nevertheless, he sees the analysis of the subjective meaning of the collectivity as an important sociological task. The work of the Chicago School had placed undoubted stress on collective action rather than structure as the real measure of community, exhibiting an emphasis, too, on various kinds of collective behaviour. Subsequent developments, often on the cusp between sociology and an emergent symbolic interactionism, demonstrated a concern with the way in which perceptions generated out of individual perspectives are modified and become adapted to each other as a collective phenomenon. Usually, however, the level of abstraction remained in the range of institutional and occupational settings. Coverage of the spontaneous integration of partial perspectives into a collective pattern at a social level remained relatively limited. The degree of difficulty of attaining a 'take-off trajectory' to collective consciousness was demonstrated, if implicitly, by the structural-functionalist school of sociology. Drawing on Durkheim, the functionalist position made it clear that values, internalised through socialisation, act to canalise motivation whilst values themselves are constitutive of a person's sense of identity. In this situation values are associated with ranges of approved action; in other words, actors are steeped in a normative order.

Habermas intimates how personality comes under pressure as motivational crises set in alongside the reification of communicative practice of everyday life, i.e., the reification of interpersonal relations in systematically distorted communication. This is the point of reference for investigating pathogenesis in Habermas's account. The fragmentation of 'everyday consciousness', where local scattered perspectives remain diffuse and unarticulated, stabilises late capitalist modernity. The fragmented structures of modern consciousness are, thus, unable to comprehend the intrusion of system imperatives. Not only is fragmentation at issue here but also the cultural impoverishment of everyday consciousness. An adequate explanatory scenario for Habermas would forgo serving a critique of ideology and seeking for the tattered remnants of revolutionary consciousness and, instead, consider the conditions for 'recoupling' an everyday communication resting on vital traditions with a rationalised culture. In his concern with universal human emancipation he has developed a sequence begining with an impoverished communicative infrastructure of the life world leading to movements to protect communities, promoting, in turn, personal identities which celebrate the particular and provincial. Latterly, Giddens (1991) has pointed out that there is a tension between what he calls 'emancipatory politics' and 'life politics'. The former involves the primary imperatives of justice, equality and participation and centres around life-chances whilst the latter is a politics of choice closely associated with a desired life-style. He refers to the reflexive project of the self, in which we 'make ourselves' as persons, in relation to life politics, but not, interestingly enough, to raised consciousness in the case of emancipatory politics. The life decisions of life politics do not concern the conditions of liberation attendant on emancipatory politics; choices can be made not withstanding extant social relations. In Archer's view Giddens's structuration theory 'does not offer a concept of collective action and has very little indeed to say about social movement, collective conflict or corporative control' (Archer, 1995, p. 252). It should be added that structuration theory is not unique in this as it would be equally true of ethnomethodology, post-Wittgensteinian philosophy and social constructionism, at very least. What they would have in common that would incline them against the prospect of collective action, or collective consciousness for that matter, is primarily twofold: the denial of the kind of continuity of consciousness and personal identity that would have a stake in 'its' future (i.e., a projected progress across time), and the closing up of the space required for the self to reflect on its social and public character. Laclau and Mouffe (1995) deny the very idea of an evolving consciousness enclosed within a dialectic of recognition with all its essentialist implications and evocation of a logic in history. Post-modernism and post-structuralism, more generally, has stressed the contingent and indeterminate nature of social existence and the relative openness of the future. Identities are worked-up discursively in relations of power with others; each identity internally validated and not seeking transcendent grounds outside it.

There can be no collectivity of whatever sort without some measure of commonality and communication of a significant difference. The paradox is that whilst individual identity emphasises difference at one level, collective identification emphasises similarity at the other and, it should be added, the recognition and prioritisation of that similarity. The ways in which one can pull against the other, as has been indicated, are various and extensive. The term identity designates either a state of being the same or what individual persons are taken, or take themselves, to be. Consciousness has a part to play in both these definitions of identity. For Hegel and Marx the ultimate aim was to get from the one, self identity, to the other, being the same. In discussing the tangible outcome of the Master–Slave dialectic, Hegel refers to the awareness of the identity of self and Other as the intuition of their specific identity with each other. The idea is one of individuals mutually throwing light upon one another. For him, the agent as individual and universal is forever fundamentally one identity. This emphasis appears to be at odds with the post-structuralist emphasis on the play of *difference*. One crucial thread that can be pulled out of Hegel's multi-textured analysis is that we each have to become the Other – to genuinely possess them – in order to be ourselves and, in so doing, we overcome in the process the ossified dualism of self and Other, i.e., when we recognise the Other is actually our self. Similarly, for Mead the self is not a self until it becomes an object for itself. The consequence of this is that we stand outside ourselves and view ourselves as would another and, in addition, come to grasp that every other person is in reality (like) us. It is with that knowledge, acquired systematically, and the achievement of standing outside of our own minds that we are best equipped to return to being in the world. Yet, in Hegel's system individuals are outwitted by the Absolute Idea as it unfolds; they remain unconscious of that with which they are, allegedly, at one. Hegel's system is inadequate as a measure of collective consciousness as, ultimately, real human beings do not figure. This *shared* consciousness is not worked-up by individuals as a collective response to their experience and practice – *it* possesses them. Whilst the knowing subject in Hegel's system appears actively engaged in historical struggle with the world, coming to see that what lies behind experience is actually themselves embodied in and by that activity, the claim that the knowing subject is thereby not a detached observer but a fully concrete human subject is ultimately only notional. Hegel' s entire system – which is contradictory as well as dialectical – decrees that individuals should be the passive instruments of events.

Consciousness as a property of the collectivity is first of all the capacity to adopt an ex-centric position. Identity, which is taken so often in the literature as the most obvious first step to a collectivity-consciousness, requires psychological distance to come into play; to be that identity and not, at the same time. This is to see an identity from above and beyond as others see it; to transcend being trapped in that identity in its immediacy. According to Plessner (quoted in Schacht, 1971, pp. 234–236) distance is required to facilitate insightful perception into the human condition – to see it as for the first time with *Other eyes*. We would have to emerge from that in which we were formerly immersed – the cultural 'zone of familiarity' – in order to see things for what they are. Anything too close and too immediate will elude the alienated grasp necessary to bring the obvious and long familiar to expression. In this there are echoes of Hegel, of Husserl and Sartre. In Schacht's account, Arnold Gehlen, too, picks up on the old Hegelian theme that it is through the attainment of distance that one is genuinely able to posses that which is immediately one's own. Not only does this require accretions of knowledge, experience and practice but also a certain stance against the world, described by Nietzsche and Heidegger in different ways, of 'man over-coming himself' with 'anxious courage', 'nobility of heart' and 'knowing resolve'. It is easy to recall at this juncture, too, Adorno's injunction to remain 'fearlessly passive'. For Spinoza, understanding the true causes of our desires was the only way to free ourselves; to supplant the exercise of the will finally by 'the intellectual virtue of confronting the facts impassively, without sentiment and without the intrusion of subjective fears and hopes; it is the virtue of objectivity, an acqui-escence in the rationally ascertained truth, however personally disagreeable the truth may seem' (Hampshire, 1962, p. 168). Then there is the breaking down of the internal and external, subjective and objective, personal and impersonal as we place ourselves dispas-sionately in the world to be understood; an immanent possibility for us if we make, as Nagel put it, that 'climb outside of our own minds'. To some extent this is indeed what is meant by 'The View from Nowhere' as discussed by Kant and refined in the last generation by Nagel who provides for it moral and political content. He says: 'It is necessary to combine the recognition of our contingency, our finitude, and our containment in the world with an ambition of transcendence, however limited may be our success in achieving it' (Nagel, 1986, p. 9).

Raised consciousness is, in the first instance, becoming self-conscious not only of how consciousness works on the ground but also of the nature of the self in plurality. Just as there is no substantive social and historical content of consciousness at this point there is no preoccupation with 'who' the self might be, but rather an intention to capture and isolate the properties of the self in themselves. Para-doxically, it may be equally politically and morally imperative to think the unthinkable and make contact with ourselves in the plural. For Ornstein: 'Raising consciousness means to become conscious of the different selves within and how they are partial, while also keeping aware of the larger venues of perception' (Ornstein, 1992, p. 277). Going through the pain barrier of coming to 'know thyself' is the inevitable prescription – though it should be more accurately to 'know thyselves'! Ornstein's tack, here, is undoubtedly along the right lines with people getting to know themselves, as *selves-*knowledge, as a prerequisite to a whole range of individual and social engagements. Additionally, Ornstein's view is of selves and con-sciousness(es) adaptive to a comparatively stable world on an evo-lutionary scale; now, the situation may be the various selves, of which we remain largely unaware, pitched against a highly unstable and rapidly changing world. Marx's model of a person hunting, fishing, shepherding and criticising after dinner, without ever becoming hunter, fisherman, shepherd or critic is a guide here. As with social, economic and political life, so with aspects of our mental life: we must be *all* of these selves and none. If, as Marx maintained, religious reflections of the real world would only vanish when the practical social relations of everday life offered men reasonable and perfectly intelligible relations with their fellow men, so, too, with conscious-ness and the self. Consciousness and the mental has been rendered a noumenal realm since the onslaught on rationalism, but it is important that our minds become transparent to us as a step towards the social world becoming transparent to us. To embark on the latter quest – out of conviction, whilst still working partially 'blind' – is the means to the realisation of both.

NOTES

3 MARX AND THE MARXISTS

1 Mészáros (1970) illustrates that Marx's usage of the concepts 'human' and 'essence', have meaning only as engendered in and through society. 'Essence' may eventually exude from within individuals – but it is not an indigenous resource; it is created in social interaction. Similarly, man is not 'human' *per se*: it is not a generic term. In Marx's terms 'human essence' is no more than the 'ensemble of the social relations' (Marx and Engels, 1968, p. 29). In indicating that Marx had no notion of human nature as 'good', 'bad', 'innocent' or 'guilty', Mészáros states that 'in only one sense may one speak of "human nature"; in the sense whose centre of reference is historical and its foundation, human society' (Mészáros, 1970, p. 171). In the Aristotelian tradition man, for Marx, is a 'zoon politikon'; not only a social animal but a creature only individualised in society.

2 Even in Marx's most succinct statement on 'human nature' contained in the 'Theses on Feuerbach', Fromm (1961) had detected a 'potentiality' view of human nature in Marx, who, he claims, did not say 'that "there is no human nature in each separate individual", but something quite different, namely: that "the essence of man is no abstraction inherent in each individual". It is the essential point of Marx's "materialism" against Hegel's idealism. Marx never gave up his concept of man's "nature" . . . it is one which can be understood only historically . . . as that in man which exists as a potentiality and unfolds and changes in the historical process' (Fromm, 1961, pp. 78–79).

3 Geras is quite unequivocal in contending that '[h]istorical materialism itself, this whole distinctive approach to society that originates with Marx, rests squarely upon the idea of a human nature' (1983, p. 74) and by a close scrutiny of the texts – particularly 'Theses on Feuerbach' – seeks to rehabilitate 'human nature'. Geras illustrates that Marx emphasised the capacities, needs and powers characteristically inherent in human nature whilst simultaneously maintaining a positive position on their social dimension, and claims that Marx saw the power of human nature, implicitly, as independent of reason, notwithstanding an identification of language and consciousness.

4 Undoubtedly there is a widely ranging variety of usage and meaning of the concept of ideology in the work of Marx and Engels, which has become exacerbated in neo-Marxist thought up to the present. Imposing uniformity of interpretation on ideology is a daunting prospect. What is not immediately relevant for this purpose is the precise utilisation of ideology in Marx and Engels in derisive fashion to refer to Hegel, the young Hegelians or idealism in general, nor the characteristic usage of ideology which utilises the concept to denote, quite

overtly, morality, religion and metaphysics for example. Here, ideology equates with a system of ideas or a view of the world and with mystification.

5 Common sense is practical and is formed from life experience and interests and could be seen to correspond to social being determining consciousness. However, although common sense is implicitly oppositional and forms resistance to the dominant culture, it is fragmented and untheoretical – any theoretical structures coming from the dominant culture itself. Additionally there is a way of thinking stemming from the dominant culture or from the past which is uncritically absorbed by the local culture of family and neighbourhood, comprised of superstitious, folkloristic conceptions of the world serving to sustain the status quo.

4   THE OVERCOMING OF CONSCIOUSNESS IN PHILOSOPHY

1 Schopenhauer wonders at how man alongside his life in the concrete perpetually lives another life in the abstract: 'In the former he is abandoned to all the storms of reality and to the influence of the present; he must struggle, suffer, and die like the animal. But his life in the abstract, as it stands before his rational consciousness, is the calm reflection of his life in the concrete, and the world in which he lives . . . In respect of this withdrawal into reflection, he is like an actor who has played in one scene, and takes his place in the audience until he must appear again. In the audience he quietly looks on at whatever may happen, even though it be the preparation of his own death (in the play); but then he again goes on the stage, and acts and suffers as he must. From this double life proceeds that composure in man, so very different from the thoughtlessness of the animal' (Schopenhauer, 1969, p. 85).

2 The best that can be read into Nietzsche's 'superman' is that such creatures do not resist their fate but go with it and face the future with no illusions (again a surprising echo of Hume), making of themselves what they are and will be. This is a building-up of individual identity not a breaking-down as in Schopenhauer. Yet ironically, and placing a premium on morality, Nietzsche also suggests a kind of fateful determinism in which each of us has to follow a pre-ordained journey. If ultimately Nietzsche's health failed this stern test it is perhaps adequate testimony to the ubiquity of the human constitution.

3 The principle of pragmatism, according to James, was first enunciated by C. S. Peirce in his attack on metaphysics with his definition of truth as 'the opinion which is fated to be ultimately agreed to by all who investigate' – a view with which Dewey also concurred (see Habermas's, 1978, discussion of Peirce). This amounts to the practical difference if one or other of alternatives were to be true, and from this point of view truth is what pays, allowing one part of experience to get into a satisfactory, successful relation with other parts. Truth, then, is what is profitable, or useful in people's lives.

4 Brentano, a direct influence on Husserl, had already introduced the idea of 'intentionality' as characterising consciousness, i.e., the direction of mind to an object in perception, in belief and judgement. Although Hume had previously made a similar case (Hume, 1962, p. 344), Brentano, in a passage quoted by James (James, in Thayer (ed.), 1982, p. 161), says that each object actually 'comes into' consciousness in a twofold way: as simply thought of and as admitted or denied believed or disbelieved (i.e., judged). When the object of thought, says Brentano,

becomes the subject of a judgement that assents to it or rejects it, consciousness steps into an entirely new relation towards it. As both, thought of and as deemed real or denied it is, in consequence, 'twice present in consciousness'. This Brentano likens to the way most philosophers (by Kant no less than by Aristotle, he remarks) have identified a relation obtaining between mere thought and desire – the desiring being a secondary and novel form of relation to the object and manner of receiving it into consciousness.

5   THE SOCIOLOGY OF CONSCIOUSNESS

1   The accomplishment of motivational understanding may be something having actually occurred in the past or envisaged in the imagination for the future and, quite crucially, may be regarded in terms of motive as origin or motive as goal. Moreover, this kind of understanding begins on the basis of established objective meaning as merely an indication of the existence of subjective meaning. Schütz says 'that it is only by studying the structure of the meaning-configuration in the stream of an ego-consciousness that we can ever come to an understanding of the deep-seated difference between objective and subjective meaning' (Schütz, 1967, p. 40).

2   Nisbet (1970) has emphasised Simmel's idea of the 'secret' as a consciously desired concealment filled with the consciousness that it *can* be betrayed and refers to the 'recesses' of individual motivation where the true idea remains hidden from the Other: 'The secret offers the possibility of a second world alongside the visible world, one in which as much truth, good, and right exist as in the manifest world, but one in which there may also be contained evil. The one world influences the other' (Nisbit, 1970, p. 104). The 'secret' is one of man's [*sic*] greatest achievements for Simmel which produces an immense enlargement of life.

3   KIuckhohn states that 'verbalizability' is a necessary test of value and considers the possibility of discovering 'implicit values' from statements (to researchers) of 'explicit values'. He holds to the idea that there is a relationship between 'verbal' values and 'real' values that influence overt non-verbal behaviour and refers to C. L. Stevenson and B. L. Whorf amongst others, on the relation between values and language but not to the work of C. Wright Mills a decade earlier (see Kluckhohn, 1951, p. 406).

4   Because Garfinkel's ethnomethodology is primarily concerned with research studies its philosophical basis remains unelucidated, though perhaps the best critical analysis of the philosophical roots of ethnomethodology can be found in Bauman (1973). For an interesting debate on the status of ethnomethodology in relation to established positions in sociology, this time in comparison with symbolic interactionism, see N. K. Denzin, 'Symbolic Interactionism and Ethnomethodology' and D. H. Zimmerman and D. L. Weider 'Ethnomethodology and the Problem of Order: Comments on Denzin' (which includes Denzin's rejoinder to them), in Douglas (ed.), (1971).

6   THE SUPERSESSION OF CONSCIOUSNESS IN SOCIAL THOUGHT

1   Unlike Habermas, Taylor sees Heidegger's view of language being both a radical representative of an identifiable tradition and embodying in itself, important practical, positive uses. He distinguishes between an 'enframing' theory of language characteristic of Hobbes, Locke and Condillac, where content precedes external means of expression with language being comprised of 'ideas, signs and their association, which precede its arising' (Taylor, 1992b, p. 249) and an 'expressive-constitutive' theory of language, as the legacy of Herder, Von Humboldt and Heidegger where language 'makes possible its own content' (Taylor, 1992b, p. 252).

2   Schütz has identified the following steps in Sartre's logic here: 'I seize the Other originally as a subject for which I am an object and objectify him in a second move, thus regaining my own subjectivity' and 'the Other as being not-me, a not-me, however, which is not an object but a subject. By looking at me, the Other makes me an object, limits my freedom, transforms me into a utensil of his possibilities. To be sure, in a second move, I may objectify again the Other-subject, regaining, thus, my own subjectivity' (Schütz, 1982, pp. 192, 197).

3   The Frankfurt School – the source of the earliest incisive criticisms of 'experience' described in earlier chapters – were critical of both Dilthey and Husserl and Dilthey's use of *erlebnis* was decried. Adorno shared Benjamin's hostility towards *erlebnis* ' . . . which had been extolled by the irrationalist "philosophers of life" in Germany because of its alleged spontaneity and freedom from overly intellectual reflection. More recent thinkers like the existentialists were no less guilty of privileging a pseudo-immediacy through what Adorno called their "jargon of authenticity". In both cases, a philosophy that wanted to break through the stultifying confines of rationality and tradition to grasp human existence in its naked form had unwittingly duplicated the irrationality and uprootedness of modern social experience' (Jay, 1984, p. 75).

4   One interesting point of juxtaposition with the Frankfurt School's pessimistic view can be found in Goldmann's idea of a consciousness of immediacy. He says: 'When men act, consciousness is always present; but there is no reason to concede – it is not even probable – that this consciousness is always perfectly adequate: it is one element of behaviour . . . What matters is that men's behaviour is functional and as such meartingful' (Goldmann, 1976, p. 95). Goldmann describes an ensemble of consciousness along with others issuing forth in behaviour. For him: 'The complete subject of the action and, implicitly, the structure of consciousness, can be comprehended only by starting with the fact that men act together – that there is a division of labor' (Goldmann, 1976, p. 97). Drawing a great deal on Piaget, Goldmann's analysis is one of the first attempts to ply the idea of a *transindividual* subject in order to overcome the ossified dualism of subject and object though he recognised both dynamic and conservative moments of this process. Notwithstanding the idea of an 'horizon' of the field of consciousness which confines or limits possible receptivity for a group, Goldman, in describing 'potential' consciousness, argues something roughly similar to Merleau-Ponty on this point – both being a resounding echo of Marx who states quite unequivocally in *The German Ideology* that consciousness comes from revolution. Indeed, Goldmann contends that rather than economic determinism, it is the collective subject that comprises the defining characteristic of Marxism.

5 Habermas contends that Marx developed in two dimensions the idea of the self-constitution of the human species in natural history: 'as a process of self-production, which is impelled forward by the productive activity of those who perform social labour and stored in the forces of production, and as a self-formative process, which is impelled forward by the critical-revolutionary activity of classes and which is stored in experiences of reflection (Habermas, 1978, p. 281). Yet, the framework which Marx developed as his materialist conception of the synthesis of man and nature remained wedded to instrumental action and could, therefore, only account for productive knowledge not reflective knowledge. In Habermas's view Marx was not able to see that ideology and power are distorted communication.

6 It should be noted in passing that in contrast to approaches which stress inter-subjectivity and transindividuality there has emerged an emphasis on the indi-vidual that almost renders the overtly social dimension surplus to requirements. Elster (1985), for example, employing rational-choice theory (which generated an ongoing debate in its own right – see Carling, 1986) tends to view individuals in terms of intentions stemming from *a priori* properties of internal psychic mechanisms. Beliefs and desires are a starting point in the analysis and do not themselves appear to stand in need of explanation. There are, in fact, further variations on the liberal-individualist interpretation of Marx. A recent variant of 'rational choice' or 'analytical' reconstructed Marxian theory, 'analytical semi-Marxism' of G. A. Cohen (1995), engages what remains of Marxism with arid debates and issues that Marx himself always found laughable – morality and bourgeois pretensions of 'timeless' justice and right which, as normative prin-ciples, were considered as all but impotent in the struggle to change the world. In fact, Cohen's ground-breaking work (1978) had already relegated corporeal human beings – in Hegelian fashion – to an equational property of thought experimentation.

7 THE NEW CRITIQUE OF CONSCIOUSNESS

1 Popper (1983), for example, concludes that he agrees with Hume that talk of a substantial self in which the properties of the self inhere does not help much. Neither does he agree with the theory of the 'pure' self – as prior to or free from experience – to be found in Kant. For Popper the self is a result of inborn disposi-tions and social experience. Not only does the latter involve the acquisition of language but also learning a sense of time, with oneself – the social self with a history – extending into the past and into the future. He stresses the role of posing problems and trying out (weeding out) our *conjectures*. He says: 'How do we obtain self-knowledge? Not by self-observation, I suggest, but by becoming selves, and by developing theories about ourselves..' He continues: 'In order to be a self, much has to be learnt . . . but this involves theory; at least in its rudimen-tary form as an expectation: there is no self without theoretical orientation, both in some primitive space and some primitive time.' (Popper, 1983, pp. 279–280). The self, then, is inextricably linked to child development, maturation and a social world of significant others – a case for social interactionism.

2 A further rehearsal of the significance of the non-social/social divide – at least to the extent of spurring Habermas (1990) to a critique – has been Luhmann's (1984) version of systems theory where consciousness, as a psychic system, is uncoupled from the social system construed in terms of communication – in

effect, a meaning-processing system. Thus, the system-environment relationship replaces that of inside–outside in the subject–object problematic of metaphysics. According to Habermas, language is so under-determined as a medium of communication for Luhmann that it is not designed to transcend the ego-centrism of the individual systemic perspective with common perspectives at a transsystemic, supra or higher level. Habermas says that in this view 'language remains secondary in relation to consciousness. The solitary life of the soul, including discursive thought, is not formed by language from the very outset. Structuring by language only articulates the spontaneous flow of consciousness by pauses and lends it the capacity to form episodes' (Habermas, 1990, p. 380). In other words, it operates in the mind prior to communication and persons are seen as the carriers of consciousness able to judge prior to being taken up in the social system.

3   Recently, Hillel-Ruben (1998) has worked up an account of the basis of social properties in which they are rendered irreducible to mental properties, whilst still leaving space for 'activity' and 'behaviour' understood in terms of consciousness. In this process he is indicating that some relations existing between persons are non-social, or reducible to non-social relations, that uninstantiated social properties exist and that social structural properties are not *only* properties of social systems.

4   The test case thought-experiment that illustrates the depth of division in the two positions outlined above is Armstrong's (1980) example of driving a vehicle. He has argued that introspective awareness is awareness of self and, further, that unless introspective consciousness monitors mental activity it will not be remembered as having occurred. He gives the examples of the 'blank-outs' whilst driving a vehicle and the shock at becoming aware of being 'absent-minded in charge of a vehicle' characterised by low levels of introspective consciousness. In effect, for him, there would be little or no memory of the self's history without introspective consciousness. Searle, too, has alluded to the 'states' of consciousness when driving a vehicle on auto-pilot and this question has featured in his exchanges with Block (see Block *et al.* (eds.), 1997, pp. 397–400: see also Carruthers's, 1998, use of this illustration).

5   Ironically, one would have thought that Archer would, in principle, be more sympathetic to the proto-realist position of Reid in his criticism of Locke whom he accuses of attributing to 'memory or consciousness, a strange magical power of producing its object, though that object must have existed before the memory or consciousness which produced it' (Reid, in Robinson (ed.), 1998, p. 310).

REFERENCES

Adorno, T. W. and M. Horkheimer (1972) *Dialectic of Enlightenment*, New York: Herder & Herder.

Althusser, L. (1969) *For Marx*, London: Allen Lane.

(1971) *Lenin and Philosophy and other Essays*, London: New Left Books.

Ameriks, K. (2000) *Kant's Theory of Mind*, Oxford: Clarendon Press.

Anderson, P. (1979) *Considerations On Western Marxism*, London: Verso.

Appelbaum, D. (1996) *The Vision of Hume*, Shaftesbury, Dorset: Element.

Arato, A. and E. Gebhardt (eds.) (1978) *The Essential Frankfurt School Reader*, Oxford: Basil Blackwell.

Archer, M. (1995) *Realist Social Theory: The Morphogenetic Approach*, Cambridge University Press.

Armstrong, D. (1980) *The Nature of Mind and Other Essays*, Ithaca, N.Y.: Cornell University Press.

(1993) *A Materialistic Theory of the Mind* (Rev.edn) London: Routledge.

Aune, B. (1970) *Rationalism, Empiricism and Pragmatism: An Introduction*, New York: Random House.

Austin, J. L. (1962) *How To Do Things With Words*, Oxford University Press.

Balibar, E. (1995) *The Philosophy of Marx*, (trans.) C. Turner, London: Verso.

Bateson, G. (1987) *Steps to an Ecology of Mind, Collected Essays*, Northvale N.J. : Jason Aronson.

Bauman, Z. (1973) 'On the Philosophical Status of Ethnomethodological Sociology', *Sociological Review* 21.

Benhabib, S. (1992) *Situating the Self*, Cambridge: Polity.

Benjamin, W. (1973) *Charles Baudelaire: A Lyric Poet in the Era of Capitalism*, London: New Left Books.

Berger, P. and S. Pullberg (1966) 'Reification and the Sociological Critique of Consciousness', *New Left Review* 35.

Berger, P. and T. Luckmann (1967) *The Social Construction of Reality*, Harmondsworth: Penguin.

Bergson, H. (1991) *Matter and Memory* (trans.) N. M. Paul and W. S Palmer, New York: Zone Books.

Berkeley, G. (1983), *Treatise Concerning the Principles of Human Knowledge*, K. Winkler (ed.), Indianapolis: Hackett Publishing Co.

Berlin, I. (1956) *The Age of Enlightenment – The Eighteenth-Century Philosophers*, New York: Mentor.

Bernstein, B. (1965) 'Social Class and Linguistic Development: A Theory of Social Learning', in A. H. Halsey, J. Floud and C. Arnold Anderson (eds.), *Education, Economy and Society – a Reader in the Sociology of Education*, New York: Free Press.

Bhaskar, R. (1989a) *Reclaiming Reality*, London: Verso.
(1989b) *The Possibility of Naturalism* (2nd edn) Brighton: Harvester.

Billig, M. (1987) *Arguing and Thinking*, Cambridge University Press.
(1991) *Ideologies and Beliefs*, London: Sage.

Billig, M., S. Condor, D. Edwards; M. Gane, D. Middleton and A. Radley (1988) *Ideological Dilemmas*, London: Sage.

Blackmore, S. (1999) *The Meme Machine*, Oxford University Press.

Block, N., O. Flanagan and G. Güzeldere (eds.) (1997) *The Nature of Consciousness – Philosophical Debates*, Cambridge, Mass.: M.I.T. Press.

Blum, A. and P. McHugh (1971) 'The Social Ascription of Motives', *American Sociological Review* 36.

Boas, F. (1938) *The Mind of Primitive Man*, New York: Macmillan.

Bottomore, T. and R. Nisbit (eds.) (1979) *A History of Sociological Analysis*, London: Heinemann.

Bourdieu, P. (1977) *Outline of a Theory of Practice*, Cambridge University Press.
(1986) *Distinction*, London: Routledge.

Bradley, H. (1996) *Fractured Identities*, Cambridge: Polity.

Brentano, F. (1948) *Psychology from an Empirical Standpoint*, (trans.) A. Rancurrello, London.

Brook, A. (1994) *Kant and Mind*, Cambridge University Press.

Bruce, S. and R. Wallis (1983) 'Rescuing Motives' *British Journal of Sociology* 34: 1, pp. 61–71.
(1985) ' "Rescuing Motives" rescued: a reply to Sharrock and Watson', *British Journal of Sociology* 36: 3, pp. 467–470.

Bruner, J. (1986) *Actual Minds, Possible Worlds*, Cambridge, Mass.: Harvard University Press.

Burke, K. (1935) *Permanence and Change*, New York: New Republic.
(1945) *A Grammar of Motives*, Englewood Cliffs, N.J. : Prentice-Hall.

Burkitt, I. (1991) *Social Selves*, London: Sage.

Burr, V. (1995) *An Introduction to Social Constructionism*, London: Routledge.

Campbell, C. (1996) *The Myth of Social Action*, Cambridge University Press.

Carrithers, M., S. Collins and S. Lukes (eds.) (1985) *The Category of the Person*, Cambridge University Press.

Carruthers, P. (1998) *Language, Thought and Consciousness*, Cambridge University Press.

Carling, A. (1986) 'Rational Choice Marxism', *New Left Review* 186.

Chalmers, D. J. (1996) *The Conscious Mind*, Oxford University Press.

Churchland, P. (1988) *Matter and Consciousness* (rev. edn), Cambridge, Mass.: M.J.T. Press.

Cicourel, A. (1964) *Method and Measurement in Sociology*, New York: Free Press.

Clarke, J. J. (1997) *Oriental Enlightenment – The Encounter Between Asian and Western Thought*, London : Routledge.

Cohen, A. (1994) *Self Consciousness: An Alternative Anthropology of Identity*, London: Routledge.

Cohen, A.P. and N. Rapport (eds.) (1995) *Questions of Consciousness*, London: Routledge.

Cohen, G.A. (1978) *Karl Marx's Theory of History – A Defence*, Oxford: Clarendon Press.

(1995) *Self-Ownership, Freedom and Equality*, Cambridge University Press.

Collier, A. (1994) *Critical Realism – An Introduction to Roy Bhaskar's Philosophy*, London: Verso.

Collin, F. (1997) *Social Reality*, London: Routledge.

Collingwood, F. J. (1961) *The Idea of History*, Oxford University Press.

Collins, S. (1985) 'Categories, concepts or predicaments', in M. Carrithers *et al.*

Comte, A. (1975) *The Positive Philosophy*, 2 Vols, London: Trubner.

Coser, L.A. (ed.) (1965) *George Simmel*, Englewood Cliffs N.J.: Prentice-Hall.

(1971) *Masters of Sociological Thought*, New York: Harcourt Brace Jovanovich.

Coulter, J. (1979) *The Social Construction of Mind*, London: Macmillan.

(1989) *Mind In Action*, Cambridge: Polity.

Coward, R. and J. Ellis (1977) *Language and Materialism*, London : Routledge and Kegan Paul.

Craib, I. (1976) *Existentialism and Sociology – a Study of Jean-Paul Sartre*, Cambridge University Press.

(1992) *Modern Social Theory – from Parsons to Habermas* (2nd edn.), Hemel Hemstead: Havester/Wheatsheaf.

(1997) 'Social Constructionism as a Social Psychosis', *Sociology* 31: 1 (Feb.).

(1998) *Experiencing Identity*, London: Sage.

Crick, F. (1994) *An Astonishing Hypothesis – the Scientific Search for the Soul*, New York: Simon & Schuster.

Crossley, N. (1995) 'Body Techniques, Agency and Intercorporeality', *Sociology* 29: 1 (Feb).

Dahlbom, B. (ed.) (1995) *Dennett and his Critics*, Oxford: Basil Blackwell.

Damasio A.R. (1996) *Descartes' Error*, London: Papermac.

(1999) *The Feeling of What Happens: Body and Emotion in the Making of Consciousness*, London: Heinemann.

D'Andrade, R.D. and C. Strauss (eds.) (1992) *Human Motives and Cultural Models*, Cambridge University Press.

Davies, M. and G. W. Humphreys (eds.) (1993) *Consciousness*, Oxford: Basil Blackwell.

Dennett, D.C. (1991) *Consciousness Explained*, Harmondsworth: Penguin.

(1996a) *Darwin's Dangerous Idea*, Harmondsworth: Penguin.

(1996b) *Kinds of Minds*, London: Weidenfeld and Nicholson.

Deleuze, G. and F. Guattari (1997) *Anti-Oedipus: Capitalism and Schizophrenia*, London, The Athlone Press.

Derrida, J. (1981) *Positions*, London, The Athlone Press.

Descartes, R. (1997) *Key Philosophical Writings*, Hertfordshire: Wordsworth.

Dilthey, W. (1979) *Selected Writings* (ed. and intro.) H. P. Rickman, Cambridge University Press.

Douglas, J. (ed.) (1971) *Understanding Everyday Life*, London: Routledge and Kegan Paul.

Douglas, M. and M. Isherwood (1980) *The World of Goods: Towards an Anthropology of Consumption*, Harmondsworth: Penguin.

Dretske, F. (1997) 'Conscious Experience' in N. Block *et al.*
Dreyfus, H.L. and H. Hall (1992) *Heidegger: A Critical Reader*, Oxford: Blackwell.
Durkheim, E. (1947) *The Elementary Forms of the Religious Life,* Glencoe, Ill.: Free Press.
   (1985) *The Rules of Sociological Method*, Glencoe Ill.: Free Press.
Eagleton, T. (1991) *Ideology*, London: Verso.
Edgell, S., K Hetherington and A. Warde A. (eds.) (1996) *Consumption Matters*, Oxford: Blackwell.
Edgley, R. (1969), *Reason in Theory and Practice*, London: Hutchinson
   (1983) 'Philosophy' in D. McLellan (ed), *Marx: the First Hundred Years*, Oxford: Fontana.
Eldridge, J. E. T. (1983) *C. Wright Mills*, London: Tavistock.
Elias, N. (1978a) *What is Sociology?*, London: Hutchinson.
   (1978b) *The History of Manners:, vol. I, The Civilizing Process*, Oxford: Blackwell.
Elster, J. (1985) *Making Sense of Marx*, Cambridge University Press.
Evans, P. and G. Deehan (1990)*The Descent of Mind* London: Paladin.
Faris, E. (1932) 'The Primary Group: Essence and Accident', *American Journal of Sociology* 25:111 (July).
Flanagan, O. (1992) *Consciousness Reconsidered*, Cambridge, Mass.: M.I.T Press.
Flew, A. (ed.) (1964) *Body, Mind and Death* , London: Collier MacMillan.
Flynn, T. R. (1984) *Sartre and Marxist Existentialism*, University of Chicago Press.
Forbes, I. (1990) *Marx and the New Individual*, London: Unwin Hyman.
Foucault, M. (1974) *The Order of Things*, London: Routledge.
   (1987) *Discipline and Punish*, (trans.) A. Sheridan, Harmondsworth: Penguin.
   (1989) *Madness and Civilization*, London: Routledge.
Frisby, D. and D. Sayer (1986) *Society*, London: Tavistock.
Fromm, E. (1961) *Marx's Concept of Man*, New York: Ungar.
Garfinkel, H. (1967) *Studies in Ethnomethodology*, Englewood Cliffs, N.J.: Prentice-Hall.
Geertz, C. (1975) *The Interpretation of Cultures*, London: Hutchinson.
Gellner, E. (1964) *Thought and Change*, London: Weidenfeld and Nicholson.
   (1974) 'The New Idealism – Cause and Meaning in the Social Sciences' in A. Giddens (ed).
   (1992) *Reason and Culture*, Oxford: Blackwell.
Geras, N. (1983) *Marx and Human Nature – Refutation of Legend*, London: Verso.
Gergen, K. J. (1989) 'Warranting Voice and the Elaboration of the Self', in J. Shotter and K. J. Gergen (eds.).
Gerth, H. and C. Wright Mills (1970) *Character and Social Structure*, London: Routledge and Kegan Paul.
Giddens, A. (ed. and intro.) (1972) *Emile Durkheim: Selected Writings*, Cambridge University Press.
   (ed.) (1974) *Positivism and Sociology,* London: Heinemann.
   (1976) *New Rules of Sociological Method*, London: Hutchinson.
   (1979) *Central Problems in Social Theory*, London: Macmillan.
   (1979) 'Positivism and Its Critics' in T. Bottomore and R. Nisbet (eds.).
   (1984) *The Constitution of Society*, Cambridge: Polity.
   (1991) *Modernity and Self-Identity*, Cambridge: Polity.
Goffman, E. (1971) *The Presentation of Self in Everyday Life*, Harmondsworth: Pelican.

(1972) *Relations In Public*, Harmondsworth: Penguin.

Goldmann, L. (1977) *Cultural Creation*, Oxford: Basil Blackwell.

Gramsci, A. (1971) *Selections from the Prison Notebooks of Antonio Gramsci*, London: Lawrence and Wishart.

Greenfield, S. (1995) *Journey to the Centre of the Mind: Toward a Science of Consciousness*, New York: W. H. Freeman and Co.

(1998) *The Human Brain*, London: Phoenix.

Habermas, J. (1978) *Knowledge and Human Interests*, (2nd Edn.) London: Heinemann.

(1979) *Communication and the Evolution of Society*, London: Heinemann.

(1984) *The Theory of Communicative Action*, Vol. I Cambridge: Polity.

(1987) *The Theory of Communicative Action*, Vol. II Cambridge: Polity.

(1989) *Moral Consciousness and Communicative Action*, Cambridge Mass.: M.I.T. Press.

(1990) *The Philosophical Discourse of Modernity*, Cambridge: Polity.

(1992) 'Work and *Weltanschauung*: The Heidegger Controversy from a German Perspective' in H.L. Dreyfus and H. Hall (eds.).

(1995) *Postmetaphysical Thinking*, Cambridge: Polity.

Hacker, P.M.S. (1997) *Insight and Illusion – Themes in the Philosophy of Wittgenstein*, Bristol: Thoemmes Press.

Hall, S. and P. du Gay (eds.) (1996) *Questions of Cultural Identity*, London: Sage.

Hamilton, P. (1974) *Knowledge and Social Structure*, London: Routledge and Kegan Paul.

Hampshire, S. (1962) *Spinoza*, Harmondsworth: Pelican.

(1992) *Innocence and Experience*, Harmondsworth: Penguin.

Hanfling, O. (ed.) (1980) (2nd edn.) *Fundamental Problems in Philosophy*, Oxford: Blackwell.

Harré, R. (1979) *Social Being*, Oxford: Blackwell.

(1983) *Personal Being*, Oxford: Blackwell.

Harré R. (ed.) (1986) *The Social Construction of Emotions*, Oxford: Blackwell.

Harré, R. and G. Gillett (1994) *The Discursive Mind*, London: Sage.

Hastrup, K. (1995) *A Passage To Anthropology: Between Experience and Theory*, London: Routledge.

(1995) 'The Inarticulate Mind' in A.P. Cohen and N. Rapport (eds.).

Havas R.E. (1992) 'Who is Heidegger's Nietzsche?' in H.L. Dreyfus and H. Hall (eds.).

Hawthorn, G. (1976) *Enlightenment and Despair: A History of Sociology*, Cambridge University Press.

Hegel, G.W.F. (1971) *Hegel's Philosophy of Mind*, (forward) J. N. Findlay, Oxford University Press.

(1977) *Phenomenology of Spirit*, (trans.) A.V. Miller Oxford University Press.

Heidegger, M. (1959) *An Introduction to Metaphysics*, Yale University Press.

(1967) *Being and Time*, Oxford University Press.

(1978) *Basic Writings*, (ed. and intro.) D. F. Krell, London : Routledge and Kegan Paul.

Heil, J. (1998) *Philosophy of Mind*, London: Routledge

Heinemann, F. H. (1958) *Existentialism and the Modern Predicament*, London: Black.

Heritage, J. (1984) *Garfinkel and Ethnomethodology*, Cambridge: Polity.

Hillel-Ruben, D. (1998) 'Social Properties and their Basis', in T. May and M. Williams (eds.) *KnowingThe Social World*, Buckingham: Open University Press.

Hindess, B. and P. Hirst (1975) *Pre-Capitalist Modes of Production*, London: Routledge and Kegan Paul.

(1977) *Modes of Production and Social Formation*, Basingstoke: Macmillan.

Hirst, P. (1976) 'Althusser and the Theory of Ideology',*New Left Review* 72.

(1994) 'The Evolution of Consciousness: Identity and Personality in Historical Perspective', *Economy and Society* 23, 1 (Feb.).

Hirst, P. and P. Woolley (1982) *Social Relations and Human Attributes*, London: Tavistock.

Hobbes, T. (1968) *Leviathan*, Harmondsworth: Pelican.

Hodges, H. A. (1944) *Wilhelm Dilthey – An Introduction*, London: Routledge and Kegan Paul.

Hodgkiss, P. (2001) 'The Intersecting Paths of Critical Relations', in J. Lopez and G. Potter (eds.), *After Postmodernism: An Introduction to Critical Realism*, London: The Athlone Press.

Hoffman, J. (1975) *Marxism and the Theory of Praxis*, London: Lawrence and Wishart.

Holstein, J. A. and J. F. Gubrium (1999) *The Self We Live By*, Oxford University Press.

Honderich, T. (ed) (1999) *The Philosophers*, Oxford University Press

Horkheimer, M. (1974), *Critique of Instrumental Reason*, New York: Seabury Press.

Horowitz, I. L. (ed.) (1967) *Power, Politics and People – The Collected Essays of C. Wright Mills*, New York: Oxford Univiersity Press.

Hughs, J. (1990) (2nd ed) *The Philosophy of Social Research*, London: Longman.

Hume, D. (1962) *A Treatise of Human Nature* (ed.) D. G. C. Macnab, Books I, II, III, Glasgow: Collins.

Humphrey, N. (1993) *A History of the Mind,* London: Vintage.

Husserl, E. (1970) *The Crisis of European Sciences and Transcendental Phenomenology*, Evanston, Ill: Northwestern University Press.

Ingold, T. (ed.) (1996) *Key Debates in Anthropology*, London: Routledge.

James, W. (1950) *Principles of Psychology*, Vols. I and II, New York: Dover.

(1961) *Psychology: The Briefer Course* (ed.) G. Allport, New York: Harper and Row.

(1971) ' "Does Consciousness" Exist?', in *Essays in Radical Empiricism* (ed.) R. B. Perry, New York: Dutton.

Jay, M. (1984) *Adorno*, London: Fontana.

Jaynes, J. (1990) *The Origin of Consciousness in the Breakdown of Bicameral Mind*, Boston, Mass: Houghton Mifflin.

Jenkins, R. (1996) *Social Identity*, London: Routledge.

Kant, I. (1959) *The Critique of Pure Reason*, (trans.) N. Kemp Smith, London: Dent.

Kean, J. (1984) *Public Life and Late Capitalism*, Cambridge University Press.

Kenny, A. (ed.) (1994) *The Wittgenstein Reader,* Oxford: Blackwell.

Kitching, G. (1988) *Karl Marx and the Philosophy of Praxis*, London: Routledge.

Kluckhohn, C. (1951) 'Values and Value-orientations in the Theory of Action' in T. Parsons and E. Shils (eds.).

Kojève, A. (1970) *An Introduction to the Reading of Hegel*, Ithaca, N.Y.: Cornell University Press.

Korner, S. (1990) *Kant*, Harmondsworth: Penguin.

Kotre, J. (1996) *How We Create Ourselves Through Memory*, New York: Simon & Schuster.

Laclau, E. and C. Mouffe (1985) *Hegemony and Socialist Strategy*, London: Verso.

Laing, R. D. (1965) *The Divided Self*, Harmondsworth: Penguin.

Larrain, J. (1983) *Marxism and Ideology*, London: Macmillan.

(1994) *Ideology and Cultural Identity*, Cambridge: Polity.

Lasch, C. (1985)*The Minimal Self*, London: Picador.

Layder, D. (1993) *New Strategies in Social Research*, Cambridge: Polity.

(1994) *Understanding Social Theory*, London: Sage.

Lefebvre, H. (1991) *The Production of Space*, Oxford: Blackwell.

(2000) *Everyday Life in the Modern World,* London: The Athlone Press.

Leibniz, G. W. (1973) *Philosophical Writings* (ed.) G. H. R. Parkinson, London: Dent.

Lenin, V. I. (1960) *Collected Works*, London: Lawrence & Wishart.

Leonard, P. (1984) *Personality and Ideology*, London: Macmillan.

Lévi-Strauss, C. (1963) *Structural Anthropology*, Harmondsworth: Penguin.

(1994) *The Savage Mind*, Oxford University Press.

Lichtman, R. (1982) *The Production of Desire: The Integration of Psychoanalysis into Marxist Theory*, New York: Free Press.

Locke, J. (1977) *An Essay Concerning Human Understanding,* (selec. and ed.) J. W. Yolton, London: Dent.

Louch, A. R. (1966) *Explanation and Human Action*, Oxford: Basil Blackwell.

Löwith, K. (1982) *Max Weber and Karl Marx*, London: George Allen & Unwin.

Luce, J. V. (1992) *An Introduction to Greek Philosophy*, London: Thames & Hudson.

Luhmann, N. (1984) *Soziale Systeme*, Frankfurt.

Lukács, G. (1971) *History and Class Consciousness*, London: Merlin.

Lycan, W. G. (ed.) (1999) *Mind and Cognition* (2nd edn), Oxford: Blackwell.

Lyons, W. (ed.) (1995) *Modern Philosophy of Mind*, London: Dent (Everyman).

Lyotard, J.-F. (1984) *The Post Modern Condition: A Report On Knowledge*, Minneapolis, Min: University of Minnesota Press.

McCarney, J. (1980) *The Real World of Ideology*, Sussex: Harvester.

McCrone, J. (1990) *The Ape that Spoke,* London: Macmillan.

McGinn, J. (1993) *The Problem of Consciousness*, Oxford: Blackwell.

Marcuse, H. (1964) *One Dimensional Man*, London: Routledge & Kegan Paul.

Mannheim, K. (1960)*Ideology and Utopia*, London: Routledge & Kegan Paul.

Marx, K. (1867)Das Kapital: Kritik der Politischen Oekonomie, Hamburg: Erster Band (First German Edition of *Capital*; 2nd edn 1872).

(1973) *Grundrisse*, Harmondsworth: Penguin.

(1992) *Early Writings*, Harmondsworth: Penguin.

Marx, K. and F. Engels (1968) *Selected Works*, London: Lawrence and Wishart.

(1976) *Collected Works*, Vol. 5, London: Lawrence and Wishart.

Mauss, M. (1970) *The Gift* (trans.) T. Cunnison, London: Cohen & West.

Mead, G. H. (1934) *Mind, Self and Society*, University of Chicago Press.

(1964) *Selected Writings* (ed.) A. Reck, Indianapolis, Ind.: Bobbs-Merrill.

Melucci, A. (1996) *The Playing Self*, Cambridge: Polity.

Merquior, J. G. (1979) *The Veil and the Mask*, London: Routledge & Kegan Paul.

(1985) *Foucault*, Harlow: Longman.

Merleau-Ponty, M. (1962) *The Phenomenology of Perception*, London: Routledge & Kegan Paul.

Mészáros, I. (1970) *Marx's Theory of Alienation*, London: Merlin.

(1971) *Aspects of History and Class Consciousness*, London: Routledge & Kegan Paul.

(1984) *Philosophy, Ideology and Social Science*, Brighton: Wheatsheaf.

Miklowitz, P. S. (1998) *Metaphysics to Metafictions – Hegel, Nietzsche and the End of Philosophy*, Albany, N.Y.: State University of New York Press.

Mill, J. S. (1991) *On Liberty and Other Essays*, Oxford University Press.

Miller, D. (ed.) (1983) *A Pocket Popper*, Oxford: Fontana.

Mills, C. Wright (1939) 'Language, Logic and Culture', *American Sociological Review*, 4:5 (Oct).

(1940) 'Situated Actions and Vocabularies of Motive', *American Sociological Review*, 5:6 , (Dec).

(1959) *The Sociological Imagination*, New York: Oxford University Press.

(1966) *Sociology and Pragmatism* (ed. and intro.) I. L. Horowitz, New York: Galaxy Books.

Montaigne, M. de (1958) *Essays* (trans.and intro.) J. M Cohen, Harmondsworth: Penguin.

Morris, B. (1991) *Western Conceptions of the Individual*, Berg: New York/Oxford.

(1994) *Anthropology of the Self-the Individual in Cultural Perspective*, London: Pluto.

Munro, R. (1996) 'The consumption view of self: extension, exchange and identity', in Edgell *et al.* (eds.)

Nagel, T. (1986) *The View From Nowhere*, Oxford University Press.

Nietzsche, F. (1969) *Thus Spoke Zarathustra* (trans. and intro.) R. J. Hollingdale, Harmondsworth: Penguin.

(1977) *A Nietzsche Reader*, (Select., trans., and intro.) R. J. Hollingdale, Harmondsworth: Penguin.

(1995) *Unfashionable Observations* (trans. and afterword) R. T. Gray, Stanford University Press.

Nisbet, R. A. (1970) *The Sociological Tradition*, London: Heinemann.

Ornstein, R. E. (1992) *The Evolution of Consciousness*, New York: Simon & Schuster-Touchstone.

Ouspensky, P. D. (1986) *The Fourth Way – the Teachings of G. I. Gurdjieff*, London: Arkana.

Outhwaite, W. (1994) *Habermas – A Critical Introduction*, Cambridge: Polity.

Pannekoek, A. (1975) *Lenin as Philosopher*, London: Merlin.

Pareto, V. (1963) *The Mind and Society*, Vols. I-IV, New York: Dover.

Parfit, D. (1987) *Reasons and Persons*, Oxford: Clarendon.

Park, R. E. (1927) 'Human Nature and Collective Behaviour', *American Journal of Sociology* 32 (March).

Parker, I. (1992) *Discourse Dynamics*, London: Routledge.

Parker, I. and J. Shotter (eds.) (1990) *Deconstructing Social Psychology*, London: Routledge.

Parkin, F. (1982) *Max Weber*, London: Tavistock.

Parsons, T. (1964), *Social Structure and Personality*, New York: Free Press.

Parsons, T. and E. Shils (1951) *Toward a General Theory of Social Action* New York: Harper Torchbooks.

Penrose, R. (1995) *Shadows of The Mind*, Oxford: Vintage.

Petrović, G. (1967) *Marx in the Mid-Twentieth Century*, New York: Anchor.

Piaget, J. (1926)*The Language and Thought of the Child*, London: Routledge & Kegan Paul.

Piepe, A. (1971) *Knowledge and Social Order*, London: Heinemann.
Pinker, S. (1994) *The Language Instinct*, New York: Harper Collins.
  (1998) *How the Mind Works*, The Softback Preview.
Pleasants N. (1999) *Wittgenstein and the Idea of a Critical Social Theory*, London: Routledge.
Plummer, K. (1983) *Documents of Life*, London: Unwin Hyman.
Polt, R. (1999) *Heidegger*, London: U.C.L. Press.
Popper, K. R. and J. C. Eccles (1983) *The Self and its Brain – An Argument For Interactionism*, London: Routledge & Kegan Paul.
Potter, J. and M. Wetherell (1987) *Discourse and Social Psychology*, London: Sage.
Poulantzas, N. (1973) 'The Problem of the Capitalist State', in J. Urry and J. Wakeford (eds.).
Rees, J. (1998) *The Algebra of Revolution: The Dialectic and the Classical Marxist Tradition*, London: Routledge.
Ricoeur, P. (1989) *The Conflict of Interpretations: Essays in Hermeneutics I*, London: The Athlone Press.
  (1990) *Time and Narrative*, 3 vols., Chicago University Press.
  (1991) *From Text to Action: Essays in Hermeneutics II*, London: The Athlone Press.
  (1992) *Oneself as An Other*, Chicago University Press.
Roberts, M. (1996) *Analytical Marxism: A Critique*, London: Verso.
Robinson, D. N. (1995) *An Intellectual History of Psychology* (3rd edn), London: George Allen & Unwin.
  (ed.) (1998) *The Mind*, Oxford University Press.
Rockmore, T. (1997) *Cognition: An Introduction to Hegel's Phenomenology of Spirit*, Berkeley, Calif.: University of California Press.
Rogers, C. (1961) *On Becoming A Person*, New York: Houghton Mifflin.
Rorty, R. (ed.) (1976) *The Identities of Persons*, Berkeley, Calif.: University of California Press.
  (1992) *Consequences of Pragmatism*, Brighton: Harvester
  (1992) 'Heidegger, Contingency, and Pragmatism', in H.L. Dreyfus and H. Hall (eds.).
Rose, A. M. (ed.) (1971) *Human Behaviour and Social Process*, London: Routledge & Kegan Paul.
Rose, G. (1995) *Hegel: Contra Sociology*, London: The Athlone Press.
Rose, N. (1990) *Governing the Soul – the Shaping of the Private Self*, London: Routledge.
Rose, S. (1976) *The Conscious Brain*, Harmondsworth: Penguin.
  (1993) *The Making of Memory*, London: Bantam.
Rosen, M. (1996) *On Voluntary Servitude*, Cambridge: Polity.
Rousseau, J.-J. (1984) *Of The Social Contract* (trans.) C. M. Sherover, New York: Harper Row.
Russell, B. (1961) *History of Western Philosophy* (2nd edn), London: George Allen & Unwin.
Ryle, G. (1963) *The Concept of Mind*, Harmondsworth: Peregrine.
Sacks, O. (1986) *The Man who Mistook his Wife for a Hat*, London: Picador.
  (1991) *Seeing Voices*, London: Picador.
Sadler, T. (1995) *Nietzsche: Truth and Redemption – Critique of the Postmodernist Nietzsche*, London: The Athlone Press.

Sapir, E. (1921) *Language*, New York: Harcourt, Brace.

Sartre, J.-P. (1957a) *Being and Nothingness* (trans.) H. E. Barnes, London: Methuen.

(1957b) *The Transcendence of the Ego*, (trans.) F. Williams and R. Kirkpatrick, New York: Noonday Press.

(1972) *The Psychology of Imagination*, London: Methuen.

(1976) *Critique of Dialectical Reason* (trans.) A. Sheridan-Smith, London: New Left Books.

Sarup, M. (1993) *An Introductory Guide to Post-Structuralism and Post Modernism*, Hemel Hempstead: Harvester/Wheatsheaf.

Sass, L. A. (1994) *Madness and Modernism*, Cambridge, Mass.: Harvard University Press.

Schacht, R. (1971) *Alienation*, London: George Allen & Unwin.

Schachtel, E. G. (1959) *Metamorphasis: on the Development of Affect, Perception, Attention and Memory*, New York: Basic Books.

Scheffler, I. (1974) *Four Pragmatists – a Critical Introduction to Peirce, James, Mead and Dewey*, London: Routledge & Kegan Paul.

Schopenhauer, A. (1969) *The World as Will and Representation*, Vol.I, New York: Dover.

Schulte, J. (1992) *Wittgenstein*, State University of New York Press.

Schütz, A. (1967) *The Phenomenology of the Social World*, Northwestern University Press.

Schütz, A. (1982) *Collected Papers, I, The Problem of Social Reality*, The Hague: Martinus Nijhoff.

Scott, M. B. and S. M. Lyman (1972) 'Accounts', In J. G. Manis and B. Meltzer (eds.) *Symbolic Interactionism: a Reader in Social Psychology*, Boston: Allyn & Bacon

Searle, J. R. (1994) *The Rediscovery of The Mind*, Cambridge, Mass.: The M.I.T. Press.

(1996) *The Construction of Social Reality*, Harmondsworth: Penguin.

(1999) *Mind, Language and Society*, London: Weidenfeld & Nicolson.

Sève, L. (1978) *Man in Marxist Theory*, Sussex: Harvester Press.

Sharrock, W. W. and D. R. Watson (1984) 'What's the Point of "Rescuing Motives"?', *British Journal of Sociology* 35:3, pp. 435–451.

(1986) 'Re-locating Motives', *British Journal of Sociology* 37: 4, pp. 581–583.

Sheridan, A. (1980) *Michel Foucault – the Will to Truth*, London: Tavistock.

Shoemaker, S. and R. Swinburne (1984) *Personal Identity*, Oxford University Press.

Shotter, J. and K. J. Gergen (eds.) (1989) *Texts of Identity*, London: Sage.

Shotter, J. (1993) *Cultural Politics of Everyday Life*, Buckingham: Open University Press.

Simmel, G. (1964) *The Sociology of Georg Simmel*, (trans., ed., intro.) K. H. Wolff, New York: Free Press.

(1971) *On Individuality and Social Forms* (ed.) D. N. Levine University of Chicago Press.

Skinner, B. F. (1938) *The Behaviour of Organisms*, New York: Appleton–Century.

Solomon, R. C. (1988) *Continental Philosophy Since 1750 – the Rise and Fall of the Self*, Oxford University Press.

Spinoza, B. (1992) *Ethics*, (trans.) S. Shirley, Indianapolis, Ind: Hackett.

Strathern, M. (1991) *Partial Connections*, Maryland: Rowman & Little.

(1995) *The Relation*, Cambridge: Prickly Pear Press.

Strauss, A. L. (ed.) (1956) *The Social Psychology of George Herbert Mead*, University of Chicago Press.

Strawson, P. F. (1959) *Individuals: An Essay in Descriptive Metaphysics*, London: Methuen.

(1980) 'Persons', in O. Hanfling (ed.).

Stuart Hughes, H. (1958) *Consciousness and Society: The Reorientation of European Social Thought 1890–1930*, Granada: London.

Tarnas, R. (1996) *The Passion of the Western Mind*, London: Pimlico.

Taylor, C. (1975) *Hegel*, Cambridge University Press.

(1985) 'The Person' in M. Carrithers, S. Collins, S. Lukes (eds.).

(1992a) *Sources of the Self – the Making of Modern Identity*, Cambridge University Press.

(1992b) 'Heidegger, Language, and Ecology' in H.L. Dreyfus and H. Hall (eds.).

Thayer, H. S. (ed.) (1982). *Pragmatism – the Classic Writings*, Indianapolis: Hacker.

Tiryakian, E. A. (1979) 'Emile Durkheim', in T. Bottomore and R. Nisbet (eds.)

Torey, Z. (1999) *The Crucible of Consciousness*, Oxford University Press.

Tucker, D. F. B. (1980) *Marxism and Individualism*, Oxford: Blackwell.

Turner, R. (ed) (1974) *Ethnomethodology*, Penguin: Harmondsworth.

Tye, M. (1995) *The Problems of Consciousness*, Cambridge, Mass.: M.I.T. Press.

Urry, J. and J. Wakeford (eds.) 1973 *Power in Britain*, London: Heinemann.

Vico, G. (1982) *Selected Writings*, (ed. and trans.) L. Pompa: Cambridge University Press.

Volosinov, V. N. (1973) *Marxism and the Philosophy of Language*, London: Seminar Press.

Vygotsky, L. S. (1962) *Thought and Language*, Cambridge, Mass.: M.I.T. Press.

Watson, J. B. (1924) *Behaviourism*, New York: Norton.

Watson, S. (1998) 'The New Bergsonism: Discipline, Subjectivity and Freedom', *Radical Philosophy* 92 (Nov./Dec.).

Weber, M. (1964) *The Theory of Social and Economic Organization*, London: Collier, Macmillan.

(1968) *Economy and Society*, vols. I, II and III, G. Roth and C. Wittich (eds.) New York: Bedminster Press.

(1978) *Economy and Society*, vols. I and II, G. Roth, and C. Wittich (eds.) Berkeley and Los Angeles, Calif.: University of California Press.

Wertsch, J. V. (1993) *Voices of the Mind*, London: Routledge.

Whorf, B. L. (1956) *Language, Thought and Reality*, Cambridge Mass.: M.I.T. Press.

Williams, B. (1973) *Problems of the Self*, Cambridge University Press.

Williams, R. (1976) *Keywords*, Glasgow: Fontana/Croom Helm.

Winch, P. (1958) *The Idea of A Social Science*, London: Routledge & Kegan Paul.

Wittgenstein, L. (1958) *Philosophical Investigations*, (3rd edn) New York: Macmillan.

(1961) *Tractatus-Logico-Philosophicus*, London: Routledge & Kegan Paul.

Wrong, D. H. (1961) 'The Oversocialized Conception of Man in Modern Sociology', *American Sociological Review* 26: 2.

Wundt, W. (1912) *An Introduction to Psychology* (trans.) R. Pinter, London: Allen & Unwin.

Zohar, D. and I. Marshall (1993) *The Quantum Society*, London: Bloomsbury.

INDEX

Luhmann, N., 247n. 2
Lukács, G., 61–3, 161

McCarney, J., 55, 63
McGinn, C., 5, 232–3
Mach, E., 8, 77–8
Mannheim, K., 8, 97, 108–11
Marcuse, H., 162, 229
Marx, K., 6, 8, 14, 41–2, 43–60, 225,
    236, 238, 241
Marxism, 7, 43, 173, 218, 231; post-
    Marxism, 160–71, 173
materialism, 44, 45, 46
materiality, 16, 40
Mauss, M., 186, 187, 191
Maya, veil of, 71
Mead, G. H., 6, 8, 98, 117, 119, 120–3,
    134, 176, 184, 190, 239
meaning, 15, 16, 245n. 1
Melucci, A., 180–1
memory, 9, 13, 14, 19, 24, 146, 221,
    223–5; in Bergson, 84–5, 223–4; as
    collective, 209; in Hobbes, 20; and
    personal identity, 26, 122; of
    traditions, 161; types of memory, 224
Merleau-Ponty, M., 8, 11, 145, 149–53,
    172, 231
Merquior, J. G., 157, 158
Mészáros, I., 243n. 1
Mill, J. S., 12
Mills, C. Wright, 3–4, 8, 98, 124–5,
    129–30
mind, 3; in action, 83, 137; autonomy
    of, 114, 116; defining reality, 12,
    103–4, 230–4; emergent property of
    brain, 205, 232, 233; as filter, 11, 24,
    81, 121, 224; Hegel's three levels, 36;
    intersubjectively constituted, 207–8;
    as mechanism, 19; meeting of minds,
    106–7, 201; as modes of action, 83;
    philosophy of, 10, 232; succession of
    perceptions, 24–5; unconscious
    teleology of, 191; see also brain;
    consciousness; memory; thinking
mind-body problem, 5, 16, 18–19, 78,
    137–8, 171, 205, 214; as same
    substance, 20, 86; unity of, as
    personality, 22
mind-independent world, 21, 34, 232–3
monism, 34

Montaigne, M. de, 28, 30, 73
moods, 12, 129, 204
moral agency, 33, 219–20
motives, 118, 124–5, 127–8, 179, 189,
    193, 211, 237, 245nn., 1, 2
Mouffe, C., 168, 238
multiple realities, 14, 107–8, 113, 231
Munro, R., 194–5

Nagel, T., 141, 171, 232–3, 240
narrative self, 8, 178–9, 180, 193,
    201–2, 211
narratives, 15, 210
natural attitude, 126–7
nature, 44, 45, 114; man's estrangement
    from, 50; as objectified reality, 47
neoplatonism, 6
neurology, 4
Nietzsche, F., 6, 8, 14, 69–70, 73–7,
    90–2, 155, 240, 244n. 2
Nisbet, R. A., 245n. 2
noumenal world, 33, 71, 232, 241; see
    also thing-in-itself

object: of consciousness, 11, 31–2; life
    as, 47
objectification, 174
objective existence, 36, 51
objectivity, 129–30, 133, 141, 240
Ornstein, R. E., 14, 221, 240–1
outer perception, 11

Pannekoek, A., 77, 78
Pareto, V., 8, 97, 100–1, 131
Parfit, D., 219
Park, R. E., 117, 225
Parker, I., 215
Parkin, F., 102–3
Parmenides, 17
Parsons, T., 117–18
passions, 19, 25
Peirce, C. S., 78–9, 244n. 3
perception, 89; and apperception, 22–3;
    consciousness of, 11; and external
    world, 27–8, 70–1; Hume on, 23–4;
    meaning from class of percepts,
    200–1; shared visual space, 154
personal identity, 21–2, 23, 238;
    continuity of, and capacity, 181–2;
    crisis, 180, 181; Giddens on, 178–9,